NATURE AND HUMAN NATURE
IN ANCIENT GREEK PHILOSOPHY AND ITS RECEPTION

sidestonepress

To Asia Minor, to Ionia, to Magnesia

Smyrnē 1922

Eternal Memory

NATURE AND HUMAN NATURE IN ANCIENT GREEK PHILOSOPHY AND ITS RECEPTION

EDITED BY
MELINA G. MOUZALA

PUBLICATIONS OF THE
NETHERLANDS INSTITUTE AT ATHENS X

Published by Sidestone Press, Leiden
www.sidestone.com
info@sidestone.nl
(+31)(0)71-7370131

Lay-out & cover design: Sidestone Press
Photograph cover: Magnesia on the Maeander: Propylaia (Ionia–Asia Minor)

ISBN 978-94-6426-376-3 (softcover)
ISBN 978-94-6426-377-0 (hardcover)
ISBN 978-94-6426-378-7 (PDF e-book)

ISSN 2452-3836 (print) | 2590-3039 (online)

DOI 10.59641/3t038uwv

Contents

Preface

In the Autumn of 2022, I contacted Emmy Mestropian-Makri, who is responsible for events and actions at the Netherlands Institute at Athens, to propose a Symposium focused on Ancient Philosophy and its reception. Speakers at the Symposium would be University Professors from the Netherlands, as well as other academics who work in the field and Professors from Greece's Universities. Some of these colleagues were already acquainted with the Netherlands Institute at Athens through previous events it has hosted. My reasoning was that the subject of the Symposium would be derived from the combination of the research interests of the guest speakers. When I first discussed with Emmy Makri, I proposed "Nature and Human Nature in Ancient Greek Philosophy and its Reception" as the title of this International Symposium, given that this subject –as something which touches on the entirety of Ancient Philosophy– could be used as an umbrella topic that would encompass the research interests of the academics and researchers we intended to invite.

Our discussions with Ms Mestropian-Makri lasted for a year, involving back-and-forth talks, contacts with invitees and the organisation of practical matters before the Symposium. Our collaboration was smooth and unhindered from the get-go, and her contribution was vital to the realisation of my vision. We also agreed to publish a volume which would include all the papers presented at the Symposium as part of the series "Publications of the Netherlands Institute at Athens".

The parallels between the origin, the genesis, the structure and operation of the universe, of the universal nature, of nature and human nature, was a crucial issue that permeated the whole of ancient Greek philosophical thought and tradition.

It would be enough to refer to two salient cases, one from the Pre-Socratics and the other from Platonic thought. In Heraclitus, *logos* implied a director for the actions of the world, and it would eventually follow that there should be a director to manage the perceptions and cognition of man. In Plato, the structure of the human soul and body is interpreted through the view of the cosmos and its soul and through inquiry into the principles as well as the structure and powers of nature.

Furthermore, nature and human nature considered both in relation to each other and separately, continue to be the primary concern of science as well as philosophy. Indeed, a careful investigation of these multidimensional concepts, which can be approached from different perspectives, may be quite useful in deciphering the various puzzles of modern life and thought. Ancient philosophy and its reception can make a significant contribution to this endeavour.

The Symposium was held on 3 October 2023, with the following speakers invited:

Frans de Haas, Claudia Marsico, Teun Tieleman, Alain Lernould, Istvan Bodnar, Alexandra Michalewski, Nicos Charalabopoulos, Father Nikolaos Loudovikos, Elias Tempelis, Melina G. Mouzala.

This volume is the fruit of that Symposium. The papers presented by the participants are included within, adapted for final publication.

Acknowledgments
I would like to express my warmest thanks to the speakers at the Symposium, as well as all those who attended and participated in the discussion; their observations provided the impetus for further development of our philosophical research. I would also like to thank all those who contributed to this volume with their papers, as well as those who read the papers and provided their invaluable commentary and observations. Many thanks also to the Netherlands Institute at Athens, Prof. Dr. Ann Brysbaert, Director of the Netherlands Institute at Athens, Prof. of Ancient Technologies, Materials and Crafts (Leiden University, Faculty of Archaeology) and of course to Emmy Mestropian-Makri for our collaboration in organising the Symposium.

Melina G. Mouzala
Athens, November 2024

Abbreviations

Abbreviations for ancient Greek authors and works follow the Greek English Dictionary by Liddell, Scott and Jones [LSJ].

in: Mouzala, M.G. (ed.) 2025: *Nature and Human Nature in Ancient Greek Philosophy and Its Reception.* Leiden: Sidestone Press, pp. 9-10.

Introduction

Melina G. Mouzala

I. Brief History of the Concept "Nature"

Φύσις is a word peculiar to the Greek language. As a result, all the key aspects of the ancient history of the concept this word signifies have developed and evolved in the Greek language.[1] Associated with its corresponding notion, the word φύσις is also notorious as a symbol of the influence of ancient philosophical thought on early Christian philosophy.[2] It derives from the verbs φύω, φύομαι; the active transitive form φύω means "to grow, to produce, to bring forth, to put forth, to beget, to engender, to generate" while the middle intransitive or passive form φύομαι bears the meaning "to grow, to spring up or forth, to come into being, to arise, to grow on, to wax".[3] Lloyd argues that the absence of the word from the earliest surviving Greek writings indicates that the corresponding notion was invented during a later period in relation with nature as a domain encompassing all natural processes.[4] In Homer the word occurs in *Odyssey* 10, 302-306, where Hermes shows Odysseus a plant and explains its φύσιν, meaning its natural properties or its natural character. We owe the development of the notion of φύσις (*nature*) and the inquiry into its meaning, along with the efforts to explain the natural phenomena, to the Greek philosophers who were called φυσικοί or φυσιολόγοι and the early medical writers.[5] The so-called Presocratics employed the term φύσις (*nature*) to convey different meanings: 1. in the sense of substance (οὐσία); 2. in the sense of natural world; 3. nature as "the being" (τὸ ὄν); 4. in the sense of genesis, coming to be; 5. in the sense of natural endowment; 6. in the sense of natural order.[6]

Burnet stresses that "in Greek philosophical language, φύσις always means that which is primary, fundamental and persistent, as opposed to what is secondary, derivative and transient; what is 'given', as opposed to that which is made or becomes" (1908, p. 13). Naddaf, based on the occurrence of the word in the phrasal structure κατὰ φύσιν διαιρέων ἕκαστον in Heraclitus' fragment DK22B1, holds that "it is clear that *phusis* means not only the *essential character* of a thing but also how a/the thing originates and develops and thus continues to regulate its nature" (2005, p. 3). According to this approach, the usual meaning that appears in the fragments of the Presocratics implies that φύσις "must be understood dynamically" as the real inherent character or constitution of a thing, considered as long as it exists with all its properties. This interpretation claims that φύσις, whether conceived of as origin, as process or as result– because all these are semantic dimensions of its original

1 Zachhuber (2016), *Real Enzyclopädie für Antike und Christentum*, Vol. XXVII, coll. 744-781, s.v. Physis.

2 Zachhuber (2016), *ibid.*

3 Liddell-Scott Lexicon, s.v.; Hofmann, *Etymologisches Wörterbuch des Griechischen*, s.v.; Naddaf (2005), p. 12.

4 Lloyd (1991), p. 418.

5 Aristotle, *Physics* 184b17; 186a20; 187a 12, 28; 205a5; 203b15; 205a26; 206b23; 213b1; 265a3. See also Lloyd (1991), pp. 419-420.

6 For the references to the relevant fragments, see the *Lexicon of Presocratic Philosophy*, Academy of Athens, Research Centre for Greek Philosophy, Athens, 1994, s.v. φύσις (pp. 406-408).

in: Mouzala, M.G. (ed.) 2025: *Nature and Human Nature in Ancient Greek Philosophy and Its Reception*. Leiden: Sidestone Press, pp. 11-20.

meaning– is never employed in the sense of something static.[7] According to a different approach to the meaning of the term, already the Indo-German root *bhū-, *bhŭ or *bheu- from which it is supposed to be derived,[8] is connected with both the meanings, "grow", "develop" and "produce" on the one hand, and "being" on the other. Therefore, the term has two basic semantic orientations that are employed in a wide range of relevant vocabulary; it is used either in relation to a process to designate becoming and growth, or in relation to the static character of the notion to designate the *ousia*, being, and the essential constitution along with the permanent essential characteristics of a thing.[9] On the one hand it denotes the *ousia* or the innate principle and character of each thing and on the other the origin or the genesis or the becoming and growth of a thing.[10] Cornford also confirms the ambiguity of the term, but accepts that its shifting senses may at least be grouped under two distinct main headings: the static and the dynamic. In its static aspect, nature has two meanings: it signifies the system of all phenomena in time and space, the total of all existing things, while the nature of a thing means its constitution, structure, essence. According to Cornford, in its dynamic aspect nature bears the connotation of an active force and a primordial upspringing energy.[11]

Heidel notes that it is reasonably certain that philosophical works were familiarly quoted as bearing the title *Περὶ φύσεως* some time before the close of the fifth century, as is evident from the Corpus Hippocraticum.[12] There are also different interpretations in relation to the use of φύσις in the titles "περὶ φύσεως", which is ascribed to the works of the majority of the Presocratics, and "περὶ φύσεως ἱστορία",[13] which means investigation or inquiry into the nature of things. According to Burnet's account of the meaning of φύσις, which opposes that of Teichmüller, the Ionian philosophers were primarily interested in searching for the primary substance and not the explanation of celestial and meteorological phenomena; therefore, their works named "περὶ φύσεως ἱστορίη" must be understood within this context, otherwise they would have been named Περὶ οὐρανοῦ or Περὶ μετεώρων.[14] However, Heidel stresses that it would not be true even of the Ionians that they restricted themselves to inquiry into the primary substance of the world; φύσις had a broader meaning, since it included the law or process of growth exemplified in all things. He maintains that the word was used in the titular phrase "περὶ φύσεως" in the sense of the sum of things as constituted by the elements and the cosmic laws and processes.[15] Long, on the other hand, puts forward that the term φύσις, "in spite of its generality, inclines us to regard something more restrictive, the physical world and in particular its beginning, because primarily *physis* means 'origin' or 'growth'" (1999, p. 11). Naddaf offers a comprehensive exposition of all these approaches, assuming that the word φύσις in the above titles of works and research interests bears four different meanings: "(1) *physis* in the sense of primordial matter; (2) *physis* in the sense of process; (3) *physis* in the sense of primordial matter and process; (4) *physis* in the sense of the origin, process, and result" (2005, p. 3). Laks, based on three sources, the Hippocratic treatise *On Ancient Medicine* (ch. 20), a fragment of Euripides from his lost tragedy *Antiope* (cf. my note 13) and a passage from the *Dissoi logoi* (90 DK) concludes that "inquiry into nature" (περὶ φύσεως ἱστορία) must be thought of as having two principal characteristics: on the one hand it was directed toward the totality of things, and on the other, it embraced a genetic perspective by tracing the history of the development of things which constitute nature from their origins.[16]

Ancient Greek philosophical thought was also oriented toward questions of *human nature* alongside philosophical inquiry that focused on questions of *nature* (φύσις) and the explanation of the ontological category or property of "natural". Lloyd emphasises in his analysis the unavoidable connection between the two philosophical realms and the inclusion of the former in the latter in the ancient Greek philosophical culture. He puts forward that where other cultures and religions may stress the gap between humans and animals, arguing that humans are not counted among the 'animals', the pre-Christian Greeks generally assumed their co-membership in a common genus: "It was, perhaps, one of the strengths of the pagan Greek view of humans that there was no question of human beings *not* being part of nature. Humans are living creatures, ζῷα, and clearly belong to the same genus as all other animals" (Lloyd, 1991, p. 424). As Lebedev puts it based on theories of Neuroscience, the animate-inanimate dichotomy is a part of "folk biology" and folk psychology and constitutes a distinction which the body-soul dualism presupposes.[17] Notoriously, not all philosophers of the sixth and the fifth century were called *physikoi* or *physiologoi*; those were mainly the early Ionians and their fifth-century followers, like Anaxagoras, Empedocles and Democritus.[18] Nevertheless, even among the Ionian philosophers research interests included

7 Naddaf (2005), p. 3.
8 Mannsperger (1969), pp. 38ff; Heinemann (2005), p. 19; Naddaf (2005), p. 12. See also Hofmann (1950); Chantraine (2000), p. 1234.
9 Heinemann (2005), p. 19.
10 Cf. Zachhuber (2016), *ibid.*
11 Cornford (1991), p. 73.
12 Heidel (1910), p. 81, n. 10.
13 See Plato, *Phaedo* 96a. Cf. the phrase "ὄλβιος ὅστις τῆς ἱστορίας ἔσχε μάθησιν" in Euripides, *Fragmenta Antiopes*, frg. 910 (Nauck).
14 Burnet (1908), pp. 13-14.
15 Heidel (1910), p. 129.
16 Laks (2018), pp. 2-4.
17 Lebedev (2019), p. 658.
18 Lebedev (2019), p. 655.

aspects of nature that reveal its relation with human nature. For example, Anaximander expounded a theory that explained the way in which the first living creatures were born, a theory of zoogony and anthropogony; he also made "a comprehensive and detailed attempt to explain all aspects of the world of man's experience".[19] Xenophanes was an intellectual of his time, "one of the first Western intellectuals", who resisted the traditional forms of thought and old conventions and examined the way in which nature and the limits of human thought determine the patterns of thought.[20] Heraclitus, who must not be reckoned as a proper *physikos*, developed a theory that, as Kahn puts it, "can only be understood as a response to the world view of the Milesians" (1979, p. 19), in which he focuses on the "identity of structure between the inner, personal world of the psyche and the larger natural order of the universe" (1979, p. 21). Distinguished from the *physikoi* or *physiologoi* and placed within a different philosophical tradition were the philosophers Aristotle called the *Italikoi*, like the Pythagoreans and the Eleatics.[21] We can find evidence for a pre-Platonic perspective of a body-soul dualism in the Early Western Greek philosophical tradition, the founder and pioneer of which was Pythagoras. There is consensus among scholars that Pythagoras emphasised in his theory the survival of the soul after death–in all probability in association with the Orphics and Pherecydes of Syros– and developed a theory of immortality based on transmigration.[22] Pythagoras' attention to the soul produced the most influential finding in the history of ancient philosophy since, as Burkert points out, it gave rise to a new general concept of a living being, the idea of ἔμψυχον (*empsychon*).[23] Kahn notes that Pythagoras' theory of the soul caused a radical break with the Homeric view of the soul.[24] Palmer, in his analysis of the idea of the persistence of the soul after death among the Presocratics, supports that their approaches evidence two main lines of thought. The first is that the fate of the soul after death is connected with certain ethical commitments during life which entail the adoption of a certain way of life that recognises the priority of the soul over the body. This idea is central to the theory of soul that originates from Pythagoras and runs through Empedocles and Philolaus. The second is the idea that the individual soul is made of the same stuff as the divine principle which operates as the soul of the cosmos, with the effect that it also somehow shares with it the same structure regarding the activity and imposition of order by intellect. This line of thought starts with Anaximenes and continues with Anaxagoras and Diogenes of Apollonia.[25] Pythagoras and Parmenides are both predecessors of Plato's Metaphysics, especially regarding his theory of immortality of the soul and his theory of Forms. Parmenides focuses on the explanation of the nature of human thought and knowledge and man's misunderstanding of truth. Although Aristotle accuses Parmenides (as well as Melissus) of being an anti-naturalist,[26] the latter is also considered to have taken a cosmological point of view as the springboard for his perspective; his theory regarding the deception of perception was based on the observation of natural phenomena within the framework of an empirically-based cosmology.[27]

A crucial scientific area related to philosophy where the notion of nature was employed and gained notable traction was medicine. Lloyd asserts that medical writers, similarly to natural philosophers, invoked *nature* on the occasions when a plausible explanatory theory emerged in connection with it and was capable of dissolving mystery or obscurity regarding diseases and natural phenomena. It is characteristic of this tendency that some Hippocratic writers emphasised the role of nature in disease, aiming to eliminate any thought of supernatural interference in the etiology and the evolution of illness and its healing.[28] Lloyd points out that we can be sure that "some early Greek medical theorising was directed to establishing the *naturalness* of diseases and to refuting assumptions of direct divine intervention there", and that in such works as *On the Sacred Disease* and *On Airs, Waters, Spaces* the emphasis is on the idea that all diseases have natural causes and there is no need to associate them with the intervention of gods or daemons, asserting that those who claim the opposite intend to cheat and swindle the infirm.[29]

The anthropocentric perspective of nature arose mainly with the sophists, who devoted an important part of their work to the study of human nature. Also, it was mainly in the framework of their own intellectual movement that the φύσει-νόμῳ antithesis[30] was thematised as a subject which formed the foundation for extended philosophical discussions on major ethical and political issues, such as justice. However, as Kerferd remarks, traces of this antithesis may be found as early as Heraclitus: in DK22B2, he castigates the majority of people for the individualisation or privatisation of their understanding; although reason is common, most people live as though they each had their own private understanding; in DK22B114 Heraclitus declares that all human laws are nourished by the one

19 Kirk-Raven (1957), p. 100; 141ff.
20 Feyerabend (1987), pp. 12ff.
21 See Aristotle, *Metaphysics* 987a 10; a31; 988a26. Lebedev (2019), p. 655.
22 Huffman (2009), p. 21; Riedweg (2005), p. 62.
23 Burkert (1985), p. 300.
24 Kahn (2001), p. 18.
25 Palmer (2019), p. 25.
26 See Aristotle, *Physics* 184b25-185a13.
27 See Popper (1998).
28 Lloyd (1991), p. 422.
29 Lloyd (1991), p. 361.
30 For this antithesis generally, see Heinimann (1945); Guthrie (1977), pp. 55ff; with reference to justice, Caizzi (1999); Barney (2006).

divine law and it is this that they should follow. In this case the divine law represents the permanent and paradigmatic, whereas human laws refer to mutable things, which are thus inferior to the divine. Human law and convention are mutable.[31] In the sphere of human behaviour, φύσις and νόμος were standard antonyms that were frequently opposed, with the latter representing customs, conventions, laws, artistic activity and products, manifestations of human civilisation, and aspects of human life that was organised in communities, with different constitutions.[32] Cornford explains that "the mere mention of 'custom' (τὰ νόμιμα, τὰ νομιζόμενα) reminds us of the active content of *Nomos*, which, before it means a prohibitive-enactment, stands for *behaving* in a certain way, behaviour that is standardised, moralised, socialised, – in a word, group-behaviour" (1991, p. 74). The criticism against tradition relating to convention relies on the theses about the fixed nature of things. Gorgias, in *Helen's Encomium* 15, stresses that "the things we see do not have the nature which we wish them to have, but the nature which each actually has" (transl. Kennedy 2001 [1972[1]]). As Woodruff notes, "appeals to nature or to the natures of things are endemic to the new learning and rule out extreme relativism or scepticism. Nature is independent of what anyone thinks it to be, so if a thinker wishes to attack popular or conventional views, what is more appropriate or natural than to appeal to nature itself as a witness against tradition?" (1999, p. 304). Within this frame of thought, nature is connected with science and knowledge, whereas *nomos* and convention must be considered in relation to opinion, belief, common or popular opinion, and, further, sociology and political philosophy; however, both terms have moral and political connotations and implications.[33] In Plato's *Cratylus* the φύσει-νόμῳ antithesis brings to the fore the problem of the origin of language and the relation between language and beings (ὄντα) or language and reality, as well as the formation of language according to the human tendency to provide conventional names for things, a subject which had already been examined by certain predecessors of Plato and the sophists.[34]

In Plato's *Phaedrus* 229d2-230d5, Socrates indirectly declares that the crux of his philosophical research and discussions is the pursuit of self-knowledge and solutions to anthropological matters. When Phaedrus addresses him in 230c6- d5, saying that he is an amazing and most remarkable person for he really does seem exactly like a stranger who is being guided about, and not like a native, since he does not go away from the city out over the border and it seems that he does not go outside the walls at all, Socrates answers: "Forgive me, my dear friend. You see, I am fond of learning. The country places and the trees won't teach me anything, whereas the people in the city do" (transl. Fowler 2005 [1914], slightly modified).[35] In Plato's *Phaedo* 96a6ff., Socrates lucidly expresses his disappointment with the inquiry into nature (περὶ φύσεως ἱστορία) which he attempted in his youth, since he found the explanations offered by the theories of the *physikoi* philosophers wholly unsatisfactory. The theory of Forms Socrates presents in the following passages of the dialogue as an alternative explanation for all the natural processes of the phenomenal world constitutes, according to him, the strongest hypothesis which offers a firm and irrefutable theory of causation for all things.[36] In Plato, φύσις generally appears in connection with all the basic elements of Platonic philosophy. Indicatively, I will put forward some examples, following Mannsperger (1969, 293ff.). In the homonymous dialogue, Protagoras thematises the antithesis φύσει-διδακτόν τε καὶ ἐξ ἐπιμελείας regarding the acquisition of ἀρετή (323c2ff.) and becomes involved in dialectic with Socrates on the teachability of virtue, whereas in the same dialogue Hippias evokes the antithesis φύσει-νόμῳ, claiming that law is a despot of mankind which often constrains us against nature (337cd; transl. Lamb 1967). In the *Gorgias* Socrates introduces the question on the relationship between rhetoric and justice, and from 482d henceforth Callicles presents his theory about the law of nature which contradicts the conventional law of humans, the latter asserting that doing wrong makes us more miserable than suffering wrong. He maintains that it is naturally just that the superior rules the inferior since the superior has the natural right to rule, whereas from 488b onwards Socrates develops his counterarguments on the antithesis between natural and conventional justice, confirming that suffering injustice is more profitable to the sufferer than doing wrong is to the inflictor. In the *Meno* (81c5ff.) Socrates introduces the antithesis φύσει-διδαχῇ with relation to ἀρετή through the reference to the theory of recollection (ἀνάμνησις). In the *Cratylus* (389a-391a) the idea of a norm that corresponds to what is φύσει πεφυκός which is equally characterised as καλόν, and indeed κάλλιστον, appears within the frame of the φύσει-νόμῳ antithesis. Φύσις is recognised as distinct for each thing (φύσει ἑκάστῳ [389d1]) and as individual φύσις (ἰδία φύσις [387d2]) but this approach is combined with the paradigmatic character of the Forms and the contemplative character of the human approach to them (389b). In *Phaedo* 97c-99d, where Socrates criticises Anaxagoras'

31 Cf. Kerferd (1981), pp. 111ff.

32 Cf. Lloyd (1991), p. 425.

33 Cf. Lloyd (1991), p. 426 and Woodruff (1999), pp. 304-305.

34 See again Heinimann (1945); Barney (1997); Barney (2001); Karfík (2021).

35 Plato, *Phaedrus* 230 d3-5: "Συγγίγνωσκέ μοι, ὦ ἄριστε. Φιλομαθὴς γάρ εἰμι. Τὰ μὲν οὖν χωρία καὶ τὰ δένδρα οὐδέν μ'ἐθέλοι διδάσκειν, οἱ δ'ἐν τῷ ἄστει ἄνθρωποι". Cf. Mannsperger (1969), p. 291.

36 On Plato's Natural Philosophy, see Lloyd (1968); Gregory (2000); Johansen (2004); Brisson (2006); Koch, Männlein-Robert und Weidtmann (2019).

theory of Nous as part of the exposition of his experience from the inquiry into nature, we can recognise this conception of nature that Burnet ascribes to Plato and his successors, namely that they identify φύσις with the best or more normal condition of a thing. Burnet points out that this thesis is due to their belief that the goal of any development is prior to the process by which it is reached.[37] In the same passage, Plato also associates this perfect condition of a thing with its being (εἶναι) itself and further puts forward the idea of *agathon* itself as cohesive power which permeates the universe and makes it coherent. In *Republic* 596b-597e, as Mannsperger and Vlastos have noted, Plato depicts a structure of beings that encompasses Forms and their images and which entails degrees of reality and a continuous gradation which penetrates all kinds of things.[38] Φύσις is the realm where the Forms as παραδείγματα, namely unique, unrepeatable and perfect patterns, are produced by the god or nature-begetter (φυτουργόν), who wanting to be a real maker of a thing that really *is*, begot each Form as one by nature (φύσει); two or more such Forms were not naturally engendered by the god nor will they be begotten (transl. Bloom 1991[2], modified). Nature coincides with this realm in which the god's creative activity takes place.[39] In Plato's *Parmenides* 132d1-2 it is also said that these Forms/ideas exist in nature as patterns (τὰ μὲν εἴδη ταῦτα ὥσπερ παραδείγματα ἑστάναι ἐν τῇ φύσει) and the other things resemble them and are imitations of them (transl. Fowler 1925). In *Theaetetus* 176e3 the ontological "topos" within which the Forms exist is recognised as the realm of Being, therefore if these passages are combined one can assume that the realm of *nature* referred to in book X of the *Republic* and *Parmenides* 132d is identical with that of Being. Also, earlier in the *Republic*, in the allegory of the divided line (509d6ff.), a different kind of gradation is illustrated, in which the animals around us and everything that grows (πᾶν τὸ φυτευτόν) and the whole class of artifacts are placed in the second order from the base of this ontological and epistemological scale, of which the upper segment of its line encompasses the intelligible forms and culminates in the Form of the Good. In *Phaedrus* 269eff. it is acknowledged that all great arts demand discussion and high speculation about nature, while the reference to medicine and Hippocrates the Asclepiad allows Socrates to thematise the relationship between knowledge of the nature of the soul and knowledge of the nature of the whole. In the *Sophist* the interlocutors search for the φύσις of each genos through the diaeretical method applied in the dialectical investigation of the ontological categories of the five *megista genē*. As Mannsperger notes, φύσις is not among these genera, but as soon as the mutual relations between them are thematised, the verbal expressions used in each case reveal that each of them must be considered as a φύσις (e.g., 245c8, 257a8, 258a7); this approach, in which the perspective of nature is predominant, endows the ideas –till then rigidly isolated and related solely to themselves– with interrelations and movement, and further opens them up to understanding of the structure of the intelligible world to which they belong in terms of a dynamocentric conception of being.[40] The *Timaeus* includes the grandiose Platonic enterprise for the comprehensive grasp of the entire cosmos and of ἀνθρωπείη φύσις through an εἰκὼς λόγος. As Proclus notes in his Commentary on Plato's *Timaeus*, "This whole dialogue, throughout its entire length, has physical inquiry as its aim, examining the same matters simultaneously in images and in paradigms, in wholes and in parts. It has been filled throughout with all the finest rules of physical theory, tackling simples for the sake of complexes, parts for the sake of wholes, and images for the sake of their originals, leaving none of the originative causes of nature outside the scope of the inquiry" (Proclus, *In Timaeum*, I, 1.17-24; transl. Tarrant 2006). In book X of the *Laws* (889bff.), Plato, within his effort to demonstrate the primacy of soul to matter, refers to the discovery of the source of the unreasonable opinions of all those humans who have ever investigated nature; according to this theory, the arguments that produce the soul of the impious have declared that the first cause of the generation and destruction of all things, i.e. the soul, is not first, but has come into being later, while what is later is earlier. This is why they have erred concerning the real existence of the gods. They have misunderstood the priority and the power of the soul, which is older than body and more than anything governs the bodies' changes and all their transformations (transl. Mayhew 2008, slightly modified). In this book of the *Laws*, what is opposed with the natural and what exists *by nature* (φύσει), is what exists *by art* (τέχνῃ), whereas the antithesis between god and nature is again repudiated, and it is finally shown that νοῦς, τέχνη and the sphere of the things which exist φύσει are in mutual correlation.[41] In parallel with the references to nature itself in the Platonic dialogues, the interest in the investigation and understanding of the ἀνθρωπίνη φύσις (human nature) and of the πάθη it has undergone, not only in terms of psychology and the partition or the internal anatomy of the soul but also in terms of physiology, epistemology, ethics, education, pedagogy, and cognitive metaphysics permeates the entire Platonic corpus.[42]

Of special interest is Aristotle's account of the meanings his predecessors and contemporary philosophers attributed to nature, as far as he exerted great influence on the theories

37 Cf. Burnet (1908), p. 13.

38 Mannsperger (1969), p. 295; Vlastos (1973), p. 62.

39 Mannsperger, *ibid.*

40 Cf. Mannsperger, (1969), pp. 170-171; 296.

41 Cf. Mannsperger (1969), p. 297; Mayhew (2008), pp. 100-101.

42 Indicatively, see *Symp.* 189d5-6; *Resp.* 514a1-2; *Tht.* 149c1. See also Koch (2019); Männlein-Robert (2019); Knauß (2019).

of the philosophers of the Hellenistic period, Late Antiquity and Byzantium. In his *Physics* II. 1, Aristotle presents three main interpretative approaches to nature. Predominant in all of these is the contradistinction between nature and art and the use of examples from the domain of artefacts and artistic activity and production. First, he speaks about those who think that the matter is the nature of each thing by referring to that which is primarily inherent in each thing, unformed *per se* (τὸ πρῶτον ἐνυπάρχον ἑκάστῳ, ἀρρύθμιστον <ὂν> καθ'ἑαυτό [*Phys.* 193a10-11]); for example, the nature of a bed is the wood from which is made, that of a statue the bronze. In *Physics* 193a9-30, Aristotle refers to those who hold that the nature and substantive existence (ἡ φύσις καὶ ἡ οὐσία) of natural products resides in their material on the analogy of the wood of a bedstead or the bronze of a statue.[43] The artificial arrangement of the material by the craftsman is merely an incident that has occurred to it, whereas its essential and natural quality is to be found in that which persists continuously throughout any change in the state of the artefact. Similarly, if the materials themselves bear to yet other substances the same relation which the manufactured articles bear to them, then, after analysis, it is in the matter that we must look for the 'nature' and essential being of each compound natural thing. For instance, if water is the material of bronze or gold, or earth of bone or timber, and so forth, then we must look to the water or earth for the *nature* and essential being of gold and each similar constituent. Aristotle stresses that within this frame of thought each thinker among the *physiologists* assumed to be primary this substance or these substances which he regarded as constituting the substantive existence of all things in general, all else being mere modifications, states, and dispositions of them. This is why some have said that it was earth that constituted the nature of things, some fire, some air, some water, and some several and some all of these elemental substances.

Therefore, one way of viewing *nature* is to interpret it as the ultimately underlying material of all things that have in themselves the principle of movement and change. However, after this definition Aristotle introduces the core of his own conception of nature. He puts forward that from another point of view, we may think of the nature of a thing as residing rather in its form, i.e., in the kind of thing it is by definition (τὸ εἶδος τὸ κατὰ τὸν λόγον [*Phys.* 193a30-31]). The main argument for this assumption relies on an analogy drawn between art and nature. As in the case of art we should not allow that what was only potentially a bedstead and had not yet received the form of bed had in it as yet any art-formed element, or could be called 'art', so in the case of natural products what is potentially flesh or bone has not yet the 'nature' of flesh or bone until it actually assumes the form indicated by the definition by which we determine what the thing in question is. Aristotle clearly states that it is the form rather than the matter which is in fact φύσις. A third interpretation of nature equates φύσις with γένεσις. According to it, nature *qua* genesis proclaims itself as the path to nature *qua* goal (ἡ φύσις ἡ λεγομένη ὡς γένεσις ὁδός ἐστιν εἰς φύσιν [*Phys.* 193b12-13]). Furthermore, Aristotle investigates different aspects of nature in his physical treatises *De generatione et corruptione*, *De caelo*, *Meteorologica*, *Parva Naturalia* as well as in his works devoted to Psychology and Biology. In parallel, Aristotle's philosophical interest in human nature is developed primarily in his ethical treatises, but significant sections of this framework are also included in his psychology, epistemology and metaphysics.[44]

Given that, as already mentioned, the term φύσις (nature) has been applied in many different ways by different people in the history of philosophy,[45] I will rely next on Proclus' account of the meanings attributed to it by the ancient philosophers, in his Commentary on Plato's *Timaeus* (*In Timaeum* I, 10.5-22),[46] for a brief introduction to its concepts and connotations in Ancient Greek Philosophy.[47] Proclus begins his exposition with three questions regarding nature: a) what is nature; b) whence it proceeds; c) how far it extends its own productive activity. The first refers to the essence of nature, the second to the ontological origin or source from which nature derives and the third to the problem of how far it extends its activity as a productive cause.[48] Some of the ancient thinkers, such as Antiphon, used the term φύσις for matter (ὕλη). Aristotle's *Physics* II.1 provides testimony regarding Antiphon's position that nature is identified with matter. In connection with his own theory about matter as the constituent which is primarily inherent in each natural thing, unformed *per se*, Aristotle reports Antiphon's argument as follows: "Some identify the nature or substance of a natural object with that immediate constituent of it which taken by itself is without arrangement, e.g. the wood is the 'nature' of the bed, and the bronze the 'nature' of the statue. As an indication of this Antiphon points out that if you planted a bed and the rotting wood acquired the power of sending up a shoot, it would not be a bed that would come up, but wood" (*Physics* 193a12-14; transl. Hardie and Gaye,

43 I follow the translation of Wicksteed and Cornford (1957) with some modifications.

44 See Colaner (2012); Segev (2017); Stevenson, Haberman, Wright, Witt (2017), pp. 99-115; Kirk &Arel (2023).

45 Proclus, *In Timaeum* I, 9. 31-32.

46 Generally, I follow the translation of Tarrant (2006). Tarrant (2006, p. 103, n. 52), in his remark that the reference to Antisthenes by Proclus is unexpected given the Neoplatonic doxography represented by his exposition, stresses that this part of his commentary finally includes material which is ultimately dependent on Aristotle's *Physics* itself. For Nature in Proclus, see Martijn (2010).

47 For the Greek concept of nature, see also Lovejoy (1909); McClure (1934); Gadamer (1985); Lloyd (1991); Naddaf (2005); Heinemann (2005); Macé (2012); Habash (2016); Gregory (2020).

48 Cf. Martijn (2010), p. 24.

1984). Other philosophers used the term φύσις (nature) for form (εἶδος), the main representative of this line of thought being Aristotle, who in his *Physics* (193a30-b18) develops a set of arguments in favour of this thesis, especially in contradistinction to the opinion that nature is matter. Other philosophers, notably some of those before Plato, used the term φύσις (nature) to denote the whole thing, calling what arises by nature (τὰ φύσει) 'natures' (φύσεις).[49] Proclus at this point refers to Plato's *Laws* 892b3-c7, where Plato mentions those who by 'nature' mean "the generation [or source] of the first things".[50] From Plato's passage one can infer that furthermore, those thinkers applied this usage of the word φύσις (nature) to the four elements, the heavenly bodies and living things, which they called 'natural' with the reasoning that they may all be reckoned among the first things.[51] Other thinkers, according to Proclus' exposition, equated nature with natural properties or natural powers, such as heaviness (βαρύτητας), lightness (κουφότητας), thinness or rarity (μανώσεις), and density (πυκνώσεις), like some of the Peripatetics and of even earlier physicists. Others called nature "god's craft" (τέχνην θεού), while others the soul and yet others something like this. As for Plato, Proclus believes that he does not claim we should call 'nature' primarily matter or the form-in-matter (ἔνυλον εἶδος) or the body or the physical properties, yet he stops short of identifying it outright with soul. In Proclus' view, Plato taught us the most accurate approach to nature by locating its essence in between the two, i.e., between soul and bodily properties. According to this approach, as Proclus interprets it, nature is inferior to the soul by its being divided about bodies and by its failing to revert back to itself, yet it excels the things that come after it by possessing the formal principles (λόγους) of all things and generating them all, and bringing them to life (ζῳοποιεῖν).

Generally, a major issue Neoplatonism attempted to answer was the status of Nature or the ontological level in which it should be placed, especially in comparison to the Soul. Ancient philosophers long debated the relation between Nature and Soul especially with regard to the question of which is the prior ἀρχὴ κινήσεως.[52] As Sorabji notes, the crucial question was whether Nature represents a self-sufficient mechanism or is dependent on higher ontological powers. Alexander of Aphrodisias' assertion, testified by Simplicius, is that Nature acts without having or contemplating such kind of models as the Platonic Forms/Ideas and without rational reflection or choice; however, it acts by a sequence of changes that have an order and a purpose. Besides, in the reproduction that takes place in Nature, the enmattered form of the parent or generally of the efficient cause serves as a model for the product.[53] According to Plotinus Nature acts without knowing.[54] Whether Plotinus conceived of Nature as a fourth hypostasis is the subject of ongoing discussion. James Wilberding, in his discussion of the older view that in certain passages Plotinus does appear to hypostatise Nature, states that the dominant scholarly view today "acknowledges on the one hand that in Plotinus' considered view Nature is not a distinct hypostasis but simply a part or power of the World-Soul, but on the other hand concedes that Plotinus' own account of Nature makes it difficult to understand in what ways, if any, Nature's relationship to the higher World-Soul and the hypostasis Soul is supposed to be different from Soul's relationship to Intellect (Nous)" (Wilberding, 2022, p. 313). He recommends an examination of Plotinus' account of Nature through the lens of his entire metaphysical theory, and in particular of his theory of procession and reversion. It is important not only to acknowledge the significance of Plotinus' statements that there are only three principles and that Nature is a power or a part of the Soul, but also to find out the common features between Nature and the hypostases of Soul and Intellect.[55] As for Proclus, Martijn clarifies that in his conception, "Nature is neither soul nor the aggregate of everything natural, but primarily a hypostasis of its own in between the two, where hypostasis is to be understood in the narrower technical sense of 'fundamental ontological level'-something that does not merely have, but also *is* a hypostasis" (Martijn, 2010, p. 24 and n. 21). As Lernould notes, Proclus introduces Nature as an intermediate hypostasis between the Soul and the corporeal. Nature is distinguished from the Soul by being inseparable from bodies. But the crucial point in this approach is the reconciliation of immanence with transcendence, since Nature operates as an ontological principle.[56] From one perspective Nature is distinguished from the Soul and Intellect in the ontological hierarchy of causes from which the corporeal derives, since in this hierarchy they come above Nature and are themselves causes of order, whereas from another perspective Nature is also Soul, Intellect, Henad, and even One.[57]

II. Overview of the contents of the volume and structure

This volume includes seven papers that explore different aspects of "Nature and Human Nature in Ancient Greek Philosophy and its Reception", which was the subject of

49 On the problem that Proclus uses plural (φύσεις) while Plato uses singular (φύσις, φύσιν), see Tarrant (2006), p. 103, n. 54.

50 I follow the translation of Mayhew (2008).

51 Cf. Mayhew (2008), p. 103.

52 Cf. Martijn (2010), p. 27.

53 Sorabji (2004), p. 33. Alexander apud Simplicius *In Aristotelis Physicorum*, 310.25-311.38.

54 Plotinus, *Enneads*, 2.3.17.4-5; 4.4.13.7-12; cf. Wilberding (2022), p. 320.

55 See Wilberding (2022), p. 331.

56 Lernould (2012), pp. 69-70.

57 On the different perspectives from which Nature is interpreted in Proclus, see Lernould, *ibid.*, pp. 70-71.

the International Symposium held at the Netherlands Institute of Athens on 3 October 2023. They all deal with philosophers, philosophical works and treatises which belong to the broad subject of the inquiry into nature, including human nature. The volume is divided into two parts. The first includes a set of papers which examine the relation between nature and human nature, focusing on the role of physiognomy, the relation between cosmic and human psychic order, the relation between individual and universal nature from a medical viewpoint, and the relation between human, divine, and "natural" will. They are organised in chronological order, beginning from Classical Antiquity (Plato and the Socratics [Phaedo]), running through Late Antiquity (Middle Platonism [Atticus], Galen), and concluding with the Latin Patristic tradition and Byzantium (Augustine, Maximus the Confessor). The second encompasses a set of papers which focus on the examination of nature and its causal roles, on the relation between the universe and the First cause as well as the cosmic order in Alexander of Aphrodisias and Peripatetic philosophy, on the examination of nature in Alexander of Aphrodisias according to certain fragmenta and testimonia related to his lost commentary on Aristotle's *Physics* as well as certain of his other treatises, and finally the parallel examination of nature and soul in Peripatetic philosophy and Late Neoplatonism, namely in the *De anima* by Alexander of Aphrodisias and in Simplicius and Philoponus in their commentaries on Aristotle's *Physics*. This set of papers is once again organised in chronological and thematic order.

Claudia Marsico discusses the role of physiognomy in the classical-era debates about human nature and explores the figure of Phaedo of Elis, the narrator of Plato's *Phaedo*. The author analyzes Phaedo's character and his philosophical views on the body and soul as outlined in the *Zopyrus*, aiming to gain insight into Phaedo's personality. She finally investigates certain aspects of Plato's *Phaedo* to shed light on Plato's choice of this companion as the central figure of the philosophical inquiry illustrated in the dialogue. The author re-evaluates Phaedo's personality, thus underscoring his importance for the Socratic milieu.

Alexandra Michalewski studies the parallel drawn by Atticus between the ordering activity of the world-soul (which is also called "nature") and that of the individual soul, by focusing on the concept of providence. She demonstrates that Atticus considers the doctrine of providence to be at the crossroads not only of cosmology, but also of ethics. He targets the Peripatetic doctrines of the immobile Prime Mover, separated from the sublunary world, and of a non-immortal soul and contrasts the Peripatetic conception of an ungenerated world, which does not depend on any benevolent cause, to the Platonic Stoicising model of a world-soul exercising providential activity that extends to caring for each individual person.

Teun Tieleman examines how exactly Galen conceived of the relation between individual and universal nature. He regarded humans as intermediate creatures, with an animal and a divine side, a view more commonly associated with ancient Platonism. He analysed human nature in terms of the mixture of elements or elementary qualities, with consequences both for therapy and for enhancement and perfecting. Human nature as well as health and illness are subjected to the same physical principles which occur in the natural world or the cosmos. This opens a religious, or theological, perspective integral to Galen's effort to develop a philosophical medicine or medical philosophy: the doctor as a servant of God and medicine as an extension of God's creative and sustaining activity.

Fr. Nikolaos Loudovikos examines the parallel in the Patristic scholarship between Augustine's and Maximus' doctrines of will and stresses their differences. According to the author, Augustine's conception of the will can be characterised as 'ecstatic', compared to that of Maximus, because he seems to understand human will as something which is to be overcome by Christ's divine will. Maximus' anti-Monothelite 'revolution' is precisely that Christ wills only through and by and according to nature(s); there is no disharmony between human and divine will. The author shows that Maximus, for whom the truth of human existence lies in achieving nature's fulfilment, employs a concept of *natural will*, which contains the entirety of natural potency and desire.

Frans de Haas examines Alexander of Aphrodisias' view of the Peripatetic theory regarding the relation between the universe and the First Cause, which is responsible for the unity and order of the universe. The author first illustrates the state of the discussion between Stoics, Platonists and Peripatetics on this issue, going on to present the main features of Alexander's approach to the challenges that arise from this discussion. Alexander introduced a divine power, which he identified with the non-rational nature at work in each natural thing and provided a Peripatetic cosmology with a new account of cosmic order, which is both top-down and bottom-up.

István Bodnár presents Alexander of Aphrodisias' view of nature as one may assume it from the fragments and testimonia on his commentary on Aristotle's *Physics* in Simplicius' *Commentary on Aristotle's Physics*, taking also into account his relevant theses in some of his shorter works and quaestiones. Within this framework, the author stresses the causal roles Alexander assigned to nature in a *scala naturae*, which incorporated both more complex natural bodies and the fundamental simplest bodies, i.e., the elements. Finally, he presents Alexander's approach to the causal role of the Prime Mover with regard both to the celestial bodies and the sublunary world.

Melina G. Mouzala examines the answers provided by Simplicius and Philoponus on the question of the distinction between nature and soul considered as principles of the natural and ensouled bodies, in their comments on Aristotle's *Physics* II. 1-3. In his attempt to explain from his perspective the relation of nature to soul, Simplicius is implicitly involved in dialectic with the theses of Alexander of Aphrodisias and the Stoics on certain aspects of this issue. The author investigates this implicit dialectic as well as Simplicius and Philoponus' interpretation of nature as ζωή, a notion which they also use as an intermediate between nature and soul.

Melina G. Mouzala
Athens, November 2024

Bibliography

Lexicons

Chantraine, P.: *Dictionnaire étymologique de la langue Grecque, Histoire des Mots.* Nouvelle édition avec supplément. Paris: Klincksieck, 1999.

Hofmann, J.B.: *Etymologisches Wörterbuch des Griechischen,* München: Verlag von R. Oldenbourg, 1950.

Lexicon of Presocratic Philosophy, Academy of Athens, Research Center for Greek Philosophy, Athens, 1994.

Liddell, H.G., Scott, R. and Jones, H.S. *A Greek-English Lexicon.* 9th edition with revised supplement. Oxford: Clarendon, 1996.

Secondary Literature

Burkert, W. (1985): *Greek Religion.* Translated by J. Raffan. Cambridge, Massachusetts: Harvard University Press.

Barney, R. (1997): "Plato on Conventionalism". *Phronesis* 42, No. 2: pp. 143-162.

Barney, R. (2001): *Names and Nature in Plato's* Cratylus. Studies in Philosophy. New York/London: Routledge.

Barney, R. (2006): "The Sophistic Movement". In: Gill, M.L. and Pellegrin, P. (eds): *A Companion to Ancient Philosophy, Blackwell Companions to Philosophy.* Oxford: Blackwell Publishing Ltd., pp. 77-97.

Brisson, L. (2006): "Plato's Natural Philosophy and Metaphysics". In: Gill, M.L. and Pellegrin, P. (eds): *A Companion to Ancient Philosophy, Blackwell Companions to Philosophy.* Oxford: Blackwell Publishing Ltd., pp. 212-231.

Burnet, J. (1908[2]): *Early Greek Philosophy.* London: Adam and Charles Black.

Caizzi, F.D. (1999): "Protagoras and Antiphon: Sophistic debates on Justice". In: Long, A.A. (ed.): *The Cambridge Companion to Early Greek Philosophy.* Cambridge: Cambridge University Press, pp. 311-331.

Colaner, N. (2012): "Aristotle on Human Lives and Human Natures". *History of Philosophy Quarterly* 29, No 3: pp. 211-226.

Cornford, F.M. (1991): *From Religion to Philosophy: A Study in the Origins of Western Speculation.* Princeton, New Jersey: Princeton University Press.

Feyerabend, P. (1987): "Xenophanes and the Homeric Gods". *The Kenyon Review*, New Series, 9, No. 4: pp. 12-22.

Gadamer, H. (1985): "Natural Science and Hermeneutics: The concept of nature in ancient philosophy". *Proceedings of the Boston Area Colloquium in Ancient Philosophy, 1*(1), pp. 39-52. DOI:10.1163/2213441785X00049.

Gregory, A. (2000): *Plato's Philosophy of Science.* London: Duckworth.

Gregory, A. (2020): *Early Greek Philosophies of Nature.* London and New York: Bloomsbury Academic.

Guthrie, W.K.C. (1977): *The Sophists.* Cambridge: Cambridge University Press. (First published as Part I of *A History of Greek Philosophy,* Volume III, Cambridge University Press 1969. Reprinted 1977).

Habash, J. (2016): *Early Greek Philosophy and the Discovery of Nature* (Doctoral dissertation, Duquesne University). Retrieved from https://dsc.duq.edu/etd/32

Heidel, W.A. (1910): "Περὶ Φύσεως. A Study of the Conception of Nature among the Pre-Socratics". *Proceedings of the American Academy of Arts and Sciences* 45, No 4: pp. 79-133.

Heinemann, G. (2005): "Die Entwicklung des Begriffs *physis* bis Aristoteles". In: Schürmann, A. (Hrsg): *Physik/Mechanik.* In: Wöhrle, G. (Hrsg): *Geschichte der Mathematik und Naturwissenschaften,* 3. Stuttgart: Franz Steiner Verlag, pp. 16-60.

Heinimann, F. (1945): *Herkunft und Bedeutung einer Antithese im griechischen Denken des 5. Jahrhunderts.* Basel: F. Reinhardt.

Huffman, C. (2009): "The Pythagorean Conception of the Soul from Pythagoras to Philolaus". In: Frede, D. and Reis, B. (eds): *Body and Soul in Ancient Philosophy.* Berlin-NewYork: Walter de Gruyter, pp. 21-44.

Johansen, T.K. (2004): *Plato's Natural Philosophy. A Study of the Timaeus-Critias.* Cambridge: Cambridge University Press.

Kahn, C. (1979): *The Art and Thought of Heraclitus, An edition of the fragments with translation and commentary*. Cambridge: Cambridge University Press.

Kahn, C. (2001): *Pythagoras and the Pythagoreans: A Brief History.* Indianapolis: Hackett.

Karfík, F. (2021): "A Theory of Language between the *Cratylus*, the *Theaetetus*, and the *Sophist*". In: Mikeš, V. (ed.): *Plato's Cratylus. Proceedings of the Eleventh Symposium Platonicum Pragense*, Brill's Plato Studies Series, vol. 8. Leiden: Brill: pp. 179-190.

Kerferd, G.B. (1981): *The Sophistic Movement.* Cambridge: Cambridge University Press.
Kirk, G. & Arel, J. (2023) (eds): *Aristotle on Human Nature: The Animal with Logos.* London: Bloomsbury Academic.
Kirk, G.S. & Raven, J.E. (1957): *The Presocratic Philosophers.* Cambridge: Cambridge University Press.
Knauß, J. (2019): "Anthropologische Grundlagen sozialer Organisation in Platons *Nomoi*". In: Koch, D., Männlein-Robert, I. und Weidtmann, N. (Hrsg.): *Platon und die Physis.* Tübingen: Mohr Siebeck, pp. 223-239.
Koch, D. (2019): "Φύσις, φύειν und ἀρετή. Zum Zusammenklang eines Verhältnisses in Platons Dialogen". In: Koch, D., Männlein-Robert, I. und Weidtmann, N. (Hrsg.): *Platon und die Physis.* Tübingen: Mohr Siebeck, pp. 49-55.
Koch, D., Männlein-Robert, I. und Weidtmann, N. (2019) (Hrsg.): *Platon und die Physis.* Tübingen: Mohr Siebeck.
Laks, A. (2018): *The Concept of Presocratic Philosophy: Its Origin, Development, and Significance.* Translated by G.W. Most. Princeton & Oxford: Princeton University Press (Title of the original edition: *Introduction à la "philosophie présocratique"*, Presses Universitaires de France, 2006).
Lebedev, A. (2019): "Idealism (mentalism) in Early Greek metaphysics and philosophical theology: Pythagoras, Parmenides, Heraclitus, Xenophanes and others (with some remarks on the "Gigantomachia about being" in Plato's *Sophist*)". *Indo-European Linguistics and Classical Philology* XXIII: pp. 651-704. 10.30842/ielcp230690152352.
Lernould, A. (2012): "Nature in Proclus: from irrational immanent principle to goddess". In: Wilberding, J. and Horn, C. (eds): *Neoplatonism and the Philosophy of Nature.* Oxford: Oxford University Press, pp. 68-102.
Lloyd, G.E.R. (1968): "Plato as a Natural Scientist". *Journal of Hellenic Studies* 88: pp. 78-92.
Lloyd, G.E.R. (1991): *Methods and Problems in Greek Science. Selected Papers.* Cambridge: Cambridge University Press.
Long, A.A. (1999): "The scope of early Greek philosophy". In: Long, A.A. (ed.): *The Cambridge Companion to Early Greek Philosophy.* Cambridge: Cambridge University Press, pp. 1-21.
Lovejoy, A.O. (1909): "The Meaning of Φύσις in the Greek Physiologers". *The Philosophical Review* 18, No 4: pp. 369-383.
Macé, A. (2012): "La naissance de la nature en Grèce ancienne". In: Haber, S. et Macé, A. (éds.): *Anciens et Modernes par-delà Nature et Société.* Presses Universitaires de Franche-Comté, pp. 47-84.
Männlein-Robert, I. (2019): "'Unsere φύσις' im Höhlengleichnis Platons". In: Koch, D., Männlein-Robert, I. und Weidtmann, N. (Hrsg.): *Platon und die Physis.* Tübingen: Mohr Siebeck, pp. 73-91.
Mannsperger, D. (1969): *Physis bei Platon.* Berlin: Walter de Gruyter & Co.
Martijn, M. (2010): *Proclus on Nature: Philosophy of Nature and Its Methods in Proclus' Commentary on Plato's Timaeus.* Philosophia Antiqua, Vol. 121. Leiden/Boston: Brill.
Mayhew, R. (2008): *Plato: Laws 10*, translated with an Introduction and Commentary. *Clarendon Plato Series.* Oxford: Clarendon Press.
McClure, M.T. (1934): "The Greek Conception of Nature". *The Philosophical Review* 43, No 2: pp. 109-124.
Naddaf, G. (2005): *The Greek Concept of Nature.* New York, Albany: State University of New York Press.
Palmer, J. (2019): "Presocratic Interest in the Soul's Persistence after Death". In: Sisko, J.E. (ed.): *Philosophy of Mind in Antiquity.* In: Copenhaver, R. and Shields, C. (General Editors): *The History of the Philosophy of Mind, Volume 1.* London and New York: Routledge, pp. 23-43.
Popper, K.R. (1998): *The World of Parmenides: Essays on the Presocratic Enlightenment.* Edited by A.F. Petersen with the assistance of J. Mejer. London and New York: Routledge.
Riedweg, C. (2005): *Pythagoras: His Life, Teaching and Influence.* Translated by S. Rendall in collaboration with C. Riedweg and A. Schatzmann. Ithaca and London: Cornell University Press.
Segev, M. (2017): "Aristotle on Nature, Human Nature and Human Understanding". *Rhizomata* 5, No 2: pp. 177-209. DOI:10.1515/rhiz-2017-0012
Sorabji, R. (2004): *The Philosophy of the Commentators, 200-600 AD, A Sourcebook*, Volume 2, Physics. Bloomsbury Academic.
Stevenson, L., Haberman, D.L., Wright, P.M., Witt, C. (2017): *Thirteen Theories of Human Nature.* New York, Oxford: Oxford University Press.
Tarrant, H. (2006): *Proclus. Commentary on Plato's Timaeus.* Volume I, Book I: *Proclus on the Socratic State and Atlantis.* Translated with an Introduction and Notes. With a General Introduction by D. Baltzly and H. Tarrant. Cambridge: Cambridge University Press.
Vlastos, G. (1973): *Platonic Studies.* Princeton: Princeton University Press.
Wilberding, J. (2022): "Nature: Plotinus' Fourth Hypostasis?". In: Gerson, L.P. and Wilberding, J. (eds): *The New Cambridge Companion to Plotinus.* Cambridge: Cambridge University Press, pp. 312-337.
Woodruff, P. (1999): "Rhetoric and relativism: Protagoras and Gorgias". In: Long, A.A. (ed.): *The Cambridge Companion to Early Greek Philosophy.* Cambridge: Cambridge University Press, pp. 290-310.
Zachhuber (2016), *Real Enzyclopädie für Antike und Christentum*, Vol. XXVII, coll. 744-781, s.v. Physis.

PART I

Classical Antiquity,
Late Antiquity and Byzantium

Phaedo of Elis, Physiognomy, and Human Nature in Plato's *Phaedo*

Claudia Marsico

University of Buenos Aires

Abstract

This paper examines the often-overlooked figure of Phaedo of Elis, the narrator of Plato's *Phaedo*, which recounts Socrates' final moments and his reflections on the immortality of the soul. While Phaedo may initially appear as a secondary figure, his presence is far more significant. The study aims to elucidate Phaedo's relevance for understanding the conceptual background of Plato's philosophical strategy in the Phaedo. The paper is divided into three main sections. First, I will explore the role of physiognomy in ancient debates on human nature, providing the contextual foundation for situating Phaedo's character. Second, I will analyze Phaedo's views on the relationship between body and soul as outlined in the *Zopyrus*, offering insights into Phaedo's personal and philosophical identity. Finally, I will examine specific passages in Plato's *Phaedo* to consider why Plato might have chosen Phaedo as the narrator of this dialogue. Through this inquiry, the significance of Phaedo's role will be reassessed, shedding new light on his intellectual position within the Socratic circle.

Plato's *Phaedo* recounts Socrates' final moments and his reflections on the immortality of the soul. Curiously, the figure of Phaedo of Elis, the dialogue's narrator, has received minimal scholarly attention. Often reduced to the image of the grieving young man whose hair Socrates touches affectionately in *Phaedo* 89b-c, Phaedo appears as a vivid yet secondary character in the narrative surrounding the death of the totemic father of philosophy. However, a closer inspection reveals a more complex and significant figure, challenging this conventional impression. This paper seeks to reassess Phaedo's role from an unconventional perspective. It will begin by discussing the role of physiognomy in classical-era debates on human nature. The analysis will then turn to Phaedo's character and his philosophical views on the body and soul, as presented in the *Zopyrus*. Finally, building on these insights, the paper will investigate key aspects of Plato's *Phaedo* to elucidate why Plato may have chosen this particular companion as the narrative's central figure.

1. The Horizon of Ancient Anthropology

Discussions on nature become especially contentious when they deal with human beings. Numerous well-known studies have examined the underlying assumptions of Homer's works, where *psykhe* and *soma* did not carry the meaning they would later acquire in the classical period. Initially, *psykhe* referred to the breath that escapes through the mouth at the

in: Mouzala, M.G. (ed.) 2025: *Nature and Human Nature in Ancient Greek Philosophy and Its Reception.* Leiden: Sidestone Press, pp. 23-34.

moment of death; only later did it evolve to denote the soul or mind. Similarly, *soma*, which originally signified corpse, came to represent the body. While both terms are rooted in the experience of death, they encapsulate interrelated yet contrasting conceptual units that seek to illuminate the mental and physical dimensions of human existence. These early notions diverge significantly from the more widespread terms used to describe mental functions and bodily parts in the context of living individuals, suggesting a complex historical process that ultimately gave rise to a dualistic framework.[1]

However, the evolutionary narrative that posits a complete and linear transformation is overly simplistic. Contrary to common assumptions, significant elements of the earlier model persist well beyond the archaic period, albeit in partial or residual forms. For instance, magical practices in the fifth and fourth centuries BCE continued to employ conceptual frameworks inconsistent with a fully developed dualism.[2] This persistence is also evident within the Socratic philosophies. Among its diverse implications, one particularly noteworthy aspect is the presence of corporal models in the thought of Aristippus and Antisthenes. In Aristippus' approach, bodily functions assume primacy, while mechanisms typically associated with the soul are regarded as derivative. Here, the individual is primarily understood as a body whose constitution is oriented towards two fundamental affections -pleasure and pain- conceived in a physicalist manner as bodily dispositions. These affections are not identified through mental reflection but through an "inner touch".[3] Beyond the five outwardly directed senses, this internal sense monitors the body, registering its interactions with external stimuli that evoke pleasure or pain. The subsequent behavioral responses are guided by the pursuit of pleasurable encounters and the avoidance of painful ones. While occasional references to the soul as the final stage of this process can be found, these do not imply a dualistic framework. Similarly, Antisthenes advocates for a metaphysical corporealism rooted in concrete, qualified realities. Within this perspective, the concept of *psykhe* retains a concrete meaning that renders the opposition between physical and mental categories largely irrelevant.

These views stand in marked contrast to Plato's perspective in the *Phaedo*, whose dualistic framework attains a high level of philosophical sophistication and has traditionally garnered the most scholarly attention. However, beyond this well-known philosophical model, there exists a more rudimentary, almost commonsensical, version of dualism closely related to this discussion. This simpler dualistic assumption emerges in physiognomy, which regards the body as a visible sign of an underlying, non-bodily dimension –such as an individual's character. Certain perspectives, including that of Phaedo of Elis, as will be discussed later, underscore physiognomy's role in revealing the inseparable connection between physical and mental dimensions.

Before delving further into this connection, however, it is worth posing a preliminary question: What is physiognomy? Commonly defined as the interpretation of bodily signs, physiognomy has ancient roots in Eastern traditions, yet its development in ancient Greece took on distinctive characteristics. In its Eastern manifestations, physiognomy primarily served as a form of divination, observing bodily features to predict an individual's future. As such, it was less concerned with human nature or with the ontological relationship between physical and mental dimensions, focusing instead on life's temporal flow and the unfolding of destiny. By contrast, Greek physiognomy dispensed with this divinatory orientation. The physical features of an individual were not examined to foretell the future but to gain insight into their character through systematic inferences from observable traits. In this sense, physiognomy intersected with the domain of philosophical anthropology, as it sought to uncover the underlying nature of the human being by reading the body as a meaningful, expressive surface.

Against this historical backdrop of physiognomy, it is difficult not to recall the Greeks concept of *kalokagathia*, which equates beauty with virtue, treating them as two sides of the same coin.[4] This notion is not a recent import from the East. It is already present in Homeric literature, where physical and mental attributes appear closely intertwined. For instance, in *Il.* 13.276-286, bravery and cowardice are discerned through facial expressions, while Thersites' boldness in *Il.* 2.211-277 is explicitly linked to his physical ugliness. However, it is crucial to distinguish physiognomy from mere physical description. The portrayal of fear, for instance, does not necessarily imply physiognomic reasoning, and attributes like beauty or refined manners often reflect social status rather than inherent character traits. Thersites' behavior, perceived as inappropriate, stems not from any physiognomic principle but from his non-noble status within a society that regarded *kalokagathia* as a defining trait of the aristocratic elite. Thus, while these associations provide contextual background, they should not be overstated or prematurely labeled as physiognomic evidence.[5] Physiognomy, as a systematic practice, emerged later and owed much to foreign influence.[6]

1 See the traditional work of Snell (1953), pp. 5-23, and the more recent explorations of Bremmer (1983) and (2020).

2 See my research on this topic in Marsico (2018).

3 See Cicero, *Acad.* 2.24.76 (SSR, IV.A.209).

4 On this notion, see Holmes (2010), Konstan (2017), pp. 80-84, Nikityuk (2019), pp. 429-442, and Stavru (2021), pp. 4-17.

5 On this view, see, e.g., Sassi (2021), p. 15. See also Tsouna (1998).

6 Although the Greeks often sought the origin of their cultural developments abroad (see Cherniss (1957), this seems to be the case regarding the birth of physiognomy.

The philosophical interest in this practice is evident in various accounts. Pythagoras, for instance, is said to have applied physiognomic criteria when selecting his disciples –a knowledge purportedly acquired through contact with Near Eastern traditions.[7] While the available testimonies are late and of questionable reliability, they nonetheless suggest that the practice was learned, used, and transmitted prior to the classical period. This interest intensified significantly in the fourth century BCE, a time of considerable philosophical innovation when physiognomy gained remarkable prominence.

While Plato's perspective on physiognomy remains the most extensively studied, it is noteworthy that the entire Socratic circle appear to have shown interest in this field. Antisthenes, for instance, authored a work titled *Physiognomic*, or *On the physiognomist sophists*.[8] Although only scant references to this text survive, its very existence suggests a theoretical engagement with the subject and hints at the existence of a "professional" profile offering physiognomic services. Unfortunately, the content of this work remains elusive, leaving scholars to rely on conjectures. Tsouna, for instance, suggests that the book might have constituted a critique of physiognomic arguments,[9] while Boys-Stones proposes a broader interpretation, considering it a philosophical investigation into the practice.[10] This ambiguity surrounding these interpretations is understandable, given that our knowledge rests on a single fragment. In this fragment, Athenaeus, while cataloging animal names, mentions the terms *delfax* and *delfakion* referring to pigs and cites Antisthenes' *Physiognomic* as stating that "the tavern girls stuff the piglets (*delfakia*)".[11] The precise function of this statement within the text remains unclear, but it may have served as part of an analogy using animal behavior to illustrate human characteristics –a common strategy in later physiognomic treatises.[12]

Moreover, physiognomy, as one of the many methods for understanding nature that flourished during the classical period, also sought recognition as a legitimate technical discipline. Similar patterns of professionalization can be observed across various fields of knowledge. This is evident in rhetoric, as exemplified by Gorgias' attempts to elevate rhetorical practice; in medicine, through numerous Hippocratic texts that emphasize methodical diagnosis; and among the mathematicians, who sought to develop more systematic explanatory frameworks.[13] Even in historical inquiry, this trend is apparent: Thucydides, for instance, stresses the importance of *tekmeria* (evidential signs) in *Histories* 1.21, advocating for precision and empirical grounding in the reconstruction of past events.[14]

Still, not all practices that sought to establish themselves as *tekhnai* succeeded. Divination, for instance, often referred to in ancient texts as *mantike tekhne*, enjoyed periods of high prestige before ultimately being dismissed as mere quackery.[15] However, dismissing such practices outright as pseudoscientific overlooks the opportunity to examine processes of incomplete technification. It also reveals anachronistic assumptions about the nature of science in antiquity, which operated under more flexible parameters than modern standards. The recognition of scientific rigor for certain practices often depended less on their inherent qualities than on the broader epistemic frameworks in which they were situated –frameworks that shifted over time.

Physiognomy represents another case of an unsuccessful bid for technical status. It sought legitimacy as a method for understanding nature but ultimately faltered in its pursuit. Why did it fail? One key factor was its conceptual overlap with other, more firmly established disciplines, particularly medicine. Medical theory, especially the humoral model, shared several of physiognomy's core premises.[16] Texts such as *Epidemics* 2.5.1 and 2.6.1, *Airs, Waters, and Places* 24, and *On diet* 1.28 demonstrate how medical approaches integrated climatic and physical characteristics to identify patterns of disease. In comparison, physiognomy emerges as the weaker, more speculative counterpart.

Its most solid attempt to codify physiognomy as *tekhne* is found in a treatise preserved in the Aristotelian *corpus*. This text focuses on physical affections (*pathemata*) as signs (*semeia*) of mental dispositions (*dianoiai*) (805a1 ff.),[17] and it provides a taxonomy of character traits based on bodily features. Although the treatise was not written by Aristotle himself,[18] it aligns with certain passages that

7 Aulus Gellius, *Noctes Atticae* 1.9.

8 Perhaps also the Magus, which dealt with oriental themes and mentions Zoroaster, could deal with these themes, especially since as alternative authors the *Suda* mentions Aristotle, as well as Antisthenes of Rhodes.

9 Tsouna (1998), p. 181.

10 Boys-Stones (2007), p. 23.

11 Athenaeus, 14.656f (SSR, V.A.62). The manuscripts attribute the fragment to Antiphanes, but Dindorf was right in changing the name to Antisthenes, which is customary now.

12 On Antisthenes' use of animal metaphors, see Marsico (2024). In this vein, it is also worth mentioning the Stoics, as they asserted to follow Antisthenes' ideas. Diogenes Laertius 7.173 attests to this link and claims that Zeno was able to infer human character from appearance, i.e., have some kind of physiognomic expertise.

13 On the case of mathematics, see Eggers Lan (1995).

14 On the history as a *tekhne*, see Hartog (2000).

15 On divination as a tekhne, see Johnston *et al.* (2009), pp. 139-144 and Addey (2022).

16 Galen, *Plac.* 4 and 7.

17 See the parallel with the link between reality, thought, and language in the beginning of *De interpretatione*. About this issue, see Sadun Bordoni (1994).

18 After this attempt, we must wait until the work of Polemon in the 2nd century AD, reconstructed in an indirect way, which increased the case studies. See Swain and van Bladel (2008).

suggest his familiarity with physiognomic reasoning. In *Prior Analytics* 2.27, 70b7-35, for example, Aristotle uses physiognomy to illustrate the enthymeme as a form of inference from signs, noting that through this procedure *physiognomonein* (physiognomic judgment) is indeed possible.[19] Similarly, in *De Generatione Animalium*, when discussing embryonic anomalies that resemble animals, Aristotle asserts that these cases involve similarity but not coexistence of different species and refers to a physiognomist who "reduces all faces to two or three animals".[20] This example functions only because Aristotle's audience was already acquainted with physiognomic practices, indicating the degree to which these ideas had permeated intellectual discourse, despite their eventual decline as a recognized discipline.

This brings us to the case of Phaedo of Elis, who led a Socratic group that remained active for many years.[21] Among his works was the *Zopyrus*, named after a Persian physiognomist who came to Athens claiming the ability to determine a person's character from their bodily features. Zopyrus is the protagonist of one of the most well-known anecdotes about Socrates. After demonstrating his skills, Socrates' friends brought him before Socrates, likely considering him a challenging subject for the physiognomist's craft. Indeed, Zopyrus concluded that Socrates was utterly vicious. The audience, consisting of Socrates' close companions –eyewitnesses of his virtuous life– responded with laughter and mockery. Yet, instead of dismissing the physiognomist's claims, Socrates agreed with them, affirming that he did, in fact, possess such vices, but had mastered them through self-discipline.

While the anecdote foregrounds the theme of self-control (*enkrateia*), it also concerns the status of Zopyrus' *tekhne*. Because Socrates does not reject the physiognomist's judgment, some scholars have suggested that Phaedo supported physiognomy.[22] In my view, however, the opposite seems more plausible. This anecdote should not be considered in isolation but within the broader context of the dialogue's philosophical aims. If Phaedo adhered to a worldview aligned with physiognomic principles, this interpretation might hold. However, the available evidence suggests otherwise. On the contrary, *Zopyrus* appears to critique physiognomy by proposing a different model centered on bodily tendencies, stressing that reason and willpower can override such inclinations. I will analyze the relevant passages supporting this approach, but first, we must consider the peculiar descriptions of Socrates' physical appearance and their relevance in this discussion.

Literary sources provide numerous examples of dissonance between bodily appearance and character. For instance, in *Iliad* 2.672-5, Nireus is described as beautiful but weak; similarly, in *Oddyssey* 8.165-77, Euryalus is depicted as handsome yet ineloquent. Comparable discrepancies appear within the Socratic circle. Alcibiades, for instance, was physically attractive but morally misguided,[23] while Theodorus was intellectually lucid despite his ugliness.[24] Socrates himself is traditionally portrayed as ugly, his outward appearance contrasting sharply with the inner virtues of his character –an apparent challenge to the assumptions underlying *kalokagathia*. As noted earlier, we must be cautious when interpreting Homeric passages through a physiognomic lens. Nevertheless, by the classical period, physiognomy was already widespread, and Socrates' unconventional appearance could have posed a direct challenge to its premises. Ultimately, Zopyrus fell into this trap, judging Socrates as a vicious man based solely on his physical features. Yet, it is worth recalling that Aristoxenus presents a markedly different portrayal of Socrates –one that is far less flattering. Aristoxenus describes Socrates as "uneducated, ignorant and lacking self-control".[25] Some scholars dismiss this testimony as the product of a hostile source. However, Plutarch cites Aristoxenus as credible, noting that after listing Socrates' negative traits, he added that "there was no injustice involved".[26] Aristoxenus' claim that Socrates was uneducated and ignorant may refer to his late intellectual development and his initial training in a manual craft. What stands out most, however, is the assertion of Socrates' lack of self-control –an evaluation that directly contradicts his traditional image as a parangon of intellectual self-mastery. Interestingly, in this view, rather than embodying philosophical intellectualism, Socrates appears as a paradigm of *akrasia*.[27]

How should this trait be interpreted? Aristoxenus, drawing on the direct testimony of his father, provides a broader outline: "This man said that he at least had not encountered many men who were more persuasive, such was both his voice and his speech and the character manifest in them, and in addition to all the things mentioned, his singular appearance. This occurred when he was not angry, but when he was inflamed by this emotion, his lack of decorum and disfigurement was terrible, for he did not refrain from any word or action".[28]

19 See Lampinen (2022), pp. 13-14 and Izaguirre (2021).

20 *De Gen. An.* 4.3, 769b20.

21 About Phaedo's group, see Marsico (2014) and Di Lanzo (2017), pp. 221-234.

22 See, for instance, Sassi (2021), pp. 15-16.

23 See, e.g., Plato, *Symposium*, 215-216. On the case of Socrates, see also Stavru (2018b).

24 See, e.g., Plato, *Theetetus*, 143e.

25 *On the malignity of Herodotus* 9.856c-d; fr. 55 Wehrli.

26 *On the malignity of Herodotus* 9.856c-d; fr. 55 Wehrli.

27 Aristotle notes that Socratic intellectualism, at least in Plato's version, could not account for *akrasia*, which makes this point curious. On this point, see Destrée (2002), pp. 139-165.

28 Fr. 54a Wehrli; Cyril of Alexandria, *Against Julian* 6.185). On the reliability of Aristoxenus as a source, see Huffman (2012), pp. 251-282 and Stavru (2018a), pp. 623-664.

This testimony underscores Socrates' singular appearance (*he tou eidous idiotes*), which is best understood not merely as ugliness but as a distinctive physical presence that defied conventional standards of beauty. His character, according to this account, aligned with a persuasive voice and speech, suggesting a certain inner harmony or at least a compelling rhetorical influence. This profile is consistent with the image cultivated in the *sokratikoi logoi*. Yet Aristoxenus also highlights Socrates' bouts of rage (*orge*)-emotional episodes that triggered *deine askhemosune*, a "terrible disfigurement", marked by uncontrolled words and actions. In modern terms, one might recall Dr. Jeckyll transformation into Mr. Hyde.

This duality lies at the heart of Phaedo's *Zopyrus*, which explores human nature and the conditions that make such transformations possible. In keeping with the dialogical format characteristic of Socratic literature, Socrates refutes his interlocutor –in this case, the Persian physiognomist– to challenge and ultimately correct his assumptions about the relationship between appearance and conduct. In this vein, Rossetti describes the dialogue as offering a personal revelation from Socrates about his way of life, considering this the primary value of the preserved fragments. Yet the two interrelated aspects deserve closer attention.[29] First, Zopyrus showcases the epistemic ambitions of physiognomy while presenting Phaedo's implicit denial of bodily determinism. The dialogue thus stages a clash between the physiognomist's technical claims and Socratic philosophical principles, ultimately demonstrating the limitations of physiognomy's predictive capacities. Second, the anecdote may have served as strategic response to accusations regarding Socrates' supposed lack of self-control. While Socratic texts rarely address such criticisms –likely because their authors sought to minimize reference to Socrates' outbursts– this silence does not preclude the possibility of such behaviors. Phaedo, by contrast, may have chosen to confront the issue directly, portraying Socrates' temperament as a natural tendency that he successfully mastered through philosophical discipline. If this interpretation is correct, then even those familiar with Socrates' occasional lapses could reinterpret these episodes as early challenges in a broader narrative of moral self-improvement. Zopyrus' verdict highlights Socrates' predisposition to vicious tendencies, while his friends attest to his virtuous character. Socrates himself resolves this tension by explaining that his virtue stems from the mastery of his baser inclinations, thus dissolving the image of Mr. Hyde and recasting him as a spiritual exemplar.

A brief passage from Xenophon's *Memorabilia* aligns with this reading. In discussing Socrates' views on violence against parents, Xenophon acknowledges that some of Socrates' statements might be construed as condoning such behavior but then offers alternative explanations to protect his reputation.[30] Similarly, the *Zopyrus* seems to address doubts about Socrates' self-control, depicting it not as an innate moral deficiency but as a persistent inclination that he ultimately overcame. If so, in my view, the introspective insights recognized by Rossetti should be understood as part of a broader apologetic strategy. Phaedo, through this dialogue, defends Socrates' character while simultaneously discrediting physiognomy's scientific pretensions, thereby affirming the superiority of philosophical inquiry over physiognomic determinism.

2. Phaedo's anthropology

Let us now analyse the testimonies about Zopyrus in order to infer Phaedo's view of human nature. The first point to note is that the figure of Zopyrus aligns with the principles of Greek physiognomy rather than with the version attributed to Aristotle by Diogenes Laertius (2.45). Diogenes mentions a Syrian magician who allegedly predicted Socrates' violent death –an account that more closely reflects Eastern divinatory practices than the systematic procedures of Greek physiognomic tradition.[31] This consistency with "technical physiognomy" supports the hypothesis that Phaedo intended to critique this discipline by offering an alternative explanation of the origins of human actions and character.

The anecdote of Socrates' encounter with Zopyrus survives in three primary versions: two transmitted by Cicero and the one by Alexander of Aphrodisias. In Cicero's accounts, nature appears as an immutable horizon, resistant to alteration and only capable of being restrained. Yet the mechanisms for such restraint differ between the two versions. In the *Tusculan Disputations*, Socrates acknowledges the presence of vicious inclinations within himself but asserts that reason enabled him to control them,[32] positioning rational insight as the decisive factor. While it might be excessive to claim a strict alignment with Plato's Socratic intellectualism –according to which knowledge of the good ensures virtuous behavior– there is nonetheless a conceptual resonance between the two perspectives. By contrast, *De fato* underscores the role of emotional education in the development of moderation and self-restraint. Here, Cicero posits that vices arise from natural causes but can be mitigated "through willpower, dedication, and discipline".[33] This framework,

29 Rossetti (2015), pp. 82-98.

30 Xen. *Mem.* 1.49.

31 The variation should not be surprising, if we think that the daimon of Socrates in Plato is a dissuasive voice, while in Xenophon functions as a private oracle that even serves as an answer for the life of Socrates' relatives. See *Apol.*, 10 and *Mem*, 1.3.

32 Cicero, *Tusc.* 4.80 (Fr. 7 Rossetti).

33 Cicero, *On Fate*, 10 (FS, 1073; Frag. 6 Rossetti).

therefore, privileges self-mastery over the intellectualist assumption that grasping the good inevitably leads to its pursuit. Alexander of Aphrodisias presents yet another interpretation. He depicts nature not as a static foundation but as a malleable disposition, capable of being altered through sustained effort. In Alexander's account, Socrates refrains from accusing Zopyrus of deceit, noting that he would indeed have been "evil if through exercise in philosophy he had not improved his nature".[34] This version shifts the explanatory focus from inherent anthropological characteristics to the deliberate, transformative intervention to reshape behavior. Unlike *De Fato*, Alexander does not emphasize the cultivation of willpower but rather underscores the role of philosophical practice in altering natural tendencies. This perspective may also suggest a broader, more dynamic conception of human nature.

Beyond these accounts, two passages from Phaedo's *Zopyrus* provide additional, though somewhat opaque, insights into his view of the soul and its capacity to overcome innate inclinations. One such passage, preserved by the grammarian Theon, recounts the story of a Persian prince who raised a lion cub. The lion, having grown up in close companionship with the boy, followed him with remarkable loyalty. The Persians, impressed by this unusual behavior, remarked that the lion loved the prince.[35] Interpreting the significance of this anecdote remains challenging due to the lack of the context. It could simply be a passing illustration with no direct connection to Phaedo's views on character formation. However, the story may also serve as an analogy for the malleability of natural dispositions. The lion, despite its instinctual wildness, exhibited behavior incongruous with its nature –an outcome plausibly attributed to its upbringing. By extension, this account suggests that human inclinations, like those of animals, can be reoriented through education. The parallel with Plato's *Alcibiades* is striking.[36] Just as the lion cub transitions from wildness to docility, Alcibiades, one a pliant student, becomes increasingly ungovernable. The symbolic resonance may not be coincidental, especially given that Zopyrus was also the name of Alcibiades' tutor.[37] If so, this dialogue might subtly invoke this transformation to underscore the pivotal role of education in shaping character.

This view aligns with other testimonies regarding Phaedo's philosophical stance, particularly his emphasis on the cathartic function of philosophy. These accounts underscore the transformative power of philosophical practice, which can effect change even in individuals considered to have a "bad nature".[38] From this optimistic viewpoint, we can infer a positive position regarding the teachability of virtue. Philosophy's purifying role, along with the influence of educators who, like unnoticed insect stings, initiate change without the subject's immediate awareness,[39] reveals a confident outlook on the transmission of moral excellence. This confidence stands in marked contrast to the more skeptical views held by other Socratic followers. However, the sting analogy raises a fundamental question: does philosophy alter the very essence of the soul, or does it merely redirect its inclinations while leaving its nature intact? The latter interpretation appears more plausible, suggesting that each individual harbors a nature dominated by irrational desires that can nonetheless be reshaped through intellectual and moral cultivation. Thus, behavior is not dictated solely by innate tendencies; rather, it can be reoriented through interventions that modify that root and strengthen the soul's authority over the body.

Although applying contemporary conceptual frameworks to ancient thought carries certain risks, doing so may illuminate the theoretical stakes involved. In this regard, we might consider the three options outlined by Boys-Stones.[40] One of these suggests that Phaedo might have endorsed a dualistic view in which the physical body stands in opposition to a soul composed of both reason and desire. Within this framework, the soul appears as a bipartite entity, with desire systematically aligned with the body in opposition to reason. Against this interpretation, Boys-Stones argues that such a view fails to sufficiently distinguish the desiring part of the soul from the body.[41] Furthermore, one might add that the focus on specific processes and associations should not take precedence over a more fundamental explanation of the relationship between soul and body.

Another possibility is that Phaedo espoused a form of emergentism, in which psychological functions, though grounded in physical processes, constitute a distinct ontological level governed by its own principles and rules. Boys-Stones dismisses this option, arguing that emergentist views did not exist prior to Aristotle, who introduced the conception of the soul as the form of the body.[42] Only within this Aristotelian framework, he suggests, did theories along these lines begin to appear. Moreover, such a view would be incompatible with the notion of independent reason,

34 Alexander of Aphrodisias, *On Fate* 6 (FS, 1075; Frag. 10 Rossetti).

35 Theon, *On the Preparatory Exercises*, 3.74.21-75.9 (FS, 1066; SSR, III.A.11; Frag. 1 Rossetti).

36 See, for instance, Aristophanes, *Frogs* 1430-1433, where Aeschylus and Euripides are contenders for the throne of the poets in Hades, and debate about what to do with Alcibiades. Aeschylus' response states that "it is not convenient to raise a lion's cub in the city, but if we let it grow up we must put up with its temper".

37 On this point, see Marsico (2022).

38 Julian, *Letters*, 59 Hertlein [= 82 Bidez Cumont] p. 445a (FS, 1079; SSR, III.A.2).

39 Seneca, *Letter to Lucilius*, XV.2 [= XCIV], 41 (FS, 1080; SSR, III.A.12).

40 See Boys-Stones (2004), pp. 13-15.

41 Boys-Stones (2004), p. 13.

42 Boys-Stones (2004), p. 13.

which is attested in sources such as Cicero's account of Socrates' explanation of Zopyrus' judgement.[43]

These arguments, however, are not entirely conclusive. There is no inherent reason why Aristotle's model could not have been preceded by related, albeit less systematic, accounts. As for the second claim, traditional epiphenomenalist emergentism –often illustrated by the metaphor of smoke trailing behind a locomotive, a mere byproduct devoid of causal efficacy– indeed excludes the agency of mental states.[44] If this were the only possible form of emergentism, it would be ill-suited to Phaedo's approach, which explicitly engages with questions of causality and agency of mental phenomena over the body. However, this is not the only variant. For instance, Phaedo's perspective may align more closely with a form of emergentism akin to property dualism, in which mental properties inhere in physical structures without being reducible to them. Still, if so, his position would resemble the soul-harmony theory more closely than the doctrine of an immortal, incorporeal soul –an interpretation that, while not impossible, would introduce a notable tension in the Plato's *Phaedo*, as Boys–Stones rightly observes.[45] Indeed, it would be peculiar for Plato to attribute to Phaedo an account that so openly conflicts with his own metaphysical framework without offering any indication of disagreement or critique,[46] especially considering that the soul-harmony argument is deeply intertwined with Orphic elements and appears to be rejected by both Plato and Phaedo.[47]

A third, intermediate possibility is also considered by Boys-Stones.[48] Within the lines of a partial emergentism, human beings are composites of rational soul and body, whith desires as epiphenomena that oppose reason and interfere with its designs. However, if the soul is reduced solely to rationality, this reading entails an overly complex structure, requiring a duplication of soul levels –one autonomous and rational, the other epiphenomenal and desiring. More problematically, the sources repeatedly insist on the role of will and effort, aspects that can hardly be reduced to pure reason. These elements also involve emotional dimensions that are activated through philosophical practice, which would be difficult to accommodate within this model.

Considering these issues, it is preferable to distance oneself from these three variants. Indeed, Phaedo's position seem to align more closely with a fourth option, one associated with a form of interactionist dualism, in which soul and body exert mutual influence. In this framework, the soul can modify the body –not in its physical appearance, but in its modes of interactions with the world. The distinction between them is preserved, thereby excluding views related to neutral monism. The soul and body remain distinct entities, and the soul retains the capacity to subsist independently after its separation from the body. This interpretation is consistent with the available testimonies, as it acknowledges both the bodily nature of human desires and the autonomy of the soul, which is rooted in reason and will. Furthermore, it accounts for the soul's ability to introduce lasting changes in behavior.

While this perspective presupposes a form of dualism, akin to Boys-Stones' first option, it does not entail a strict portioning of the soul into discrete parts and the association of one of them with the body. Rather, it emphasizes the dynamic relationship between bodily dispositions and patterns of the soul, a connection that justifies the discussion of physiognomy. However, it simultaneously argues that this link is not fixed and that the soul remains independent, often in a state of tension with the body. This interactionist framework makes possible Phaedo's contribution to the distinctively intra-Socratic discussion of self-control (*enkrateia*), which, in this view, emerges as the resolution of the conflict between body and soul through the soul's dominance over the bodily desires that express its material inclinations.

This interpretation is particularly significant because it positions Phaedo as a distant precursor to the debates later revisited by Descartes, particularly concerning the interaction between body and mind despite their ontological disparity. In this light, Princess Elizabeth of Bohemia's famous objection to Descartes –how can an immaterial entity exert influence on a material body?–[49] could also be posed to Phaedo's position. However, unlike Descartes, Phaedo does not provide a mechanistic account, such as the theory of the pineal gland, to explain this interaction. The absence of any such explanation in the extant sources suggests that, had such a theory existed, later authors would likely have referenced it. Nonetheless, Phaedo's perspective remains a valuable contribution to ancient anthropology. If this interpretation holds, it follows that physiognomy is inadequate for explaining this framework. That is why the *Zopyrus* cannot be construed as a justification of physiognomic practice, nor can Phaedo be regarded as an advocate of such activities. The fundamental presupposition of physiognomy –namely, a fixed correspondence between bodily traits and moral character– fails to account for the moral conflict at the heart of Phaedo's argument. That conflict can only be resolved through *enkrateia*, which, within this dualistic

43 See Sharples (2001), pp. 143-173 and Caston (1997), pp. 309-354.

44 See Chan (2003), pp. 56-59.

45 Boys-Stones (2004), p. 14.

46 On the soul as harmony, see Gottschalk (1971), pp. 179-198 and Taylor (2001), pp. 51-97.

47 On Orphic and Pythagorean ideas in the *Phaedo*, see Casadesús (2013), pp. 153-176 and Ebrey (2017), pp. 1-30.

48 Boys-Stones (2004), p. 14.

49 See Rozemond (1999) and Garber (2013).

model, emerges from the interaction between soul and body. Physiognomy, by contrast, lacks the conceptual tools to grasp the complexities of human nature. In line with Alexander's testimony, only philosophy provides the means to achieve self-mastery and to comprehend the nature of moral conduct itself.

3. Phaedo in the *Phaedo*

Against this background, let us now consider why Plato might have attributed to Phaedo of Elis the account of Socrates' final philosophical exercise, which is concerned precisely with human nature. To begin with, it is worth examining his biography. Several sources recount a lurid story of his early life: a young nobleman from Elis, captured in war, turned into a prisoner and subsequently subjected to human trafficking, enslaved in a brothel for ephebes until he was finally freed through Socrates' intervention.[50] These events alone justify the prominent role assigned to him in the dialogue. The work underscores the distinction between soul and body as a means of accessing the intelligible realm, insisting on the disruptive and enslaving nature of the body and the senses. Having a former slave –one whose own body literally suffered abuse– articulate this argument lends it far greater force. Phaedo experienced firsthand the dehumanizing effects of bodily enslavement and, in turn, recognized that this condition is not, as one might assume, unique to those in bondage. Most people are similarly enslaved –ruled by the tyranny of their own bodies, driven by desires and whims. The question, then, is whether Phaedo's role in the dialogue is merely symbolic or whether his portrayal carries deeper significance. Is he included simply as a vivid narrative device, or is his presence essential to the dialogue's philosophical architecture? I will argue that it is the latter.

Plato's dialogues are populated with intellectual figures, yet Phaedo is the only one among those who later founded their own philosophical groups whom Plato not only mentions but elevates to the role of narrator. Antisthenes, Aeschines, Simon the Shoemaker, and Aristippus are entirely absent, while Euclid reserves only a brief reference.[51] This makes Phaedo an excepcional case. Given that his enduring fame would have been difficult to predict at the time, his presence in the dialogue is intriguing and invites explanation. A plausible hypothesis is that his philosophical contributions were highly relevant to the discussion of human nature and immortality. Plato may have perceived his ideas as significant rival positions -akin to Gorgias' tenets about the rhetoric in the *Gorgias*- or as perspectives with potential affinities to his own. Resolving this question, however, is fraught with the risk of circular reasoning. Our knowledge of Phaedo's own philosophy is limited, and Plato's views on psychology and anthropology remain far from settled. In this regard, Boys-Stones' suggestion that the Phaedo can serve as a reliable source for reconstructing Phaedo of Elis' ideas seems overly ambitious. How can we discern traces of Phaedo's ideas if we lack certainty about Plato's own position? A more cautious approach is to rely on independent sources, however fragmentary they may be.

Since this task has been undertaken in the previous section, we can now take a step further by recalling what has been said about other Socratic philosophies and their strong corporealist background. The scene in the *Phaedo* is particularly significant because it gathers many members of the Socratic circle for Socrates' final moments. These figures can be divided into three groups: those who remain silent or are merely mentioned, those who engage in direct philosophical dialogue with Socrates –such as Simmias and Cebes–, and those who interact with him on a more personal level, such as Crito and Phaedo, with the later recounting the episode. Crito, for his part, appears largely uninterested in theoretical questions. Even after Socrates' elaborate efforts to prove the immortality of the soul, Crito remains focused on the practical matter of his friend's burial. Yet his role is nonetheless significant: he represents care and loyalty, both towards Socrates and the broader Socratic circle. Notably, he was the one who secured Phaedo's liberation from slavery.[52] This connection between Crito and Phaedo suggests that Plato sought to underscore a distinct subgroup within the Socratic milieu.

What unites Simmias, Cebes, and Phaedo? They all reject corporealist views of human nature, making them well-suited as interlocutors who could support the dialogue's central theses. Let us look more closely at Phaedo's case. It is plausible that his dualistic anthropology aligned with the overarching aim of the dialogue –defending the immortality of the soul, understood as a disembodied essence in which personal identity resides. As we have seen, Phaedo's *Zopyrus* promotes philosophy as a means of caring for the soul. The same principle underlies Plato's *Phaedo*. Given the internal tensions within the group, Plato may have strategically associated himself with Phaedo to reinforce his own perspective, emphasizing their shared commitment to a non-corporealist anthropology. However, this does not imply that Phaedo adhered to the theory of Forms –an idea absent from the surviving testimonies– nor does it suggest that he and Plato were close associates within the group. Athenaeus, who held a highly negative view of Plato, often mocks the animosities he allegedly inspired among his peers. Among his anecdotes, he claims that Phaedo later denied having said what Plato attributed

50 See, e.g., Diogenes Laertius 1.105 (SSR, III.A.1, FS 1040) and Origen, *Contra Celsum* 1.64 (SSR, III.A.2, FS, 1043).

51 On the cross-mentions within the Socratic circle, see Marsico and Illarraga (2021).

52 On Crito's role within the Socratic circle, see Harte (1999), p. 140.

to him or even having participated in such discussions.[53] Athenaeus also accuses Plato of exploiting Phaedo's former enslavement, alleging that he "was caught in the act of instituting against Phaedo the lawsuit in which Phaedo was charged with being a slave"[54] –a cryptic claim that suggests some unknown conflict. Yet these accounts, whether exaggerated or reflective of genuine hostility, do not undermine the significance of Plato's choice. Regardless of their personal relations, Plato's decision to place Phaedo at the heart of the dialogue serves to highlight that his own philosophical stance was neither isolated nor without support. Moreover, this phenomenon –the construction of Socratic dialogues among figures who, in reality, may have profoundly disliked one another– remains one of the more intriguing aspects of the Socratic tradition.[55]

In the case of Simmias and Cebes, their association with Philolaus and Pythagoreanism firmly places them on the anti-corporealist side. While they were not heads of Socratic groups, they belonged to an influential intellectual circle in Italy, and Diogenes Laertius attests that they wrote dialogues, although none of these works have survived.[56] At the same time, Xenophon states in *Mem.* 3.11.17 that they frequently visited the *hetaira* Theodote. This anecdote underscores their entanglement with bodily desires and sexuality, a theme that also plays a central role in Phaedo's biography. If Crito was responsible for Phaedo's liberation, then these figures all seem to be linked by a shared concern with the problem of controlling bodily impulses.

Thus, the association of these characters in the *Phaedo* to portray an anti-corporealist Socrates is fully justified. If Plato's aim to emphasize the soul's independence from the body and its capacity to function beyond it, Phaedo's inclusion serves to reinforce this argument. It is ultimately irrelevant whether Phaedo's specific conception of the soul was identical to Plato's –we cannot ascertain how complex or nuanced his views were, nor whether he explicitly thematised its parts and functions. What mattered was to depict Socrates in dialogue with companions who all agreed on the immaterial nature of the soul. Simmias and Cebes function as the main interlocutors, while Phaedo serves as additional reinforcement for this consensus. Through this strategy, Plato presents himself not as an isolated figure attributing novel or idiosyncratic ideas to Socrates but as part of a broader intellectual group within the Socratic circle that shared a fundamental anti-corporealist perspective. Even though Plato was ill and absent during Socrates' final moments, those who were present –the main participants in the discussion– were sympathetic to his views. Furthermore, Phaedo's role as the narrator ensures that these ideas would continue to circulate beyond the immediate Socratic circle. Of course, this basic agreement concerning human nature is intertwined with Plato's theory of Forms, which Phaedo himself does not seem to have endorsed. This divergence could explain his later detachment from the *Phaedo*, as suggested in Athenaeus' testimony.

In Plato's *Phaedo*, a notable exchange occurs in 89b, where Socrates shows his closeness to Phaedo, his disciple, through an evocative reference to hair-cutting: "Today I too will cut off mine and you these, if the *logos* dies on us and we are not able to revive it." This curious statement, rich in interpretive possibilities, has elicited extensive scholarly debate. Beyond its various readings, the passage underscores Socrates' association of Phaedo with the shared endeavor of demonstrating the soul's immortality. Rather than merely illustrating Socrates' personal interest, this moment can also be understood as Plato stressing the significance of this philosophical question for Phaedo himself. Indeed, Phaedo's meticulous recounting of the discussion to Echecrates attests to his deep engagement with the subject. Through this reference, Plato positions Phaedo of Elis not merely as a passive observer but as an active participant who shares, at minimum, the purpose –if not certain convictions- that the dialogue attributes to Socrates.

This interpretation gains further traction when Phaedo responds to Socrates' call to revive the faltering argument. He cautions against the formidable challenge posed by Simmias and Cebes, remarking: "against two not even Heracles is capable" (89c). Socrates, in turn, invokes the myth of the Hydra, a creature whose menacing heads Heracles defeats only with the aid of his nephew Iolaus. This allusion is not unique to the *Phaedo*; Plato employs a similar scene in *Euthydemus* 297b-d to depict the struggle against eristic sophistry. The intertextual resonance suggests that objections to the soul's immortality –such as those raised by Simmias and Cebes– represent a comparable philosophical threat, one that demands a concerted effort to overcome. Significantly, when Phaedo offers himself as Socrates' Iolaus, Socrates responds with a nuanced distinction: "I call you, but not as Heracles, but as Iolaus to Heracles" (89c). This reply elevates Phaedo's role, casting him as a vital collaborator rather than a subordinate figure, a departure from the marginal status typically ascribed to him in the narrative. Two interpretive possibilities emerge from this exchange. On one hand, Socrates' remark might be a playful jest, marked by exaggerated humility and a whimsical elevation of a randomly chosen member of the group. On the other, it could reflect Plato's deliberate intent to foreground Phaedo's alignment with the dialogue's central problem, thereby acknowledging his intellectual investment in the

53 Athenaeus, 11.505e (SSR, III.A.5, FS 1050).

54 Athenaeus 11.507c (SSR III.4; FS, 1048)

55 On this point within the phenomenon of Socratic dialogue, see Marsico (2010).

56 Simmias is said to be the author of twenty-three works and Cebes of three in Diogenes Laertius 2.124-5.

question of the soul's nature. The latter reading aligns with Phaedo's role as the dialogue's narrator and suggests that Plato subtly credits him with a philosophical stature that complements Socrates' own.

It is further noteworthy that the well-known passage on the *misologoi* (89d-90e) –those who come to despise rational discourse– unfolds in the dialogue between Socrates and Phaedo. Here, Phaedo aligns himself with Socrates' cautionary stance against the perils of reckless application of dialectic, which risks fostering disillusionment with philosophical inquiry itself. Although this passage is commonly interpreted as a broad critique of sophistry, it also resonates with Socratic current tied to figures like the Megarians and Antisthenes.[57] In contrast to their approaches, Phaedo distinguishes himself by his proximity to Socrates, both in his anthropological outlook and his methodological commitments.

Plato's portrayal of Phaedo extends beyond this exchange, revealing additional dimensions of his character through recurring remarks on human nature and the interplay between soul and body. For instance, at 58e, when Echecrates presses Phaedo for details about Socrates' final moments, Phaedo's response foregrounds Socrates' physical demeanor. He focuses on Socrates' body. Adopting what might be described as a quasi-phenomenological perspective, Phaedo eschews expressions of pity or sorrow –emotions one might expect given the imminent death of his friend– and instead focuses on Socrates' outward expressions of tranquility and joy. As we have seen, Socrates' appearance contrasted with his virtuous character. Now we can add that his attitude contrasted sharply with conventional expectations of a condemned man, underscoring a disjunction between his physical state and his virtuous disposition. Far from succumbing to the violence of his circumstances, Socrates' serene conduct suggests an inner resilience that transcends bodily affliction, hinting at a deeper principle governing his behavior. Indeed, at 59a, Phaedo observes that Socrates' demeanor suspends the anticipated emotional responses among his companions, eliciting a complex blend of laughter and tears– a reaction echoed elsewhere, such as in 62e and 77e, where Phaedo highlights his moments of rejoicing. This atypical presentation, reminiscent of the anecdote involving Zopyrus, confounds onlookers and underscores the enigmatic quality of Socrates' character.

The role of the body is prominent in 60b-c, where Socrates reflects on the sensory confusion induced by the removal of his shackles. He notes that the cessation of pain manifests as pleasure, despite the absence of any inherently pleasurable stimulus. This observation frames pleasure and pain as two facets of a single bodily experience, a duality that the soul, in its capacity for discernment, can recognize as illusory. Such a perspective posits the soul's ability to distance itself from corporeal influence– a theme resonant with Phaedo's account that the lack of a cause for pain appears as a pleasure, although there is nothing intrinsically pleasant. Therefore, the body makes pleasure and pain appear as two sides of one coin, while the soul can recognize this trait as an illusion. In this sense, the soul can take distance from the body. This is the same tenet we found in Phaedo's *Zopyrus*, which could suggest that Plato may have crafted his *Phaedo* with an eye to his companion's philosophical inclinations, leveraging Phaedo's ideas to bolster his own arguments. Further support for this interpretation appears in 82c-d, where Socrates described the ghosts lingering near tombs as souls transformed into material entities -an idea compatible with Phaedo's conception of distinct ontological dimensions. While Phaedo's anecdotes, such as those involving Zopyrus or the child and the lion, imply that the soul can achieve autonomy from bodily constraints, Plato's Socrates introduces a complementary possibility: that a soul, if sufficiently enfeebled, may lose its independent character and succumb to material influence. Together, these elements illuminate Phaedo's role not merely as a narrator but as a figure whose intellectual contributions enrich Plato's exploration of the soul-body relationship.

Another pivotal passage that foregrounds Phaedo's significance is the concluding scene of Socrates' death, encompassing the administration of hemlock and the disposition of his body (115b-118a). At 115b, Socrates advocates self-care –a theme central to the preceding discussion– within the framework of a dualistic soul-body paradigm. Consistent with this perspective, he later chastises Crito for his concern over funeral arrangements, declaring, "Once I have drunk the poison, I will no longer stay with you", and shortly afterwards "You bury my body only" (115d). Phaedo's narration then shifts to the reactions of those present, with particular attention to the physical progression of Socrates' death. In 117e-118a, the prison attendant confirms the poison's effect by noting Socrates' loss of sensation, a process culminating in the checking of his belly. At this moment, Socrates utters his enigmatic final words: "Crito, we owe a cock to Asclepius, so pay it and don't neglect it" (118a). While interpretive debates surrounding this statement -ranging from the notion that Asclepius cures Socrates of life to Wilamowitz's rejoinder that "neither life is a disease nor Asclepius cures evils of the soul"- are well-trodden, I will not linger on these competing speculations here, as they remain inconclusive.[58]

57 See Zilioli (2014), Brancacci (2023), and Chame (2024).

58 Among them, that it is a reference to Plato being cured of the illness that kept him away from this last meeting, or that it is a good thing that the poison did not bring complications. For a list of traditional and recent interpretations, see Ricciardone (2019) and Bossi (2019).

Instead, let us consider a plausible connection to Phaedo that emerges from this scene. The cock, symbol traditionally linked to transitions such as birth due its association with daybreak, aligns fittingly with Asclepius, the deity presiding over the passage from illness to health – a role not unrelated to Persephone and the underworld.[59] One might argue that Plato invokes the cock simply to underscore the irony of a man condemned for impiety dedicating his final words to a god. Yet a deeper resonance with Phaedo's earlier exchange with Socrates at 89b offers a more compelling reading. There, Socrates, grasping Phaedo's hair, jests that he would cut it in mourning "if the argument dies on us and we are not able to revive it". In his final moments, Socrates may recognize that the argument for the soul's immortality has been successfully "healed", allowing him to depart with equanimity, assured that only his body perishes. Asclepius, in this light, merits gratitude for overseeing the restoration of this philosophical discourse – a notion reinforced by the earlier allusion to Heracles and Iolaus at 89c, where Phaedo emerges as Socrates' vital collaborator. The constellation of references to Apollo, recalled in 58b, Heracles, and Asclepius, far from being discordant, frequently cohere,[60] mirroring the collective effort of Simmias, Cebes, and Phaedo alongside Plato to champion the soul's primacy.

In sum, Phaedo's prominence in the dialogue may reflect Plato's strategic alignment with a kindred thinker. If Phaedo indeed espoused a dualistic theory of the soul, as fragmentary evidence suggests, Plato's emphasis on him could represent a unification of philosophical voices affirming human nature's immaterial dimension and the soul's immortality. Although Phaedo's own works survive only in scant references, these traces indicate meaningful convergences with Platonic thought. Such affinities might account for the anthropological distinctions between the *Phaedo* and the *Republic*, potentially signaling that, in the former, Plato's intent to bridge divergent Socratic perspectives was at the foreground. Phaedo emerges as an ally in countering corporealist tendencies within the Socratic circle, earning him the role of narrator and spokesman. His account accentuates the shared commitments of these non-materialist positions, aligning Plato and Phaedo on the same philosophical front. This alignment may also explain why Athenaeus, or his source, familiar with Phaedo's writings, depicts him as distancing himself from the Platonic narrative – a portrayal that could reflect Phaedo's independent voice within a broader coalition. Thus, Phaedo's role serves as a tactical reinforcement of the non-corporealist "bloc" within the Socratic tradition, bolstering its stance on the relationship between nature and human existence.

Bibliography

Addey, C. (2022): "Introduction: divination and knowledge in ancient Greek and Roman cultures". In: Addey, C. (Ed.): *Divination and Knowledge in Greco-Roman Antiquity*. New York: Abingdon, pp. 1-20.

Bossi, B. (2019): "Back to the cock: On gratitude and care". In: Cornelli, G. *et al.* (eds.): *Plato's* Phaedo. Sankt Augustin: Academia Verlag, pp. 74-83.

Boys-Stones, G. (2007): "Physiognomy and ancient psychological theory". In: Swain, S. et al. (eds.): *Seeing the face, seeing the soul: Polemon's physiognomy from classical antiquity to medieval Islam*. Oxford: OUP, pp. 19-124.

Brancacci, A. (2023): "Language, definition and being in Antisthenes". *Rhizomata* 11, No 2: pp. 227-249.

Bremmer, J. (1983): *The early Greek concept of the soul.* Princeton, NJ: Princeton University Press.

Bremmer, J. (2020): *The World of Greek Religion and Mythology: Collected Essays II*. Tübingen: Mohr Siebeck.

Casadesús, F. (2013): "On the origin of the Orphic-Pythagorean notion of the immortality of the soul." In Cornelli, G. et al. (Eds): *On Pythagoreanism*. Berlin: De Gruyter, pp. 153-176.

59 On the rooster, see Cruccas (2016).

60 See Olivier Hekster (2002).

Caston, V. (1997): "Epiphenomenalisms, ancient and modern". *Philosophical Review* 106: pp. 309-354.

Chame, S. (2024): "Bryson of Heraclea and Polyxenus, Megarian philosophers". *Phronesis* 69, No 2: pp. 1-28.

Chan, M. (2003): "The challenge of materialism". In: Chan, P.: *The Mystery of Mind, A Systematic Account of the Human Mind Toward Understanding Its Own Realization*. New Hampshire: Iuniverse, pp. 56-59.

Cruccas, E. (2016): "Ὁ περσικὸς ὄρνις: The symbology of the rooster in the cult of the Kabiroi". In: Johnston, P. *et al.* (eds.): *Animals in Greek and Roman Religion and Myth*. Sankt Augustin: Academia Verlag, pp. 171-188.

Destrée, P. (2007): "Aristotle on the causes of akrasia". In: Bobonich, C. *et al.* (eds): *Akrasia in Greek Philosophy*. Leiden: Brill, pp. 139-165.

Di Lanzo, D. (2017): "Phaedo of Elis: The biography, Zopyrus, and his intellectual profile". In: Moore, C. *et al.*: *Socrates and the Socratic dialogue*. Leiden: Brill, pp. 221-234.

Ebrey, D. (2017): "The Asceticism of the Phaedo: Pleasure, Purification, and the Soul's Proper Activity". *Archiv für Geschichte der Philosophie* 99, No 1: pp. 1-30.

Eggers Lan, C. (1995): *El nacimiento de la matemática en Grecia*. Buenos Aires: Eudeba.

Garber, D. (2013): "Understanding Interaction: What Descartes Should Have Told Elisabeth". In:

Graukrober, S. et al. (eds.): *Debates in Modern Philosophy*. London: Routledge, pp. 35-53.
Gottschalk, H. (1971): "Soul as *Harmonia*". *Phronesis* 16, No 2: pp. 179-198.
Harte, V. (1999): "Conflicting Values in Plato's Crito". *Archiv für Geschichte der Philosophie* 81: pp. 117-147.
Hartog, F. (2000): "The Invention of History: The Pre-History of a Concept from Homer to Herodotus". *History and Theory* 39, No 3: pp. 384-395.
Hekster, O. (2002): "Of Mice and Emperors: A Note on Aelian *De natura animalium*". *Classical Philology* 97, No 4: pp. 365-370.
Holmes, B. (2010): *The Symptom and the Subject: The Emergence of the Physical Body in Ancient Greece*. Princeton/Oxford: Princeton University Press.
Huffman, C. (2012): "Aristoxenus' life of Socrates". In: Huffman, C. (ed.): *Aristoxenus of Tarentum. Discussion*. London: Transaction, pp. 251-282.
Izaguirre, J. (2021): "Persuasion's physique: Revisiting sign-inference in Aristotle's rhetoric". *Rhetoric Review* 40, No 4: pp. 349-362.
Johnston, S. & Reynolds, J. (2009): "Ancient Greek divination". *Aestimatio: Sources and Studies in the History of Science* 6: pp. 139-144.
Konstan, D. (2017): *Beauty: The Fortunes of an Ancient Greek Idea*. Oxford: OUP.
Lampinen, A. (2022): "Difference and essentialism: The polemics of physiognomy in the later Roman Empire". In: Krötzl, C. *et al.* (eds.): *Negotiation, Collaboration and Conflict in Ancient and Medieval Communities*. London: Routledge, pp. 13-48.
Marsico, C. (2010): *Zonas de tensión dialógica*. Buenos Aires: del Zorzal.
Marsico, C. (2014): *Filósofos socráticos II. Antístenes, Fedón, Esquines y Simón*. Madrid : Losada.
Marsico, C. (2018): "Materiales mágicos. Conjuros, hechicería, necromancia y otros dispositivos de economía antropológica en el pensamiento griego". *Studia Antiqua et Arqueologica* 24, No 1: pp. 51-70.
Marsico, C. (2022): "Walls, heavy seas, and lion's cubs: The Socratics beyond the soul-body dualism". In: Marsico, C. (ed.): *Socrates and the Socratic Philosophies*. Sankt Augustin: Academia Verlag, pp. 225-250.
Marsico, C. (2024): "Antístenes, the Cyclops, and Plato's healthy city". In: Pentassuglio, F. *et al.* (eds.): *Socratica V. Selected Papers*. Berlin: De Gruyter.
Marsico, C., & Illarraga, R. (2021): "Behind the witness' voice: Xenophon as a source of the Socratic philosophies". *Xenophon Conference 2021*. Liverpool.
Nikityuk, E. (2019): "Kalokagathia: To a question on formation of an image of the ideal person in antiquity and during modern time". *Studia Antiqua et Archaeologica* 25, No 2: pp. 429-442.
Ricciardone, C. (2019): "What is the meaning of Socrates' last words? A multifaceted approach". *Ancient Philosophy* 39, No 2: pp. 267-293.
Rossetti, L. (2015): "Phaedo's Zopyrus (and Socrates' confidences)". In: Zilioli, U. (ed.): *From the Socratics to the Socratic Schools*. London: Routledge, pp. 82-98.
Rozemond, M. (1999): "Descartes on mind-body interaction: What's the problem?". *Journal of the History of Philosophy* 37, No 3, pp. 435-467.
Sadun Bordoni, G. (1994): *Linguaggio e realtà in Aristotele*. Roma-Bari: Laterza.
Sassi, M. (2021): "Physiognomy from antiquity to the Renaissance: An introduction". In: Devriese, L. (ed.): *The Body as a Mirror of the Soul: Physiognomy from Antiquity to the Renaissance*. Louvain: Presses Universitaires de Louvain, pp. 1-30.
Sharples, R. (2001): "Dicaearchus on the soul and on divination". In: Forenbaugh, W. & Schutrumpf, E. (eds.): *Dicaearchus of Messana. Text, Translation and Discussion*. New Brunswick, NJ: Transaction, pp. 143-173.
Snell, B. (1953): *The Discovery of the Mind. The Greek Origins of European Thought*. Oxford: Blackwell.
Stavru, A. (2018a): "Aristoxenus on Socrates". In: Stavru, A. *et al.* (eds.): *Socrates and the Socratic Dialogue*. Leiden: Brill, pp. 623-664.
Stavru, A. (2018b): "Socrates' physiognomy: Plato and Xenophon in comparison". In: Danzig, G., Johnson, D. & Morrison, D. (Eds.): *Plato and Xenophon: Comparative Studies*. Leiden/Boston: Brill, pp. 208-251.
Stavru, A. (2021): "La kalokagathia in Senofonte: un'eccellenza eminentemente socratica". *Caliope* 42: pp. 4-17.
Swain, S., & van Bladel, K. (2008): "Seeing the face, seeing the soul: Polemon's physiognomy from classical antiquity to medieval Islam". Oxford: OUP, pp. 225-233.
Taylor, C. (2001): "The Arguments in the Phaedo Concerning the Thesis that the Soul is a Harmonia". In Wagner, E. (Ed.): *Essays on Plato's Psychology*. Lanham: Lexington, pp. 51-97.
Tsouna, V. (1998): "Doubts about other minds and the science of physiognomics". *Classical Quarterly* 48, No 2: pp. 399-409.
Zilioli, U. (2014): "The circle of Megara". *Philosophy* 103: pp. 74-118.

Ordering the Soul:

Ethical and cosmological perspectives on Atticus' doctrine of providence

Alexandra Michalewski

CNRS-Centre Léon Robin (UMR 8061)

Abstract

The aim of this paper is to study the parallel drawn by Atticus between the ordering activity of the world-soul (which is also called "nature") and that of the individual soul, by focusing on the concept of providence. Atticus was a Middle Platonist who was strongly opposed to harmonising the theses of Plato and that of Aristotle. According to him, the fundamental point of disagreement lies in the doctrine of the soul, which he interprets as an incorporeal and self-moving substance. The concept of motion plays a key role in this polemic: the regulating movement of the world-soul, which depends on the benevolent action of a creator god, not only guarantees the cosmological order, but also sets the basis for the development of ethics by making the connection between the divine and the human beings. By contrast, the Peripatetic universe, which is ungenerated and not ruled by providence, is presented by Atticus as supporting the development of an atheism at least as great as that of the Epicureans. Firstly, I will show how the world-soul results from the demiurge's ordering of the pre-cosmic soul, and how the regulating activity of the soul has an impact on both cosmological and ethical levels. Thus, in a second part, I develop the hypothesis that, since the world-soul and human souls are structurally the same, when individuals act virtuously they take over from the world-soul, establishing as much order as possible both in themselves and in their surroundings.

Atticus was a deeply anti-Aristotelian exegete who opposed the tendency to harmonise the doctrines of Plato and Aristotle that emerged in the 2nd century AD. For him, this incompatibility manifests itself to the highest degree at the cosmological level: the Aristotelian universe is ungenerated and deprived of providence, whereas Plato, in the *Timaeus*, described the generation of the world as the result of the activity of a benevolent and providential god. At the heart of this cosmological system, the soul, as motion and principle of motion, plays a key role. Within the framework of Atticus' cosmogenesis three types of soul are to be distinguished: (1) the pre-cosmic soul, which moves in a disorderly fashion before the generation of the world and becomes (2) the world-soul when it receives the rationality stemming from (3) the soul of the demiurge. The world-soul, which Atticus also calls *physis*, is an intermediary entity between the demiurgic intellect

in: Mouzala, M.G. (ed.) 2025: *Nature and Human Nature in Ancient Greek Philosophy and Its Reception*. Leiden: Sidestone Press, pp. 35-44.

and the sensible world,[1] through which the god can exercise his providential activity, i.e., is able to put everything in order, to keep the universe perpetually safe, and to take care of each individual.[2] The doctrine of providence is thus at the crossroads not only of cosmology, but also of ethics. Indeed, according to Atticus, becoming aware of a link connecting the god to the human beings motivates them to act virtuously.[3] To the Platonic Stoicizing model of a world-soul exercising providential activity that extends to caring for each person in particular, he contrasts the Peripatetic conception of an ungenerated world, which does not depend on any benevolent cause, and brings the Aristotelian position closer to that of the Epicureans. In a nutshell, by means of the notion of providence, Atticus addresses both the cosmological and the ethical question of the demiurge's activity and its connection to worldly affairs.

In the first part of this chapter, I will examine the cosmological foundations of Atticus' definition of providence. In the second part, I will focus on the intermediary role played by the world-soul, which is the link between the demiurge and the physical world, before concluding with an analysis of the ethical implications of Atticus' doctrine. My hypothesis is that the unifying element of Atticus' theory of providence is the concept of motion. To the immobility of the Prime Mover, which is a separate intellect, he opposes the providential movement of a creator-god who is an intellect associated with a soul, i.e. an intellect that expresses its care (κηδεμονία) for the universe and the human beings[4]. Correspondingly, human beings, by believing in the doctrine of providence, will not only connect their soul to the divine, but also reproduce, in their own domestic or civic life, the ordering activity of the demiurge.

1. Providence as a motion of the Demiurge

a. The scope of divine providence

The interpretation of Plato Atticus elaborated was a means of defending a theory of divine providence as concerned with worldly affairs. He argues that the narrative of the generation of the world in the *Timaeus* is meant to remind us that the γένεσις τοῦ κόσμου is the first expression of divine benevolence. His analyses concerning providence are to be found in the treatise *Against those who profess* [to interpret] *Plato's doctrines by means of Aristotle's doctrines*, some fragments of which have been preserved by Eusebius of Caesarea in the *Praeparatio Evangelica* (*PE*). Atticus' treatise, directed against those Platonists who are tempted by a harmonising interpretation of Plato and Aristotle, was written with specific intention of stressing their radical incompatibility.[5] It is well known that the defence of the extension of providence to cover the details of human affairs lies at the heart of Atticus' polemics against Peripatetic theology. This polemical perspective was of great interest to the Apologetic Fathers. Thus, Eusebius considered Atticus to be the best figure to show how the philosophy of Plato followed that of the Hebrews when it comes to the most essential points: Indeed, Plato and Moses both maintain that the world is generated by a providential God and demonstrate the soul's immortality. By contrast, Aristotle is presented has having gone in the opposite direction, rejecting both the doctrine of providence and that of the soul's immortality.[6] In fact, the two are closely connected: to deny the soul's immortality is to abandon the belief that it can be rewarded or punished after death. This is why Aristotle's denial of these two Platonic doctrines places him in the camp of the atheists, along with the Epicureans, as Atticus argues in *PE*, XV.5.7-8. Moreover, in the introductory paragraph of this fragment, Eusebius claims that Aristotle limited the scope of divine providence to the heavens only and did not extend its government to cover the sublunary world:

> Again, Moses and the Hebrew prophets, and indeed Plato, who is in agreement with them in these matters, have set out their views on universal providence with great clarity. But Aristotle brings the realm of the divine to a halt at the moon and keeps the remaining parts of the cosmos fenced off from God's care.[7]

In the following generation, Theodoret of Cyrrhus, who draws on the *PE* in his work *A Cure for Pagan Maladies*, gathers, in summarized form, the two main arguments deployed by Atticus to reveal the fundamental opposition between Plato and Aristotle.

> Plato, for instance had asserted that the soul is immortal, Aristotle called it mortal. Plato had maintened that God exercices providence over the universe. Aristotle, to judge by his words, excluded the world from divine government, for he said that God's ride over the universe extended as far as the moon and

1 Eusebius, *PE*, XV.12-1-4.

2 Eusebius, *PE*, XV.5.2.

3 Eusebius, *PE*, XV.5.3-5.

4 Eusebius, *PE*, XV. 5. 9; 11; 13.5.

5 The heading Πρὸς τοὺς διὰ τῶν Ἀριστοτέλους τὰ Πλάτωνος ὑπισχνουμένους is given in *PE* XI.1. Karamanolis (2006), pp. 151-153 has provided a detailed analysis that calls into question the hypothesis according to which this could be the exact title of Atticus' treatise.

6 Eusebius, *PE*, XV, 5.1; 9.

7 Eusebius, *PE*, XV.5.1.

that the rest came under the way of destiny. Aristotle has introduced other novelties of which it seems to me superfluous to talk at the moment.[8]

Atticus' criticism of the Aristotelian denial of providence prompted Alexander of Aphrodisias to respond.[9] Indeed, when at the end of *Quaest.* 2.21, Alexander claims "that those who profess Plato's [doctrines], and have strongly persuaded themselves that Aristotle had nothing to say about providence, do not say anything with attention or reflection" (Alexander, *Quaestio* II. 21, 70, 33-34. transl. R. Sharples slightly modified), he seems to alluding to Atticus' treatise. The *Quaestio* which has the form of an incomplete dialogue, echoes another of his treatise, of which an Arabic version survives, namely the treatise *On Providence*,[10] which claims that divine providence *does* extend to the sublunary world, but is concerned only with species and not with individuals.[11]

b. The temporal generation of the world and the interpretation of *Tim.* 30a

Atticus subordinates the doctrine of the generation of the world to that of divine providence. For him, providence can only exist if the demiurge exercises a causal power in relation to the world comparable to that of a craftsman who calculates and deliberates about how to produce and preserve his creation. Indeed, Atticus argues that what is ungenerated is self-sufficient and does not need an external cause to subsist. In other words, if the world were ungenerated, it would be totally self-sufficient and divine providence would be unnecessary.[12]

> First of all, while Plato was looking into the question of the generation of the cosmos, he also had it in mind that this great and beneficial doctrine of providence (τὸ τῆς προνοίας τὸ μέγα τοῦτο καὶ πολυωφελὲς δόγμα) needed thorough investigation. He realised that there was no need to posit an agent of creation or preservation for something that did not come into being in good order; so to make sure he did not deprive the cosmos of providence, he did away with the idea that it was ungenerated.[13]

Atticus thus affirms that it was in order to reveal the prominence of demiurgic providence that Plato, in the *Timaeus*, described the world as a temporally generated reality. In doing so, it is possible that Atticus was targeting Taurus' reading of the *Timaeus*. Following in the footsteps of the Academics, Taurus holds that although Plato describes the world as *geneton* (*Tim.* 27c5), he actually takes it for ungenerated. According to him, if Plato did this, it was essentially for two theological reasons – the first is that most people spontaneously think that a created world is ruled by divine providence, and the second is that the causal relation is best understood in temporal terms.[14] But if Plato adopts this pedagogical strategy, this does not mean that the universe had a beginning in time, as Plutarch, for example, maintains. Thus, Taurus points out that it is necessary to ascend to the level of a sempiternalistic reading of the Platonic dialogue which reveals the true, deeper meaning of providence. The world is said to be *γενητόν* not because it came into being at a certain moment in time, but because it depends perpetually on its divine cause.

From this perspective, F. Petrucci has suggested that Atticus' emphasis on his Greek identity, through the evocation of the Attic clarity of Plato's wording in *Tim.* 30a ("a Greek speaking to Greeks"), was a response to the "subtleties" of Platonists like Taurus, who, because he was a native of Beirut, was not able to grasp the real meaning of the cosmological dialogue.[15] However, if Taurus is certainly targeted by Atticus' criticisms of the interpretation of *Tim.* 28b, it is not out ruled out that other exegetes are associated with him, especially Severus.[16] Indeed, the latter developed a very different interpretation of *Tim.* 30a,[17] linked to a nuanced interpretation of the temporal generation of the universe, based on a distinction between the cosmos in absolute terms, which is everlasting, and the cosmos which began from a particular starting-point.[18]

> They should forgive us if, when it comes to Plato's beliefs, we put our faith in what he explained to us and set out with complete clarity of expression as a Greek speaking to Greeks. 'God' he says 'took hold of all that was perceptible, which was agitated, and in confused unordered motion, and he brought it to order out of disorder, thinking the one a much better state than the other'.[19]

---

8 Theodoret, *Curatio*, 5.47. transl. Th. Halton.

9 See Sharples (1994), p. 121. For more on this, I refer to Michalewski (2017), pp. 134-136.

10 For a detailed presentation of this text, see Thillet (2003).

11 These problems have already been discussed extensively in scholarly literature. I limit myself to refer to Sharples (1982) and (2003); Rashed (2007), pp. 294-304.

12 On this aspect, see Michalewski (2014), pp. 84-86.

13 Eusebius, *PE*, XV.6.2. Unless otherwise indicated, I follow Boys-Stones' translation (2018).

14 Philoponus, *De aet. mundi* 187. 4-15.

15 Petrucci, *Taurus of Beirut, The Other Side of Middle Platonism*, London, Routledge, 2018, p. 58-59.

16 Karamanolis (2006), p. 185; Michalewski (2024), pp. 71-72.

17 Porphyry, *On principles and Matter* (*PM*), 86-87.

18 Proclus, *In Tim.* I.289.7-9 (Diehl).

19 Eusebius, *EP* XV.6.3-4.

The association between the defence of providence and a temporal reading of the generation of the world is already to be found in Plutarch' texts[20]. But what is new with Atticus is that he articulates the doctrine of the generation of the world in terms of an in-depth theory of cosmological principles that is presented in a scholarly manner. His theory is based on the exegesis of several sections of the *Timaeus*, and particularly of *Tim.* 30a, which Atticus considers a key passage in Plato's cosmological edifice. According to him, in this section, Plato explains how the demiurge fashioned the world by making the pre-cosmic matter move with regularity. We also find indirect evidence for the connection between the generation of the world and *Tim.* 30a both in the summary of the Porphyrian arguments against Atticus provided by Proclus in his *Commentary on Plato's Timaeus* (I, 391-3-396, 26) and in the final doxography of the *PM*.[21]

c. The doctrine of cosmological principles

The testimonies concerning Atticus preserved in the *PM* not only confirm, but also clarify, what we already knew about Atticus' cosmology, namely that Plato admitted four principles: the creator-god, the intelligible Forms, matter, and soul – that is to say, a self-moving mover[22].

> Atticus, in the first treatise on the teachings of Plato, sets out the following concise and summary fashion the doctrine of Plato concerning First Principles: By exact definition, they are divided into four principles: the one that is the Father and Creator of everything; the other that is the Form and Idea, according to which he formed everything; then Matter, which is receptive to all beings; and movability, or motion, which co-existed with Matter (and) which moves by itself. That which moves by itself he calls 'Soul'.[23]

These four principles are grouped in pairs so as to form a general dualism – god and the Forms are opposed to matter and soul. Thus, Atticus, far from defending the legitimacy of the *Dreiprinzipienlehre*[24] – as many scholars believed for a long time[25] – in reality stresses its inadequacy. Actually, according to Atticus, the Platonists who claim that there are only three principles in Plato's cosmology fail to grasp the key role played by the pre-cosmic soul.

> Some people do not comprehend that Plato also puts Soul among the First Principles, and thus he set three principles: Matter, God, and Form. But it does not seem that he postulates this. For he says: 'Taking over all existing things, which were in a discordant and disorderly state, God brought them to order from disorder'. It is clear, then, from the words of Plato that Matter, which (God) took over, was neither unmovable nor unqualified[26].

Thus, the typical Middle-Platonist triad "God, Forms, Matter" is not able to account for the crucial role that the disorderly state of animated matter plays in the doctrine of providence. In fact, it is because matter is primarily moved by an irrational soul that the demiurge can exercise its benevolent action in bringing the world into order. And this is precisely what is at stake in *Tim.* 30a. As a result, Atticus distances himself from the interpretations of his Middle-Platonist colleagues: By substituting for the triad "God, Form, Matter", the triad "(God)being, Matter-motion", he points to what is missing in the *Dreiprinzipienlehre*, namely the activity of the pre-cosmic soul.

But what is striking in Atticus' account of the demiurgic formative activity is that it is the motion of the pre-cosmic soul that gives rise to god's ordering motion. Thus, the production of the world results from the subordination of one motion by another, namely the subordination of the disordered motion of the pre-cosmic soul, which Atticus identifies with the *anagkè* of the *Timaeus*, to the ordering movement of the god.[27] Atticus' god is indeed an intellect in a soul, which, as Porphyry indicates in his *Commentary on Plato's Timaeus*, "was watching for the readiness of matter" to be ordered.[28] Once the demiurge has mastered and regulated the motion of the *anagkè*, no other external cause can disturb the beautiful organization of the universe.

In the *PM*, after having addressed the way of grouping the principles, Atticus deals with the craftsman model of divine causality. With the help of the argument from design, he deduces from the regularity of the natural order the necessity of the existence of a supreme craftsman who organized the world: "And if there is the one who creates, it is by all means necessary that there is also that which comes to be, is created, and formed. But it is also necessary that God have a certain movement through the gazing at which he creates (Porphyry, *PM*, 79)". It is clearly asserted that the demiurgic activity implies motion – and motion is due to the presence of a soul. Thus, by means of his divine soul, the demiurge takes hold of the disorderly motion of the pre-cosmic soul and produces the world-soul, which, in turn, makes primordial matter into the organized substratum of the universe.

20 See e.g. Plutarch, *De Sera numinis vindicta*, 550d.
21 Porphyry, *PM*, 73-86.
22 On this issue, see Michalewski (2024), pp. 109-128.
23 Porphyry, *PM*, 73.
24 Dörrie (1995), p. 458.
25 For a *status quaestionis*, I refer to Michalewski (2017a), p. 120.
26 Porphyry, *PM*, 75.
27 Eusebius, *PE*, XV.6.16.
28 Proclus, *In Tim.* I.394.17-19 (Diehl).

2. World-soul and individual Soul

a. The ordering of the world

In order to understand more precisely the link between the ordering motion of the god and the doctrine of providence, we must grasp the nature of the intermediary role played by the world-soul. To the Aristotelian separation of the supralunary and the sublunary realm, Atticus opposes the Platonic vision of a unified world that is a living organism[29]. The world is a single totality animated and ruled by the world-soul. The latter is produced by the demiurge who gives it order and measure through the intelligible Forms located in his divine soul. By ordering the pre-cosmic soul, that is, by associating it with the intelligible Forms, the demiurge turns the chaotic soul into the rational world-soul. Once the latter is produced, it becomes the relay for divine causality.

In fact, it is the world-soul that ensures the regularity of cosmic cycles and the preservation of the universe. And it is at this level that we can perceive the providential activity of the demiurge on the universe. This is why, as G. Boys-Stones points out,[30] Atticus tends to blur the distinction between what belongs to the activity of the god and what belongs to that of the world-soul. Thus, in *PE*, XV.5.2, Atticus begins a paragraph by referring to the regularity of the celestial motions caused by the world-soul: "Plato sees all things in relation to god and as derived from god, for he says that god holds the beginning and middle and end of all things, and accomplishes his purpose directly as he revolves (*PE*, XV.5.2.16-18)"[31]. Then, in the next sentence, he goes on to talk about the activity of the demiurge: "And again he says that he is good, and there is in the good no envy about anything, and he made everything outside himself as good as possible [...] bringing it to order from disorder" (*PE*, XV.5.2.19-22). Finally, he makes the following addition to the Platonic quotation: "he cares for everything, including men, and has taken the trouble to bring as much order as possible to everything" (*PE*, XV.5.2.22-24). The part of the sentence that begins with "he cares for everything, including men" is an insertion made by Atticus which is presented as a continuation of the Platonic quotation, serving to introduce the motif of particular providence. But how do we understand that "the god cares for men"?

In *PE*, XV.5.2, Atticus puts Epicureans and Aristotelians in the same camp, because they sever the link, the community (κοινωνία) between gods and men. Both profess that there is an ἀμέλεια on the part of the gods towards men. The indifference of the gods towards human affairs, along with the doctrine of the non-immortality of the soul, does not encourage men to be virtuous. On the contrary, it leads to a sense of impunity: "Both alike think the gods have no concern for men, and provide the unjust with the same freedom (ἄδεια) from fear of the gods"[32]. In describing the attitude of the Peripatetics, Atticus frequently employs terms that evoke the privative value of *alpha*. The Aristotelians deprive humanity of a link between god (who, for them, is not producer of the world) and human beings – the Prime Mover being an unmoving principle that is indifferent to the events of the world.

Twice, in *PE*, XV.5, we find indications that both Aristotle and Epicurus turn away from the doctrine of providence (*PE*, XV.5.7-9). By pointing out that the attitude of rejection of providence is common to Aristotle and Epicurus, Atticus jointly denounces them as atheists. If the soul truly is immortal, then it is subject to rewards and punishments in the afterlife, and this retributive operation is precisely the work of divine providence. However, in *PE*, XV.5.11, Atticus observes that Epicurus is less arrogant than Aristotle, as what he "renounces (ἀπογνοὺς)" is the idea that the gods could refrain from exercising care towards men (τῆς ἀνθρώπων κηδεμονίας) if they remained connected to them. This is why he banishes the gods to the inter-worlds. By contrast, Atticus, who seems to have fairly sound knowledge of Epicureanism, recognises that simulacra constitute a kind of material link between gods and men.[33] Thus, aside from the rhetorical tactic of distancing Aristotle from Plato by using Epicurus as a foil, Atticus sees the notion of a link between gods and men, which provides the foundation for any doctrine of providence, as being more real in Epicureanism than in Aristotelianism.[34]

In Atticus' perspective, not only does divine providence descend to earth, but it also concerns every rational being that possesses an immortal soul: "We are looking for a providence that is distinguished by its concern for us – and that is not available for anyone who denies that daimons and heroes and souls in general are able to survive (*PE*, XV.5.10)"[35]. While the Epicurean gods care about the preservation of their own goods, but not about human affairs (πᾶσαν κηδεμονίαν ὑπὲρ τῆς σωτηρίας τῶν οἰκείων ἀγαθῶν εἰσφερομένων), the Platonic god is said to be the κηδεμών (protector) of the universe and of rational beings.[36] This feature of the demiurge is linked to his perpetual contemplation of the Forms, which are the eternal models of sensible things. Hence, in contrast to the Peripatetics, who isolate god from the world, Atticus substitutes the conception of a universe which is an organic whole, produced by the god who gazes at the intelligible realities.

29 Eusebius, *PE*, XI.2.2.
30 Boys-Stones (2016), p. 329.
31 Eusebius, *PE*, XV.5.2.
32 Eusebius, *PE*, XV.5.8.
33 Eusebius, *PE*, XV.5.9.
34 See Michalewski (2024), pp. 49-50.
35 Eusebius, *PE*, XV.5.10.
36 Eusebius, *PE*, XV.13.9.

b. World-soul as nature

In order to understand the claim that god cares about human affairs, we have to look at Atticus' definition of the world-soul. In *PE*, XV.12, Atticus indicates that 'nature', which is the other name for the world-soul is an animating power (δύναμις ἔμψυχος)[37] that pervades everything and holds all things together:

> Again, Plato says that the soul puts everything in order 'pervading everything' (τὴν ψυχὴν διακοσμεῖν τὰ πάντα, διήκουσαν διὰ πάντων); that it is that which everyone else too can agree puts each thing in order (διοικεῖσθαι); that nature is nothing other than soul; and that soul is clearly not irrational. From all this he infers that everything comes about according to providence – if, that is, everything comes about according to nature. But Aristotle agrees with us about none of this[38].

In order to develop his doctrine of the providential activity of the world-soul, Atticus takes up a range of concepts stemming from Stoic physics – concepts which were themselves initially borrowed from Platonism: διακοσμέω[39]refers to the formation of the world through the actions of an artisan god and, in ancient Stoicism, to its regular reformation following the conflagration;[40]διήκω, to the way in which the god, as an active corporeal principle, extends and spreads himself through matter; [41]διοικέω, to the idea of the governance of the world.[42] This Stoic doctrine builds on the *Timaeus*, in that it takes up its conception of the world as a living whole, but makes an immanent world-soul into its principle of unity: the world-soul (or *logos*), which is omnipresent in every particle of matter, is a corporeal principle that confers unity on the government of the universe.[43] By establishing an equivalence between the world-soul and nature, Atticus shows, against Aristotle, that the only true *physis* is a world-soul, as the Stoics assert. But, against Stoic corporealism, he makes it an incorporeal reality. From the Stoic model, he retains the idea that the god's causality extends into the detail of each individual thing, and rules everything by means of the soul.

This definition of nature should probably also be understood against the backdrop of the polemics waged by the Epicureans against the Platonists with regard to the question of providence, as evidenced by the newly discovered fragments from Diogenes of Oinoanda which make use of the Aristotelian lexicon of *physis*. Indeed fragment 155 indicates that "Plato is right in claiming that the world had a beginning, although he did not create the world in the right way, because he did not employ nature as a craftsman (καλῶς Πλάτων ὁμολογήσας γενητὸν εἶναι τὸν κόσμον, εἰ καὶ μὴ καλῶς ἐδημιούργησεν αὐτόν, τῇ φύσει δημιουργῷ μὴ χρησάμενο{ι}ς)".[44] The reference to a demiurgic nature is an allusion to Aristotelian formulas which are intended to provide an alternative to the Platonic notion of a transcendent and benevolent demiurge[45]. In other words, since Atticus wishes to underline the incompatibility between the doctrines of Plato and Aristotle, he highlights the proximity between the craftsman model of divine causality defended by the Platonists and the Stoics, contrasting them with the shared position of the Epicureans and Peripatetics, who are united in their rejection of providence. Against Stoic corporealism, however, he turns nature into an incorporeal soul, receiving its structure and rationality from the demiurge. Furthermore, Atticus' world-soul ensures that the cosmos remains perpetually safe. In fact, it is through the regular activity of the world-soul that the demiurge makes the world unperishable. At the same time, the causality of the world-soul becomes merged with that of the demiurge. Thus, in *PE* XV.6, Atticus claims that the integrity of world will be always preserved, because it depends on the "cause which proceeds from God", and this preserving activity is nothing other than the expression of god's good will:

> Yet when one has established as the chief cause that which proceeds from God, one must take this as guide in all things, and show it to be a cause on no point inferior to any others. For it is ridiculous that, because a thing has come into existence, it must therefore perish, and yet not perish, if God so wills.[46]

c. Ethical perspectives

After having examined the causality of the world-soul, I would like to provide an overview of the ethical implications of Atticus' views on providence. Atticus indicates that providence, which represents an essential doctrine (δόγμα)[47] within the Platonic system, is also an article of faith or of conviction (πεῖσμα).[48] Belief in providence is the best way to achieve happiness – ethics and cosmology are inextricably interconnected within the organic structure of Platonic philosophy. Indeed, both ethics and cosmology depend on the doctrine of the soul's immortality, which is the keystone of the whole Platonic edifice: To live a virtuous life is to bring one's

37 Eusebius, *PE*, XV.12.3.
38 Eusebius, *PE*, XV.12.1.
39 Plato, *Phlb.* 28e; *Phdr.*246e; *Phd.* 97c; 98c; *Crat.* 400a; *Tim.* 37d; 53a.
40 *SVF*, II, 1052.
41 *SVF*, II, 634; 1029; 1035.
42 Plato, *Phdr*. 246c; *Leg.* 896d; *SVF*, II, 1042; 1076; 1155.
43 On how the *Timaeus* has been the object of several re-appropriations between the two traditions, cf. Reydams-Schils (1999), p. 127.

44 Erler (2017), p. 52.
45 See e.g. Aristote, *De Gen. An.*, 731a24.
46 Eusebius, *PE*, XV.6.11. transl. Gifford.
47 Eusebius, *PE*, XV.6.1.
48 Eusebius, *PE*, XV.5.2. (τοῦ περὶ τῆς προνοίας πείσματος).

soul to contemplate the intelligible and to maintain hope of being rewarded after death. But to acknowledge providence is also to recognise that we are bound to the demiurge, just as the demiurge is concerned with our human affairs.

As regards to the use of the rather rare term πεῖσμα, F. Frazier has shown how Atticus, as a masterful rhetorician, plays on the homonymy that exists between πεῖσμα, meaning "persuasion", and πεῖσμα, meaning "mooring rope", both of which derive from the same Indo-European root (*bheidh*), meaning "to bind".[49] To be rationally persuaded, to be convinced that a providence concerned with human affairs exists, is already to be connected to god, who, as the first and universal cause, connects everything to him (πάντα ἀνάπτει).[50] To be a Platonist means seeking to live in accordance with the divine order of the universe. By contrast, neither the Epicureans nor the Aristotelians are concerned with this connection between god and human beings, professing only an atheistic ἀπόγνωσις of providence. The refusal to believe (ἀπιστεῖν) in the doctrine of providence goes hand in hand with a complete atheism (παντάπασιν ἄθεος).[51] Atticus twice employs the verb ἀποικίζω to underline the absence of a link between the divine and human beings in Aristotle's universe. In *PE* XV.5.4, this verb is used to illustrate the delusion of the Peripatetics, who think that they can live at a remove from the gods during their lives (and even escape them after death), and in *PE* XV.5.14, to indicate that Aristotle refuses to extend the scope of divine providence beyond the supralunary realm, thus leaving the gods stranded far from men. This claim echoes Epicurus' banishment of the gods to the inter-worlds (εἰς ἀλλοδαπὴν ἀπῴκισε), so as to distance them from human concerns, making all communication impossible.[52] By contrast, by adhering to the Platonic doctrine of providence, one connects with god.

But how should we understand this claim? Atticus gives only few indications, but some insight can nevertheless be gained. The hypothesis I would like to develop here is the following: Connecting with God involves not only receiving benefits from the providential order, but, above all, reproducing on an individual level the organising action that the world-soul carries out at the scale of the universe as a whole. In other words, belief in providence does not entail a passive attitude in which one simply waits for divine justice, but rather it implies that individuals take on an active role in bringing about order and intelligible rationality around them. Recognising the existence of a providence that is concerned with human affairs is what makes it possible to fulfil this central imperative of Middle Platonism, taken from *Theætetus* 176d – namely to try, so far as possible, to flee to the supra-sensible realm in order to "become like god".

49 Frazier (2019), p. 435.

50 Eusebius, *PE*, XV.5.2.8.

51 Eusebius, *PE*, XV.5.14.

52 Eusebius, *PE* XV.5.11.

It is worth noting that Atticus holds that the human soul has a similar structure to that of the world-soul, although it differs in the proportion of its ingredients, making it weaker.[53] Proclus reports that Atticus understands that, in *Tim.* 41d, Plato talks about a "double mixing bowl".[54] It means that the demiurge first composed the world-soul and then he mixed the rest of the ingredients in a second krater to create individual souls. This similarity of nature can be seen, for example, in the way in which Atticus, in *PE*, XV.9.4, blurs together the role of the world-soul and that of the human soul, by switching in a single sentence from one to the other and quoting the Platonic formula from the *Phaedrus* 246c according to which "every soul" takes care of what is inanimate: "and the natural world has the ability to be well ordered through the soul's organisation. For, he says, all soul cares for every inanimate being, and ranges through the whole heaven, in different forms at different times" (*PE*, XV.9.4).

But this ordering power that belongs to the individual soul is even more striking on the ethical level. In *PE*, XV.4, Atticus indicates that Plato "tries to draw the souls of the young upwards towards the divine". In other words, ethical activity consists in straightening out the motions of the self-moving soul of young people, so that they are able to elevate themselves to the contemplation of intelligible Forms. More precisely, it seems to me that Atticus conceives of ethical activity as primarily concerning collective wholes. Indeed, if we look at the beginning of *PE*, XI.2, where Atticus defines the role of ethics, we find the idea that the good and virtuous man has the aim of reforming households or cities so as to set them on the right path (ἕκαστον καλὸν καὶ ἀγαθὸν καὶ τοὺς οἴκους ὅλους εἰς τὸ ἄριστον ἐπανορθοῦντος (*PE*, XI.2.1)". In *PE*, XV.5.1, Atticus argues that the faith on providence is "what keeps human life on the right track (τὸν ἀνθρώπινον βίον ὀρθοῖ)". The term ἐπανόρθωσις has a long history: In Plato and Aristotle, it is limited to an almost exclusively epistemological use, where it means "to correct an error". In the Stoic tradition, the term takes on different meanings: correcting or emending a text, straightening one's own mentality, reforming the city[55]. At the level of the regulating power of the world-soul it is used to denote the process by which god may punish human beings in order to convert individuals towards a more virtuous way of life.[56] Depending on the context, Plutarch brings one or other of these significations into play: e.g.

53 Baltes (1983), pp. 52-53; Boys-Stones (2018), p. 264. What could support this view, is that Atticus' doctrine of the soul is heavily indebted to that of Plutarch. Indeed, in *De virtute morali* 441f-442a, Plutarch claims unambiguously that the individual soul is a part or an imitation of the world-soul (ἥ τ' ἀνθρώπου ψυχὴ μέρος ἢ μίμημα τῆς τοῦ παντὸς οὖσα). See also *De An. Proc.* 1026d-e. On this, see Opsomer (2012), pp. 313-315.

54 Proclus, *In Tim.* III. 247.12-15 (Diehl).

55 Boys-Stones (2007), p. 88.

56 Alexander of Aphrodisias, *De fato*, 35, 207.4.15-19.

in the *Parallel Lives*, when he describes how great men, such as Agesilaus or Phocion, do correct the bad habits of their companions,[57] or in the educational treatises, when he explains the way in which poetry or philosophy can lead young people to ethical improvement.[58] In such writings, the term ἐπανόρθωσις is generally employed to "denote a process of moral reform"[59]. But whereas for Plutarch, the term is mainly related to individual behavior, for Atticus, it is also related to collective reform. Thus, when Atticus specifies that the reforms undertaken by the virtuous man concern the whole city, this is perhaps an echo on the human level of the demiurgic activity: the good man, just like the demiurge, corrects an initially disordered situation and aims, as far as possible, to produce the best order on the civic level.

To conclude, we have seen how the doctrine of providence relies on the notion of motion: The movement of god brings the pre-cosmic soul into order. Once this soul has become the world-soul, it exercises a regulating activity over the universe, an activity which is perceptible even in the details of individual affairs. From this perspective, *Tim.* 30a is taken by Atticus as a key section, which accounts for the generation of the world and reveals the existence of providence. Atticus thus targets the Peripatetic doctrines of the immobile Prime Mover, separated from the sublunary world, and of a non-immortal soul. In opposition to this, he highlights the organic unity of the Platonic cosmos (a unity to which corresponds the unity of philosophy, all of whose parts are linked).[60] In this context, the definition of happiness is deeply connected to that of providence, which, in turn, is based on the acceptance of the immortality of the soul and the existence of intelligible Forms. Indeed, according to Atticus, in order to lead a good life and to attain happiness, it is necessary to try to assimilate oneself to the divine, that is to say, to contemplate the Forms. Just as on the cosmic level, providence is the ordering activity of the world-soul, on the individual level, every human being must achieve order by unifying their soul, their home and their city as much as possible.

Bibliography

Arzhanov, Y. (2021): *Porphyry, 'On Principles and Matter'. A Syriac Version of a Lost Greek Text with an English Translation, Introduction, and Glossaries. Scientia Craeco-Arabica* 34. Berlin: De Gruyter.

Baltes, M. (1983): "Zur Philosophie des Platonikers Attikos". In: Blume, H.D. & Mann, F. (eds.): *Platonismus und Christentum.* Festschrift für Heinrich Dörrie. Münster: Aschendorf, pp. 38-57.

Boys-Stones, G. (2007): "*Fallere sollers*. The ethical pedagogy of the Stoic Cornutus". *Bulletin of the Institute of Classical Studies. Supplement,* No 94: pp. 77-88.

Boys-Stones, G. (2016): "Providence and Religion in Middle Platonism". In: Eidinow, E., Kindt, J. and Osborne, R. (eds.): *Theologies of Ancient Greek Religion.* Cambridge Classical Studies. Cambridge: Cambridge University Press, pp. 317-338.

Boys-Stones, G. (2018): *Platonist Philosophy 80 BC to AD 250. An Introduction and Collection of Sources in Translation.* Cambridge: Cambridge University Press.

Dörrie, H. (1995) : "Ammonios, der Lehrer Plotins". *Hermes* 83: pp. 439-477.

Erler, M. (2017): "Diogenes against Plato. Diogenes' Critique and the Tradition of Epicurean Antiplatonism". In: Hammerstaedt, J. *et al.* (eds.): *Diogenes of Oinoanda, Epicureanism and Philosophical Debates*. Leuven: Leuven University Press, pp. 51-65.

Frazier, F. (2019): *Quelques aspects du platonisme de Plutarque*. Leiden: Brill.

Halton, Th. (2013): Theodoret of Cyrrhus, *A Cure for Pagan Maladies*. New York: Newman Press.

Karamanolis, G. (2006): *Plato and Aristotle in Agreement? Platonists on Aristotle from Antiochus to Porphyry.* Oxford: Oxford University Press.

Michalewski, A. (2014): *La puissance de l'intelligible. La théorie plotinienne des Formes au miroir de l'héritage médioplatonicien*. Leuven: Leuven University Press.

Michalewski, A. (2017): "Faut-il préférer Épicure à Aristote ? Quelques réflexions sur la providence ". In: Baghdassarian, F. & Guyomarc'h, G. (dirs.) : *Réceptions de la théologie aristotélicienne d'Aristote à Michel d'Éphèse*. Leuven: Peeters, pp. 123-142.

Michalewski, A. (2017a): "Atticus et le nombre des principes. Nouvel examen de quelques problèmes textuels du fragment DP 26 (= Proclus, *in Tim*., I, 391, 6-12) ". In: Gavray, M.-A. & Michalewski, A. (dirs.): *Les principes cosmologiques du platonisme. Origines, influences et systématisation*. Turnhout: Brepols, pp. 119-141.

Michalewski, A. (2024): *Le dieu, le mouvement, la matière. Atticus et ses critiques dans l'Antiquité tardive*. Paris: Les Belles Lettres.

57 Plutarch, *Agesilaus*, VIII, 600 ; *Phocion*, VII, 744.

58 Plutarch, *De profectibus in virtute* 79C2 ; *De liberis educandis* 2C13 ; *De audiendo* 42a7-8, 46e7

59 Xenophontos (2016), pp. 38-40.

60 Eusebius, *PE*, XI.2.2.

Opsomer, J. (2012): “Plutarch on the division of the soul”. In: Barney, R. *et al.* (eds): *Plato and the Divided Self.* Cambridge: Cambridge University Press, pp. 311 – 330.
Petrucci, F. (2018): *Taurus of Beirut, The Other Side of Middle Platonism.* London: Routledge.
Rashed, M. (2007): *Essentialisme, Alexandre d’Aphrodise entre logique, physique et cosmologie.* Berlin: De Gruyter.
Reydams-Schils, G. (1999): *Demiurge and Providence. Stoic and Platonist Readings of Plato’s Timaeus.* Turnhout: Brepols.
Sharples, R. W. (1982): “Alexander of Aphrodisias on Divine Providence: Two Problems”. *The Classical Quarterly* 32, No1: pp. 198-211.
Sharples, R. W. (1994): Alexander of Aphrodisias, *Quaestiones* 2.16-3.15. Ithaca, New York: Cornell University Press.
Sharples, R.W. (2003): “Threefold providence: the history and background of a doctrine”. In: Sharples, R.W. & Sheppard, A. (eds.): *Ancient Approaches to Plato’s Timaeus.* London: Institute of Classical Studies, pp. 107-127.
Thillet, P. (2003): Alexandre d’Aphrodise, *De la Providence*, introduction, édition et traduction. Paris: Verdier.
von Arnim, H. (1903-1905): *Stoicorum veterum fragmenta*, 3 vol (*SVF*). Leipzig: Teubner.
Xenophontos, S. (2016): *Ethical Education in Plutarch: Moralising Agents and Contexts.* Berlin: De Gruyter.

Galen on Human Nature: Individual and Cosmos

Teun Tieleman

University of Utrecht

Abstract

The doctor-philosopher Galen of Pergamon (129-ca. 216 CE) regarded humans as intermediate creatures, with an animal and a divine side. This was a more common view associated with Platonism in particular. But in Galen this takes a special form reflecting his experience as a doctor. I start from Galen's view of human nature in terms of the mixture of physical elements, with consequences both for therapy and for enhancement and perfectioning. This also entails that human nature, its health and illness are subjected to the same physical principles that obtain in the cosmos as a whole. Humans are part of this greater whole. I will then address the question how exactly Galen conceived of the relation of individual and universal nature. This opens a religious, or theological, perspective integral to Galen's project of developing a philosophical medicine or medical philosophy: the doctor as a servant of God and medicine as an extension of God's creative and sustaining activity.

1. Introduction: Galen's Notion of Nature and its Sources

Galen of Pergamon (129-c.216 CE) reflected on human nature and our place in the cosmos not only in light of the philosophical tradition; his work in this area is deeply informed by his experience as a doctor, i.e. both a medical scientist and a practicing physician. His distinctive, if not unique, double-role as a doctor-philosopher was not a matter of him alternating between the two disciplines, let alone of being a doctor who dabbled in philosophy. He worked towards a particular form of synthesis, or merger, between the two fields, developing the ideal of a philosophically informed medicine aimed at human well-being, both physical and mental. Being of a pragmatic mindset, he considered those parts of philosophy that fall outside this ideal as the ones that are useless for scientific and moral progress anyway: this is the domain of speculation on insoluble issues, which are the ones which often determine the division between schools, with all the sectarian behaviour that goes with it.[1] Galen was sensitive to the limits of knowledge but firmly believed that we are capable of grasping the most important facts about individual human nature and how it relates to universal or cosmic nature.

1 Galen saw his ideal embodied by the founder of medicine, Hippocrates, who illustrated the need for the perfect Hippocratic doctor to be knowledgeable about all three parts of philosophy (physics, logic and ethics), as he argued in his tract *The Best Doctor is also a Philosopher*. For a recent presentation of the text, with accompanying essays, see Das, 2023. For Galen's response to the schools, or sects, on sects see the pioneering study by Frede 1981; cf. Tieleman 2023b; for Galen on insoluble and useless issues see Tieleman 2018, pp. 454-459.

in: Mouzala, M.G. (ed.) 2025: *Nature and Human Nature in Ancient Greek Philosophy and Its Reception*. Leiden: Sidestone Press, pp. 45-54.

Galen's independent outlook did not mean that he was not interested in projecting back into the past his own intellectual pedigree, in line with a more common intellectual habit, Galen anchored his philosophical medicine, or medical philosophy, in two past masters, which he presented as having founded the tradition of sound philosophy-cum-medicine: Hippocrates and Plato. His *On the Doctrines of Hippocrates and Plato* (hereafter abbreviated *PHP*) is devoted to showing them to be essentially correct and in harmony on the main issues of philosophy and medicine including the structure of the human soul and its seat in the body, demonstrative method as well as the physical elements or elementary qualities (discussed in *PHP* book VIII). Another work that illustrates this anchoring strategy is his commentary on the Hippocratic *On Human Nature* (abbreivated *HNH*).[2] Galen starts by explaining the term 'nature' in its title: it refers to the most fundamental level of 'substance' (οὐσία) or physical reality viz. the physical elements. In a secondary sense, it refers to the lowest *perceptible* level of reality: perceptible nature in the sense of properties and their powers. This level corresponds to what since Aristotle were called the 'elements in relation to perception', i.e. homoeomeric or uniform parts such as flesh and bone, which, he claims, Plato called 'first-born'.[3] These constitute the 'first' nature relative to the body-parts and organs (hands, legs, liver, uterus, etc.); or, conversely, these are 'secondary' to the homoiomerous parts.[4] In fact, Galen ascribes to Hippocrates the Aristotelian analysis of elements into qualities and underlying matter and when he identifies the elementary level as nature in its primary sense this can be paralleled from Aristotelian passages such as *Metaphysics* book V chapter 4, where Aristotle distinguishes between the different senses of 'nature' (φύσις). It includes the organic level, i.e. animals and their parts. The core idea is that nature refers to the essence of those things which contain within themselves a principle of motion.[5]

In *HNH*, then, Galen synthesizes a view of nature on behalf of Hippocrates while drawing on notions from Plato and Aristotle too. In the case of Plato he avails himself of one of his favourite passages, *Phaedrus* 270c-d where Plato praises Hippocrates for his method of analysing (i.e. applying the method of diaeresis to) the nature of individual things by starting from 'the whole' so as to get at their essence (οὐσία) (*HNH, Prooem.* 4.18-5.9 Mewaldt = XV. 4-5 Kühn), which he takes to refer to the Hippocratic On Human Nature.[6] Here, however, Galen links 'nature' to οὐσία as opposed to attributes: qualities, but also actions, i.e. as essence which is not quite the same as the first substance (πρώτη ουσία) in the sense of the first, or most basic, material level, with which he started his explanation of the title of Hippocrates' work. This is truer to Plato's intention, who makes Socrates argue that that just as Hippocrates used this method in studying the body so, too, he should apply the method in studying the soul, which is central to the philosophical informed art of rhetoric he is adumbrating. Although a lot of ink has been spilled over the sense of "the whole", i.e. whether it refers to the whole individual thing under scrutiny or to the cosmos as a whole, it seems most natural to read it in the former sense and this is certainly how Galen took it.[7]

2. Cosmic Optimism

Galen's engagement with Plato's *Timaeus* was intense and spanned his entire career. He appeals to this dialogue in explaining his view of nature in the final (preserved) book of his great work on the *Doctrines of Hippocrates and Plato* (hereafter *PHP*):

> But Plato declared that the cause that made us, the god who is the craftsman (δημιουργός) of the universe, commanded his children by speech to fashion the human race, receiving from him the substance of the immortal soul and inserting in it the part that is generated [cf. *Tim.* 41a-d]. But we must recognize this fact, that there is no similarity in kind between proving and positing that we were made in accordance with the providence of some god or gods, and knowing the substance of the maker, or even of our own soul. My earlier remarks make it clear that the fashioning of our bodies is a work of the highest wisdom and power;

2 *HNH Proem.* pp. 7.15-8.28 (XV. 9-12 Kühn). (the first eight chapters of which Galen took to be written by Hippocrates himself or alternatively by the latter's pupil and son-in-law Polybus who, he believes, followed Hippocrates in everything).

3 *HNH Prooem.* p.6.14-22 (XV. 7-8 Kühn); for Aristotle's notion of uniform parts see e.g. *Cael.* III.3: 302a30-b3, *GA* I.18: 724a29-31, *HA* I.1: 486a5-14. For the "first-born" things in Plato, see *Plt.* 288e, 289a, but here the term πρωτογενής is used in a different sense; similarly, Gal. *QAM* 37.2-5 Müller (IV. 773 K.). The fact that Galen tweaks the Platonic text may stand as a witness to his wish to trace back the concept in question to Plato.

4 *HNH Prooem.* P.6.15-20 (XV. 7-8 Kühn).

5 For the Aristotelian backdrop of Galen's conception of physis see Kovacic (2001) pp. 92-94, who rightly notes that in Aristotle and Galen the senses of physis correspond to different causes.

6 See *HNH Prooem.* P.30-32 (= XV. 12 K.). On Galen's use of *Phaedrus* 270c-d see further Tieleman (2020), pp.28-32.

7 Concept of nature: physis as ousia, elements: Gal. *HNH*, Preface: XV.1-9 K. = 3-7 Mewaldt on the different senses of 'nature': basic material substance: nature in the primary (higher, more general) sense vs perceptible nature (properties with powers: XV 3.4 K = 3-4 M. for the visible structure (uniform parts), essence of individual things (cf Plato, *Phaedr*. 270c-d). For nature as a combination of elements according to Hippocrates: cf. *Elem Hipp* 9.18 De Lacy, *Hipp. Aph.* XVIIB. 565 K. ibid. 529: 'primary and most important sense', used by Hippocrates: mixture of elements (cf. ibid. 9.21, p.134 4, where this is associated with the physiologia or study of nature, by Hippocrates. Physis as *idea* (form) of a body: *Hipp. Aph* XVIIB 532 (cf. *Hipp. Epid.* I, 1,2, II p. 604.7ff Littré). Cf Jouanna (2003) 230-232. Works On nature: Cf. Elem. Hipp. I, 9.27 De Lacy = I. 487 K. and HNH XV 5 = p. 5 Mewaldt

> but the statements of the most divine Plato about the substance of the soul and of the gods who formed us, and still more all that he says about our whole body, extend only to the point of being plausible and reasonable, as he himself pointed out in the *Timaeus* when he was first about to enter upon an account of the natural world, and again when he inserted the statement in the middle of the account (*PHP* IX, 9.1-3, pp. 596.30-598.11 De Lacy; transl. De Lacy).

This passage invites comparison with the second chapter of one of his final works, *On My Own Opinions*:

> I declare I do not know whether the universe is uncreated or created and whether or not there is anything outside it. Since I disclaim knowledge of such things, it will be clear that I do so also with regard to the nature of the craftsman (δημιουργός) of everything in the universe, i.e. whether he is corporeal or incorporeal, and still more with regard to the place in which he resides. So about the gods, too, I profess doubt (*ἀπορεῖν*), as Protagoras [cf. fr. B 4 DK] did, or I say also in their case that I do not know what their substance is like but that I do know that they exist from their actions. They are the designers of the constitution of all animals. They warn us about future events through significant utterances, omens and dreams. The god who is revered in my own birthplace Pergamon [scil. Asclepius] showed his power and providence on many occasions but also by curing me once. I know from experience both the providence and the power of the Dioscuri at sea. However, people are in my opinion in no way hindered by the fact that they are ignorant of the substance of the gods, but I decided to honour them following ancestral tradition and in line with the advice given by Socrates to obey the orders of the Pythian one [scil. Apollo] [cf. Xenoph. *Mem.* I, 1,11-16]. This is the attitude I take towards religious matters (*Prop. Plac.* ch. 2 Boudon-Pietrobelli. Transl. mine).

This passage is another witness to Galen's indebtedness to Plato's *Timaeus* with its explicit reference to Plato's divine Demiurg or Craftsman, who creates the best of all possible worlds. As in the passages from *PHP* book IX Galen found a special attraction in Plato's qualification of his creation story as likely (or as Galen also put it, plausible, πίθανος), which made it possible to reconcile Plato's account with the epistemological standards applied by Galen: those issues that do not admit of empirical verification must remain at the level of greater or lesser plausibility, e.g. the nature of God or the soul. It is however possible to infer from the purposefulness and beauty of the cosmos (including human anatomy) the existence and providence of God. There is a smooth transition here to the notion of gods in the plural, who appear here as the multiple manifestations of the one supreme divinity. They are credited with the creation of animals, which also reflects the job given to the traditional pantheon, identified as the children of the Demiurg, in Platonic *Timaeus*, whose existence is to be accepted and believed on the authority of ancestral tradition and custom (*Tim.* 40d-41a).[8] Galen's point that the gods' (of God's) existence and providence can be inferred from the design of all animals is illustrated on a grand scale by another of his main works, *On the Usefulness of Parts*, where he systematically discusses the parts of the human body with a view to showing God's (or Nature') wonderful design, witness passages such as the following:

> Do not be so amazed by the beautiful arrangement of the sun, the moon and the whole choir of the stars, or so impressed by their size, beauty, ceaseless motion, and ordered revolutions, that things here on earth seem trivial and disorganized by comparison. Here too you will find displayed the same wisdom, power, and providence. Consider well the matter of which the thing is made and entertain no idle hope that you could construct from menses and semen an animal that would be immortal, free from pain, endowed with everlasting motion, and as radiantly beautiful as the sun. You should rather estimate the art of the Creator of all things just as you judge the art of Phidias (*UP* 3.10, i 174,19-175,8 Helmreich. Cf. 175.23-176.3 Helmreich. Transl. Hankinson).

In the same chapter we find an oft-quoted passage about anatomical research as true piety, which is worth recycling here:

> I think that this is true reverence: not offering Him countless hecatombs of bulls or burning ten thousand talents' worth of incense of cassia, but when first of all I come to understand His wisdom, power and excellence myself, and then expound them to others. I take it to be an indication of perfect excellence to seek to order everything that is capable of being ordered, and to begrudge no benefit to anything. Let Him then be praised as good for this. We discover His consummate wisdom in the fact that He has ordered everything for the best, and His supreme power in his doing everything that He chooses to do. (*UP* 3.10, 174,8-19 Helmreich; transl. Hankinson.)

---

8 That Galen seems to feel no tension or contradiction here may be due not just to the fact that Plato's creation story accommodates the gods of traditional religion but reflects an at the time more common religious outlook bridging monotheism and polytheism: henotheism. *Prop. Plac.* 2 is studied from this perspective by Frede (2010) pp. 75-81.

Thus Galen's project in *On the Usefulness of Parts* has strong religious overtones; it makes a philosophical and theological point.[9] The doctor in so far as he engages in the study of nature and, given the context, that of the human body in particular first grasps God's wisdom and then makes it known to others-which is what Galen does in his great work. It is a way of singing God's praises, of paying him tribute in a more effective manner than through traditional means. One may wonder how Galen squared this attitude with his experience as a practicing physician who is constantly confronted with the limits of God's goodness, with failing Nature.[10] I will return to this issue presently. Here suffice it to note that Galen places himself in the role of a religious devotee, a servant of God as well as his missionary.

After a full account of the human body from tip to toe, the entire work culminates in the so-called epode, which constitutes its seventeenth book. Here Galen waxes positively hymnic:

> Is there any part of the universe more insignificant than that around the earth? Yet even here some intelligence (νοῦς) manifestly comes down from the bodies above; anyone who sees this is immediately forced to admire the beauty of their substance, pre-eminently that of the sun, and after the sun that of the moon, then of the stars. It is reasonable to assume that the intelligence that lives in them is as much better and more perfect than that in the earthly bodies as their bodily substance is purer. For when animals are engendered in mud and slime, in marshes and in rotting plants and fruits[11], which yet display a wonderful indication of the intelligence which constructs them, what must we think of the bodies above? (*UP* 17.1, ii 446.11-23 H. Tr Hankinson).

Galen goes on to point to the superior intelligence in the likes of "Plato, Aristotle, Hipparchus and Archimedes", who, like all humans, are composed of such ordinary substances as fleshes, blood, phlegm and yellow and black bile we share with other animals,[12] before concluding that sun, moon and stars must be of pre-eminent intelligence. addition, This intelligence trickles down, or, as Galen argues, pervades the air surrounding us and partaking of the sun's light and power.[13]

3. Limitations and Constraints: Matter

Plato's cosmic optimism shared by Galen is not blind to the element of disorder and imperfection displayed by the world. It is referred to by Plato as "Necessity", the "Receptacle", the "Place" and the "Mother of Becoming". The good Creator has the best intentions but he faces the task of imposing order upon a resistant matter-like entity (*Timaeus* 47e3-69a5), which was identified with the material cause by Aristotle and the early Peripatetics as well as Galen himself. Plato's Receptacle provides an explanation and justification for imperfection in a world of prevalent order and purposefulness. God does not create out of nothing but faces certain constraints, which provide a way of avoiding the problem of theodicy. This is clear from Galen's response to the biblical account of creation from *Genesis* I:

> It is precisely this point in which our own opinion and that of Plato and the other Greeks who follow the right method in science differs from the position taken by Moses. For the latter it seems enough to say that God simply willed the arrangement of matter and instantaneously it was arranged; for he believes everything to be possible with God, even should he wish to make a bull or a horse out of ashes. We however do not hold this; we say that certain things are impossible by nature and that God does not even attempt such things at all but that he chooses the best out of the possibilities of becoming (*UP* XI, ch. 14 = ii.158-60 H. Tr. May).[14]

God, then, has to strike compromises, with often truly admirable results, as Galen demonstrates in *On the Usefulness of Parts*. But the material the divine craftsman has to work with remains noticeable. This will have been especially clear to Galen who as a doctor had to deal with failing health. His role too has its limitations:

9 Thus, he even calls his project in *UP* a form of theology in the strict sense (ἀκριβής) exceeding all of medicine: *UP* 17.1, ii 447,16-25 H. *UP* is useful for the doctor but even more so for the philosopher as a more effective initiation ritual than that offered by the mystery religions: *UP* 17.1, ii 447,25-448,9 H. Galen not only toys with the term theology in its sense of a story about the gods such as offered by mythological poets such as Hesiod but also its philosophically purged meaning in Aristotle as the science of the supreme being: see Arist. *Metaph.* VI.1: 1026a19; XI.1: 1064b3.

10 Cf Vegetti 1981, van der Eijk 2017.

11 Galen here echoes Aristotelian passages on spontaneous generation such as *GA* I.1: 715b2-5, III.11: 762a, 761a; cf. III.8: 758b7-759a8.

12 The picture found in the epode of *UP* has been taken to reflect the idea of the Stoic world-soul (cf. May, p. 730, n.10) but there are also strongly teleological passages in Aristotle and it is no use specifying one specific source of influence; on the role of reason or intelligence (νοῦς) here cf. also *GA* II.3: 736b28-10 on divine intelligence entering bodies 'from outside' and shaping them. On this passage from the epode of UP in relation to disease see also Van der Eijk (2017), pp. 234-235.

13 *UP* XVIII.1, ii p.447.9-16 H. (= III. 359-360 K.); on this passage see Vinkesteijn (2024), pp. 119-120; Frede (2003), pp. 85, 102, 107-113.

14 For a discussion of this passage and further related ones see Tieleman (2015), with further references.

> Some constitutions are right from birth so weak that they cannot reach the age of sixty, even if Asclepius himself were to attend them (*San. Tu* 1.12.15, p. 29 Ko. = VI. 63 K. Tr. mine).

It is striking that Galen justifies the doctor's limitation by reference to the God of healing himself. As we shall see later on, Asclepius can be understood as an aspect of the all-encompassing demiurgic God (see below, p. **51**). At the same time, God's influence can be recognized even in lower forms of life, natural processes including even disease (see below, p.**51**) or seemingly insignificant body parts. The optimist spirit of Aristotle's *On the Parts of Animals* is echoed and surpassed by Galen in his *On the Use of Parts*.[15] The Aristotelian dictum "Nature does nothing in vain" finds even more radical application in Galen's hands.[16] Thus, he criticizes Plato and Aristotle for having overlooked the wonderful design manifested by the human nail (*UP* I.8, vol. I, pp.11.21-12.13 Helmreich = III.16-17 K.). But we may compare the radical teleology of *On the Use of Parts* with the statement made by Galen in his late tract *On the Formation of Embryos*, from an aporetic context:

> When one of my Platonist teachers[17] said that the soul that stretches through the entire cosmos[18] shapes the embryos I considered the artistic skill and power [scil. manifested in this process-TT] worthy of that soul but I could not bring myself to accept that scorpions, spiders, flies, mosquitoes, vipers and worms, intestinal worms and roundworms are formed by it because, I believed, an assumption like that came close to impiety. But on the other hand, it does not seem to me reasonable that the soul of matter has reached such as degree of artistic skill. I believe I can only declare about the cause that shapes living being that her skill and wisdom are very great (*Foet. Form.* 32-33, p.104.25-106.5 Nickel = IV.700-701 K.).

Galen has been wavering but in the end he cannot but acknowledge there is artistic skill (τέχνη) even in the design of such repellent or harmful creatures – a twist that recalls a similar statement made by Aristotle.[19] In his *On My Own* Opinions he writes that this is also the considered opinion Plato disclosed to a select readership in the *Timaeus* (*Prop. Plac.* ch. 13, p.130.1-132.14 Polemis-Xenophontos). The idea of a "soul of matter" alongside and apart from the governing world-soul reflects the *Timaeus* exegesis of what we call Middle Platonists, as is of course also suggested by Galen's reference to his Platonist teacher: Galen is here taking part in a Platonist debate, it seems.[20]

4. The Human Being as an Intermediate Creature

Galen's anthropology is deeply informed by Plato too. One could say that it represents a medical and anatomically-based version of the famous doctrine of the tripartition and trilocation of the psyche. Consider this summary:

> I have proved that an animal after birth is governed by three principles (ἀρχῶν), one located in the head, whose work is by itself to provide imagination and memory and recollection, knowledge and thought and ratiocination, and in its relation to the other parts of the animal to guide the sensation of the sensory parts and the motion of the parts that move voluntarily. A second principle is seated in the heart; its work is by itself to provide the 'tone' of the soul, to be constant and unyielding in the things that reason commands, and in states of emotion to provide the boiling, as it were, of the innate heat, as the soul at such times desires to avenge itself on the supposed wrongdoer, and this kind of thing is called anger; in its relation to other things its work is to be the source of warmth for the several parts and of pulsing motion for the arteries. The remaining power, seated in the liver, has as its work all the things that have to do with nutrition in the animal, the most important of which in us and in all sanguineous animals is the production of blood. To this same power belongs also the enjoyment of pleasures, and when it is moved by this enjoyment more than it should be, it produced intemperance and licentiousness (*PHP* VII 3.2-3, pp. 438.28-440.8 De Lacy. Tr. De Lacy, modified; cf. Plato, *Tim.* 69c-71e).

---

15 Cf. Aristotle's insistence in *Parts of Animals* that even in lowly and repellent creatures one can find admirable and divine features and his anecdote in the same work on Heraclitus quipping "there are gods even here" while warming himself at the stove, *PA* I.5:645a12-24. On *Parts of Animals* as a source of inspiration for Galen see Moraux (1985). *UP* represents Galen's answer to Aristotle's *PA*, which deals with the parts of animals in general while Galen in *UP* focuses almost exclusively upon the human physique.

16 On this dictum see below, n. **38**. On Galen's teleology see Hankinson (1988), (1989), (2021).

17 On Galen's early study with Platonists (and other philosophers) see *Aff. Dign.* 3-4, p.28.9-15 De Boer (Gaius T 3 Gioè), *Lib. Prop.* II 1, p.140.15-17 Boudon (= Albinus T1 Gioè, T 10 Göransson); with Tieleman (2020), pp.26-28.

18 See Plato, *Tim.* 34b, 36e.

19 See above n.**15**.

20 See the parallel passage from the preceding context where Galen also refers to ensouled matter, rejecting the position of "certain philosophers" that this creates living beings by contemplating the Ideas and expressing a preference for the assumption that it is one and the same soul that creates us and governs us during life: *Foet. Form.* 24-25, 100.24-29 Nickel (IV. 696-697K.). For the Platonist view referred to cf. Plut. *De an. procr. in Tim.* 24, 1024C. Platonist who thought along these lines started from Plato's account of the precosmic erratic motions in and of the Receptacle: *Tim.* 52d4-53a2.

The fact that we human thus combine a rational ("divine") and a non-rational a"animal") aspect is made in the following passage:

> The human race, sons, has something in common with both the gods and the non-rational animals, with the former in so far as it is rational, with the latter in so far as it is mortal. It is therefore preferable to take notice of the better part of this communion and cultivate education (*Protr.* 9.4, p.101.2-12 Boudon = I. 21 K. Tr. mine.)[21]

The idea of the human being as occupying a middle position in the scale of nature is how many Platonists in later antiquity read Plato: we are composite beings, rooted through our rationality in the divine realm but through our bodies having an animal side also.[22] It also has Aristotelian credentials.[23] Interestingly, Galen also identifies a specific human type as occupying the midmost position in our own species:

> Animal, for instance is genus; horse, ox and dog are species. Furthermore, the human being is middle, in its mixture, within the genus of animals as a whole [...] And, within human beings, the middle one is the so-called 'well-fleshed' (εὔσαρκος)[24] human being. This is the individual whom we cannot call either thick or thin, nor either hot or cold, nor refer to by any of those terms that indicate imbalance (*Temp.* 1, I. 541 K. = p. 21 Helmreich; transl. van der Eijk & Singer).

> [...] which human being has the best mixture[25] of all? We should place this human being in the middle with respect to all existent objects, and even more so in relation to human being and other elements; and using him as a kind of standard and yardstick should call all others hot, cold, dry or wet by comparison with him. Many indicators must point in the same direction here. For indeed, when one conducts the examination in relation to all existent objects, it must be apparent that such a person is in the middle, and this must be the case even more so in relation to human beings and animals. Now the common indicators that apply to all existent objects have been stated already; those applicable to animal species, on the other hand, are assessed on the basis of the perfection of the activity appropriate to each. It is appropriate for a human being to be very intelligent; for a dog to be both very docile and very brave; for a lion to be very brave only; for a sheep to be very docile. Moreover, that the activities of the body should be appropriate to the character of the soul has been shown by Aristotle in the *Parts of Animals*, and no less by us too[26] (*Temp.* I. 565-566 K. = pp. 35-36 Helmreich; tr. van der Eijk & Singer).

Such, then is the best-mixed man in respect of his body; in respect of his soul, similarly, he is precisely in the middle between boldness and cowardice, hesitancy and rashness, pity and envy. Such a person will be cheerful, affectionate, generous, intelligent (*Temp.* I. 576 K. = p. 42 Helmreich; tr. Van der Eijk & Singer). This application to morality offers Galen a nice opportunity to borrow Aristotle's famous doctrine of the right mean.

5. Galen's Role as a Doctor

Man's intermediate place in the cosmos comes with an interesting consequence for the practicing physician in particular: his role can be conceived as an extension of the creative and ordering activities of God. Creation is here viewed not (or not only) as a unique event by which the world started but as an ongoing process, with God providentially sustaining the world, i.e. what has come to be known as *creatio continua* ('continuous creation').[27] This is God's role as immanent demiurgic Nature.[28] It then becomes possible to see the doctor's healing activity as an extension of God's activity of effecting order in disorderly matter as far as possible. God's (i.e. in particular Asclepius') interventions through dreams guiding Galen's medical decisions are just one manifestation of this belief. But Galen's whole practice as a doctor makes him, in his own words, a servant of Asclepius.[29]

21 Cf. *ibid.* 2.1. *QAM* IV, c. 11, pp. 814-815 K. = pp. 78.4-80.2 Bazou.).

22 The key passage is *Timaeus* 42a1-3, on man's double nature (φύσις διπλή) from Plato's account of the creation of living beings (41a3-45b2). Cf. Alcinous, *Handbook of Platonism* (*Didaskalikos*), a work roughly contemporary with Galen, ch. 16, p.36.38-37.19 Whittaker (171-172 Hermann). On our being rooted in the divine realm (represented in this cosmos by the stars, the temporary abode of disembodied souls in the cycle of reincarnation) and having a divine spirit (δαίμων) within see also Pl. *Tim.* 89d4-90d7; cf. *Resp.* X.611e2; animals are marked by the lack of insight and philosophy: ibid. 91d6-92c3 (which perhaps should not be read as denying all rationality to animals). Cf. Nemes. *Nat. Hom.* 1, p. 2 Morani.

23 See esp. Arist. *EN* X.7: 1177b27-1178a8, esp.1177b28-29.

24 On the 'well-fleshed' and well-mixed (εὔκρατος) man see also *San. Tu.* VI. 27 K.

25 For Galen's physical explanation in terms of the blend or mixture of physical elements, as presented most notably in his treatise *On Mixtures*, see further Van der Eijk (2014) and (2015)

26 See e.g. Arist. *PA* III.1: 661b28-36; Gal. *UP* I, 1-2.

27 See *Prop. plac.* ch. 2 quoted above, p.47. Here it is clear that Galen avoids taking sides in the debate as to whether the creation story in the Platonic *Timaeus* should be taken literally, as referring to a unique event, or in the sense of a creatio continua. However, he is clear that this world is providentially governed.

28 On Nature (φύσις) = Demiurg as the active and creative principle in the whole of things see Kovacic (2001), pp.210-215. Cf. *UP* V 5, vol.i, p.268.25-28 Helmreich (III. 366-367K). On the link between creating and healing with reference ot nature see *Thrasyboulos* V. 853 K., 865-866 K.. Cf. *Nat. Fac.* II. 10 K

29 See below, n.43 with text thereto.

As we have seen in the second chapter of *On My Own Opinions* (above, p.**47**), there is not reason to suppose any fundamental difference, let alone contradiction, between Galen's appeal to an all-encompassing and all-pervasive Creator-God inspired by Plato's Demiurg on the one hand and Asclepius as one of the gods of the polytheistic pantheon on the other. In fact, there are clear signs that by Galen's time Asclepius became increasingly associated with Zeus, the supreme deity: Zeus-Asclepius. This may certainly have facilitated Galen's view of healing as an aspect of the highest god.[30]

The idea of healing as a form of creation is facilitated by the Hippocratic idea of Nature's own healing power, on which the physician builds. Thus we find Galen invoking as a Hippocratic principle that the doctor should *imitate* Nature. He actually appeals to it right at the end of his great work *On the Usefulness of Parts*:

> A third[31] advantage offered by this work [...] is its testimony against the sophists[32], who do not concede to us that crises in diseases are the work of Nature and who deny her any providence where animals are concerned. For when they frequently suggest that the usefulness of the parts (of which they know nothing) does not exist, they suppose that they are thus doing away with the skill (τέχνη) of Nature. And then they deride Hippocrates, who thinks it right to imitate what Nature is accustomed to do in crises. We ourselves are then forced to survey the usefulness of all the parts, even if they do not contribute towards the diagnosis of an illness or the prognosis of future ones. But in fact, the physician will derive the greatest benefit from this work, just as he does from a work on activities [scil. of body parts]. Indeed, when he is cutting into parts that for some reason are in bad condition, when he is cutting around them or excising them, or when he is removing arrows or darts, if he understands the usefulness of the parts, he will know which ones he should cut into freely and which he should spare (*UP* XVII.2, vol. ii, pp. 450.26-451.18 H. = III. 364-365K. Transl. May, modified).

Crisis in the ancient medical sense stands for the decisive moment after which the patient's condition will either deteriorate or improve and so is of special importance to the practicing physician. Apparently the idea is that the good Hippocratic doctor will attune his therapy to the patterns discernible in the natural course of a disease, notably in crises and remissions.[33] We come across Hippocrates' advice to imitate nature during crises more often in the Galenic corpus.[34] But in fact the idea of the doctor (or the art he represents) imitating nature is of wider application in the Galenic corpus.[35] In the second part of the passage he makes a point very similar to that put forward as the second benefit conferred upon the readers of *UP*: knowledge of the use of the body parts helps the doctor focus his therapy upon the correct organ or part; in other words, the impaired function indicates the bodily seat and enables him to avoid damaging unaffected parts and functions.[36] With all this, it is worth noting that the fact that diseases present particular patterns (expressible in terms of time: crisis on the seventh day etc.) and hence orderliness is taken as revealing the hand of God: they are not entirely governed by irrational matter. Providential nature manifests itself even at this level.[37] The practitioner of the rational art of medicine finds even here indicators and clues, even if – as we have seen – this art is stochastic and uncertain of its results. This robust view of providential

30 Galen's native city Pergamum was the undisputed centre of the Asclepius cult: see e.g. Gal. *Comp.Med.Loc.* XIII. 272K., Lucian, *Icaromenippus* 24 = Asclepius T 569 Edelstein. The Roman consular and senator Rufinus built a new sanctuary for "Zeus Asclepius the Saviour" in Pergamum around 145 CE: see Gal. *AA* I.2: II. 224-225 K. with Schlange-Schöningen (2003) pp.74-75; cf. Ziegenau and De Luca (1968-1984); Nutton (2013) p. 283

31 In the preceding context Galen has mentioned that his work is useful, first, because it drives home, against certain philosophers, the providential influence of the power (i.e. God) responsible for the usefulness of parts-which he calls a more general, not medical, issue. The second advantage is that it helps the doctor cure diseases of parts lying deep within the body: one can infer from the impaired function to the organ at which the therapy should be directed. The philosophers in question include the atomist philosophers and physicians (Epicureans, Asclepiades of Bithynia) and individuals such as Anaxagoras, who are also attacked for the same reason at the beginning of the entire work: see *UP* I.22, vol. I, pp. 58-60 H. (for Anaxagoras see I.3, vol. I, p.4 H.)

32 Galen's qualification, with its Platonic and pejorative ring, has a broad application to all those who engage in mischievous reasoning to deny obvious facts. Here it refers to Methodist and anti-Hippocratic physicians such as Thessalus of Tralles in particular. For Thessalus 'and his own sophists' see Gal. *MM* VI.3 = X. 406K. On his attack on Hippocrates see *MM* 1.2.1, X. 7-8K.

33 On the notion of crisis see Gal. *In Hipp. Progn.* III,1 = XVIII, 2, pp. 231-232 K. Cels. *Med.* 3. 4. 11. Cf. Langholf (1990), pp. 79-135; G.E.R. Lloyd (2003), pp. 124-125.

34 Gal. *In Hipp. Epid. I comm.* ii.48, 73.14-74.5 Wenkebach (XVIIA. 142-143 K.); *In Hipp. Aph.* XVIIB. 358K., 655K. XVIIIA. 24K. A few passages from the Hippocratic *On Regimen* refers to imitation in a relevant way, though without reference to crises in particular.

35 Cf. *MM* III.5: X 197 K. (imitating the nature of the skin). For a non-clinical and indeed non-medical example see *UP* VII.13, vol. I, p. 408 H. = III. 561 K. Galen mentions the tongue of a pipe as the invention of a clever craftsman who knew how to imitate nature's work, i.e. the human tongue. Galen argues that nature is superior to art or craft (τέχνη) and so a model to imitate. That art imitates nature is an Aristotelian motif: see *Phys.* II.2: 194a21.

36 Cf. above, n. 31.

37 On the 'acts of nature' in disease see also Van der Eijk (2017), p. 237.

Nature is quite in line with Galenus' emphasis on the Aristotelian dictum that Nature does *nothing* in vain.[38]

It is worth noting that the idea as it took shape in the medical tradition is reconcilable with Plato's call in the *Timaeus* to model our lives on the order and beauty of the cosmos (*Tim.* 89d4-90d7). In addition, Galen merges the Platonic idea of a divine Craftsman with Nature as artistic, as did Aristotle and the Stoics, but for which Galen appeals to Hippocrates. In this context divine Nature is not just the artistic creator of our bodies but also artistic in the medical sense of a healing force. On this point *UP* XVII.3 may be usefully compared with *PHP* IX.9.22-27. Here Galen first uses his version of the argument from design proving the existence of the Demiurg for anyone in his right mind (just as nobody would ascribe a ship or a house to chance because the builder is unknown, *ibid.* 22-24). Then he moves smoothly to Nature as the cause that fashioned us, which is illustrated by Hippocratic statements about Nature as a *healing* power, though without reference to crises (*ibid.* 25-27):

> Hippocrates [...] wrote the words: "Nature being well-instructed does what is needed without being taught"[39], and elsewhere he put it another way: "Our natures are the physicians of our diseases"[40]. And this statement amounts to the same thing: "Nature will wholly suffice"[41]. Sometimes he calls nature just (δικαίαν)[42] and the physician, he says, is its servant (ὑπέρετην) and imitator (μιμητήν)[43]; and everywhere in the discussion of particulars he extols and admires its power. He does not go so far as to declare what the substance (οὐσία) is of the nature that forms and governs us but gives the name "nature" to the cause that crafted us (τὸ ... δημιουργικὸν ἡμῶν αἴτιον), as is the custom among all men (*PHP* IX.8.26-27, p. 596.21-29 De Lacy; transl. De Lacy, modified).

Galen goes on to refer to *Tim.* 41a-d, the passage where the Demiurg entrusts his children with the creation of humans, pointing out that there is crucial difference between positing or proving "some God's, or the gods'" (where note again the interchangeability of the singular and plural) providence on the one hand and knowing the substance of him who made us (or the substance of the soul for that matter) on the other (*PHP* IX.9.1-3, pp. 596.30-598.5 De Lacy).

Conclusion

Galen did not work from scratch: he placed himself in a tradition that went back all the way to Hippocrates and Plato as its fountainheads but was enriched by the contributions of Aristotle in particular. While the dominant influence remains Plato Galen still is in a position to present his view of the cosmos as essentially Hippocratic, e.g. by exploiting to the full passages such as *Phaedrus* 270c-d. This having been said, it is noteworthy that he succeeds in combining all these sources of inspiration into a synthesis that might be called a medical philosophy or philosophical medicine. This also includes a particular view of his own role as a doctor in the context of the cosmology-cum-theology he developed.

---

38 On Nature doing nothing in vain, see e.g. *UP* III. 737, 751, IV. 56 K., *Sem.* IV 529, *PHP* 6.4.5 De L., *Nat. fac.* II 91, 175, *AA* 9.4, II 727 K.; cf. Arist. *Cael.* 271a33 (God and Nature), 291b13 (neither in vain nor unreasonably), *De an.* 432b, 434a, *GA* 741b4, *Incess. Anim.* 704b15, 711a18, *PA* 658a9, 695b19, *Pol.* 1253a9. On variant formuleas in Galen (nature does nothing superfluous, without good reason, coincidentally) see Kovacic (2001), p.213.

39 Hipp. *Epid.* vi.5.1: V 314.7-8 L.

40 Hipp. *Epid.* vi.5.1: V. 314.5 L.

41 Hipp. *Alim.* 15: *CMG* I 1, p.80.11 Heiberg = p.141.24 Joly.

42 Cf. Hipp. *Artic.* 10: IV. 102 L. cited *PHP* IX 4.2 where however δίκαιος means "even" or "symmetrical" and said of our arms and legs (cf. *LSJ* s.v. B.1). At *PHP* IX 8.12 Galen tweaks this statement as saying that the *body* is symmetrical.

43 Cf. Gal. *In Hipp. Epid. I comm.* ii.48, 73.21-23 Wenkebach (XVIIA. 143 K.): Hippocrates considers the doctor servant and imitator of nature; cf. *ibid.* ii.54 p.77.12-15 W. (XVIIA. 151 K.); cf. Hp. *Epid.* I, II. 636L, where however modern editors follow mss that give (servant of) "the art" (τέχνης) instead of "nature" (φύσιος). Galen says that he presented himself as servant (θεραπευτήν) of Asclepius, his "ancestral god" at *Lib. Prop.* III 5, p.142.16-17 Boudon (XIX. 18-19 K.). It has sometimes been supposed that Galen refers here to some cultic function he fulfilled in his native Pergamum or elsewhere; but the passages associating this appellation to these Hippocratic passages show why Galen can speak this way without any role in the Asclepius cult being involved; see Schlange-Schöningen (2003), pp. 78-79; Tieleman (2013) p. 110; Brockmann (2013), p. 55; Tieleman (2016), pp. 23-24. For art (or its practitioners) *imitating* nature there is no exact Hippocratic parallel, but Galen may have in mind, and find support in, a few statements in *On Regimen* which refer to imitation in a relevant way: *Vict.* I, c.11, p. 134.21-23 Joly (VI. 486 L.), c.16, p.138.5 Joly (VI. 490L.).

Bibliography

Brockmann, C. (2013): "Galen und Asklepios". ZAC17.1: pp. 51-67.

Das, A. (ed.) (2023): *Galen's Humanistic Medicine. The Essay* Quod Optimus Medicus. SAPERE XLIII. Tübingen: Mohr Siebeck.

Flemming, R. (2000): *Medicine and the making of Roman women: gender, nature and authority from Celsus to Galen*. Oxford: Oxford University Press.

Frede, M. (1981): "On Galen's Epistemology". In: Nutton, V. (ed.): *Galen. Problems and Prospects*. London: Wellcome Institute for the History of Medicine, pp. 65-86; repr. in *Essays in Ancient Philosophy*, Oxford: OUP 1987, pp. 279-298.

Frede, M. (2003): "Galen's Theology". In: Barnes, J. & Jouanna, J. (eds.): *Galien et la philosophie* Entretiens Hardt XLIX. Genève: Fondation Hardt, pp. 73-126.

Frede, M. (2010): "The Case for Pagan Monotheism in Greek and Greco-Roman Antiquity". In Mitchell, S., Van Nuffelen, P. (eds): *One God. Pagan Monotheism in the Roman Empire*. Cambridge: Cambridge Univ. Pr., pp. 53-81.

Hankinson, R.J. (1988): "Galen Explains the Elephant". In: Mathen, M. & Linsky, B. (eds.): *Philosophy and Biology. Canadian Journal of Philosophy*. Suppl. Vol. 14: pp. 135-157.

Hankinson, R.J. (1989): "Galen and the Best of All Possible Worlds". *Classical Quarterly* 39: pp. 206-227.

Hankinson, R.J. (2021): "God and the Material World: Biology and Cosmology in Galen's Physiology". In: Salles, R. (ed.): *Cosmology and Biology in Ancient Philosophy. From Thales to Avicenna*. Cambridge: CUP, pp. 190-208.

Havrda, M. (2017): "Body and Cosmos in Galen's Account of the Soul". *Phronesis* 62, No 1: pp. 69-89.

Jouanna, J. (2003): "La notion de nature chez Galien". In: Barnes, J. & Jouanna, J. (eds.): *Galien et la philosophie. Entretien sur l'antiquité classique*, Tome XLIX. Vandoeuvres-Genève: Fondation Hardt, pp. 229-268.

Kovacic, F. (2001): *Der Begriff der Physis bei Galen vor dem Hintergrund seiner Vorgänger*. Stuttgart: Franz Steiner Verlag.

Langholf, V. (1990): *Medical Theories in Hippocrates*. Berlin-Boston: De Gruyter.

Lloyd, G.E.R. (2003): *In the Grip of Disease. Studies in the Greek Imagination*. New York: Oxford University Press.

Moraux, P. (1985): "Galen and Aristotle's *De partibus animalium*". In: Gotthelf, A. (ed.): *Aristotle on Nature and Living Things: Philosophical and Historical Studies Presented to David M. Balme on His Seventieth Birthday*. Pittsburgh: Mathesis – Bristol Classical Press, pp. 327-344.

Nutton, V. (2013): *Ancient Medicine*. 2nd Edition. London: Routledge.

Schmalzriedt, E. (1970): *Peri Physeos. Zur frühgeschichte der Buchtitel*. München: Wilhelm Fink.

Schlange-Schöningen, H. (2003): *Die römische Gesellschaft bei Galen*. Berlin: De Gruyter.

Tieleman, T. (2013): "Miracle and Natural Cause in Galen". In: Alkier, S. & Weissenrieder, A. (eds.): *Miracles Revisited. New Testament Miracle Stories and their Concepts of Reality*. Studies on the Bible and its Reception, vol. 1. Berlin: De Gruyter, pp. 101-115.

Tieleman, T. (2015): "Galen and Genesis". In: van Kooten, G.H. (ed.): *The Creation of Heaven and Earth: Re-Interpretations of Genesis 1 in the Context of Judaism, Ancient Philosophy, Christianity, and Modern Physics*. Themes in Biblical Narrative vol. 8. Leiden-Boston: Brill, pp. 125-145.

Tieleman, T. (2016): "Religion and Therapy in Galen". In: Etzelmüller, G.& Weissenrieder, A. (eds.): *Religion and Illness*. Eugene OR: Wipf and Stock, pp. 15-31.

Tieleman, T. (2018): "Galen and Doxography". In: Mansfeld, J. and Runia, D.R. (eds): *Aetiana IV. Papers of the Melbourne Colloquium on Ancient Doxography*. Leiden and Boston: Brill, pp. 453-472.

Tieleman, T. (2020): "Galen's Self-Understanding and the Platonic *Phaedrus*". In: Delcomminette, S., d'Hoine, P. and Gavray, M.-A. (eds.): *The Reception of Plato's* Phaedrus *from Antiquity to the Renaissance*. Berlin: De Gruyter, pp. 27-39.

Tieleman, T. (2023a): "Galen on Human Perfection and Enhancement: Morality, Medicine, Cosmology". In: Leemans, J., Roskam, G. and van Deun, P. (eds.): *Longing for Perfection in Late Antiquity*. Proceedings of the Conference at Leuven 26-28 May 2021. Leiden: Brill, pp. 345-360.

Tieleman, T. (2023b): "Galen on Disagreement: Sects, Philosophical Methods and Christians". In: Joosse, A. & Ulacco, A. (eds.): *Dealing with Disagreement. The Construction of Traditions in Later Ancient Philosophy*. Monothéismes et Philosophie. Turnhout: Brepols, pp. 45-58.

Van der Eijk, P.J. (2014): "Galen on the Nature of Human Beings". In: Adamson, P., Hansberger, R. & Wilberding, J. (eds.): *Philosophical Themes in Galen. BICS* Suppl. 114. London: Institute of Classical Studies, pp. 89-134.

Van der Eijk, P.J. (2015): "Galen on the Assessment of Bodily Mixtures". In: Holmes, B. & Fischer, K. (eds.): *The Frontiers of Ancient Science: Essays in Honor of Heinrich von Staden*. Berlin: Walter de Gruyter, pp. 675-698.

Van der Eijk, P.J. (2017): "The Place of Disease in a Teleological Worldview: Plato, Aristotle, Galen". In: Rocca, J. (ed.): *Teleology in the Ancient World. Philosophical and Medical Approaches*. Cambridge: Cambridge University Press, pp. 217-241.

Vegetti, M. (1981): “Modelli di Medicina in Galeno”. In: Nutton, V. (ed.): *Galen: Problems and Prospects.* Cambridge: Cambridge University Press, pp. 47-65.

Vegetti, M. (1999): “De caelo in terram. Il *Timeo* in Galeno (*De Placitis, Quod Animi*)”. In: Brancacci, Aldo (ed.): *La filosofia in età imperiale: le scuole e le tradizioni.* Atti del colloquio, Roma, 17-19 giugno 1999. Naples: Bibliopolis, pp. 69-84.

Vinkesteijn, R. (2020): “Mixing Body and Soul: *Galen on the Substance of the Soul* in *QAM* and *De Propriis Placitis*”. *Phronesis* 64, No 2: pp. 224-246.

Ziegenau, O. & De Luca, G. (1968-1984): *Das Asklepieion von Permamum.* Altertümer von Pergamon. XI. Berlin: De Gruyter.

Vinkesteijn, R. (2022): *Philosophical Perspectives on Galen of Pergamum. Four Case-Studies on Human Nature and the Relation between Body and Soul.* Leiden: Brill.

Vinkesteijn, R. (2024): ‘Galen’s *Timaeus*’, forthcoming. In: J.W. Prins and E.V. Thomas (eds.): *Plato’s* Timaeus *and the Foundations of Medieval and Renaissance Thought*, Brill Studies in Intellectual History. Leiden: Brill, pp. 105-132.

Nature and Will in Maximus the Confessor and Augustine

Fr. Nikolaos Loudovikos

University of Ioannina

Abstract

Augustine's spiritual history, likewise Origen's, (though the latter was more sensitive than Augustine concerning the issue of freedom – but, nonetheless, he also was a *spiritualist*) did not allow him to understand human essence apart from a profound identification of it with soul, as an independent self-existing entity, which simply uses the body. Even when he assigns plausibility to bodily existence, he remains deeply pessimistic concerning its reality. Thus, he operates with an *ecstatic* understanding of the will, while Maximus, for whom the truth of human existence lies in its *whole,* that is, soul and body in a becoming of achieving nature's fulfilment, employs a concept of *natural will,* which contains all natural potency and desire.

Brian Daley, an otherwise prominent Patristic scholar, in his essay 'Making a Human Will Divine: Augustine and Maximus on Christ and Human Salvation',[1] not only draws a parallel between Augustine's and Maximus' doctrines of will, but he also makes the hypothesis that Maximus read Augustine, while he was in Africa, though as he also recognizes, there is no clear textual evidence in Maximus' work for this.[2] In fact, there exists an essential difference between the two doctrines, which indeed opens new paths in our consideration of the will. Augustine's conception of the will can be described as 'transcendental', or 'ecstatic', compared to that of Maximus'. Firstly, because, as it is well-known, Augustine submits the will to 'the virtues of the mind',[3] thus pushing it to overcome the ignorant material nature, flying toward the divine things. Secondly, because, in his Christology, seems to understand human will as something which is to be overcome by Christ's divine will. One of his foremost texts, in which this claim is launched is also quoted by Daley:

> 'How did our Lord marry two wills so that they became one in the humanity he bore? In his body, the Church, there would be some people who, after wanting to do their own will, would later follow the will of God. The Lord prefigured these people in himself.

1 A. Papanikolaou and G. Demacopoulos eds. (2008), pp.101-126.

2 It has become a sort of peculiar fashion for some Western theologians to search not just for theological affinities, but indeed for dependence of some eminent Greek Fathers upon eminent Western theologians, usually Augustine and, perhaps less, Scotus or Aquinas. One cannot see the theological purpose of such, sometimes so finely elaborated intellectual acrobatics! Some of these authors (not Brian Daley!) even become, at times, aggressive and scornful – and thus even more unconvincing.

3 *De lib. Arb.II,XVIII,50.*

in: Mouzala, M.G. (ed.) 2025: *Nature and Human Nature in Ancient Greek Philosophy and Its Reception.* Leiden: Sidestone Press, pp. 55-58.

He wanted to show that though they are weak, they still belong to him, and so he represented them in advance in his own person. […] He revealed the human will that was in him, but if he had continued to insist on that will, he would have seemed to display perversity of the heart. If you recognize that he had had compassion on you, and is setting you free in himself, imitate the next prayer he made: "Yet not what I will, but what you will be done Father" '.[4]

In this text, the bishop of Hippo tries to show how the two wills of Christ became one, exemplifying it through the oscillating will of some faithful, who hesitate to immediately choose God's will, instead of theirs. Thus, he insists that Christ 'prefigures' this wavering, by wrestling with his own human will, until he overcame it (as if it were sinful in itself) and abandoned it for the favour of the Father's will. However, in this way Augustine seems to ignore the possibility of *opening* Christ's human will to his divine will, instead of transcending it. This of course is almost the opposite of what Maximus asserted, concerning Christ's *natural will.* As I wrote recently:

'[…] Maximus saw in Gesthemane's condescension precisely the expression of Christ's *human* will. If we see Christ's human will as somehow necessarily denying divine will, then this precisely results in the Monothelite position, which subsequently needs a hypostatic will in Christ to solve his problem. The union of the two wills is thus revealed in the relationship of the Son with his Father, as it is *humanly realised*, through a free human will, open – since it is Christ's will – to the natural tri-hypostatic will of God, manifested in the hypostasis of Christ, who wills naturally and freely both as man and as God. Christ's human hesitation, natural fear and repugnance of death, *etc.*, as described by the Patristic tradition, were not, according to the Confessor, 'against' his divine will, since they represent human 'blameless and natural passions', *which, as the sinful inclination is not present in Christ, they are not in natural opposition, but in a certain convergence (συμβαίνοντα) with Him.*[5] Thus, these blameless passions do not represent any human volitional antithesis to the divine will, being also ultimately deified 'through the absolute union with divinity'.[6] Maximus' anti-Monothelite 'revolution' is precisely that Christ *wills only through and by and according to nature(s), which cannot be conceived as by nature opposing each other*. Thus, the only possible reason of disharmony between human and divine will in Christ, for Maximus, would be *sin.* And, since Christ is clear of sin, it is impossible for Him to have his two natural wills in disharmony[7].'[8]

As I have claimed in my *Analogical Identities: The Creation of a Christian Self,*[9] by his concept of 'natural will', Maximus wanted to express the inner life of nature. Let me repeat some little parts of what I wrote:

'This is precisely what Saint Maximus did. In his work on this particular subject, he seeks to define the concept, but to do so in an entirely existential, direct, non-abstract manner: "will" (as θέλησις and not βούλησις) is, in the first place, a universal, non-metaphysical, personal and profoundly direct desire to open up to the complete Being. Indeed, while the tradition before him abandoned the will, (as βούλησις), as prey to the intellect or the passions (or to a conflict between the two, he existentializes the will (as θέλησις), as "a simple, reasonable and vital appetite",[10] in contrast to the (for example Aristotelian) προαίρεσις,[11] deliberate choice, which is not, of course, a passive attraction to an object, but a mental, metaphysical attraction, intellectual and abstract, as "the companion of appetite, deliberate choice and judgement". The combination of the reason with the vital and existential allowed the Confessor to introduce the will as θέλησις into ontology itself, thus shaping, for the first time, an eschatological ontology […] In his letter to Marinus[12] he provides us with a comprehensive definition of the natural will (φυσικόν θέλημα). Through its will, the being seeks the full entity of its nature, the complete "according to nature" realization of all its essential component parts. The will holds the being together and because of it the being exists, lives and moves. Intellect and sensation follow, in contrast to all received psychology. But here we are in the sphere of ontology: the will-horizon of the Being makes it eschatological since it introduces into the Being the process of becoming an entity entire. In other words, it does so by directing action, which every being has, naturally and by reason of its nature, towards the eschatological realization of its complete Being, which begins from now […] This is why beings are linked to their principle "by appetite", as a desire for a process of becoming which completes their truth eschatologically by opening them up fully towards it. The introduction of the will as a θέλημα— *a burning desire* beyond reason,

4 *Enar.in Ps.*93,19, M.Boulding trans.(2002), p.395.

5 Ad Marinum (PG 91:236).

6 *Ibid.* (PG 91:237A).

7 *Disputatio cum Pyrrho* (PG 91:292AB).

8 See Loudovikos (2019), p.325.

9 Loudovikos (2019), Part II, ch.1.

10 *To Marinus*, PG 91, 13A.

11 *Nicomachean Ethics*, VI, 1139a 22-b5.

12 Cf. *To Marinus*, 12 CD.

encompassing not only reason but also sentiments, desires, the bodily dimension, and also perhaps what a modern psychologist would call *the unconscious*— into ontology makes it eschatological, then; in other words makes it the ontology of the freedom of the natural from its entirely "given" nature: nature "becomes", through a free desire, and in dialogue with the divine θέλησις/*desire*, and it not merely "is".'

Thus, what Maximus seems to ask is rather a gnomic/personal *opening* of this natural will to God's will (instead of overcoming it), in order for nature to acquire divine and eternal life: this is the absolute abolition of any sort Platonism, Christianized or not. And it is crucially important that even the modern Orthodox personalists, who, although they deal with Maximus, are not aware of the true meaning of his concept of natural will, they understand nature in a negative way, as a burden of necessity, as an irrational darkness; what is immensely important is that, in this case, *it is utterly impossible to work with and on this nature, through a dialogue of two wills or two acts/energies, divine and human.* Thus, even if we admit a final resurrection of this fallen nature, as these theologians rightly do, this is absolutely impossible to result to salvation, in the properly Biblical sense of the term, which implies not only the divine will of giving eternal life to creatures, but also their conscious will and intention/prohairesis to receive it, and to dialogically assimilate it – this is precisely the content of what has been called *ascesis* in the Patristic thought. In a different case, and according to the Maximian understanding of *apokatastasis*, it is impossible for creatures to be saved indeed. As I wrote in the past:[13]

'According to St Maximus, the Church recognizes three sorts of *apokatastasis* (restoration). The first is that of each being when it fulfils the inner principle of virtue. The second is the restoration of all created nature, in incorruption and immortality, through the resurrection. The third (which Maximus thinks Gregory of Nyssa has misused) is the restoration of the powers of the soul to their prelapsarian natural state. They will lose the memory of evil, but they will not participate in God; they will not be deified. Souls will receive their original powers "in terms of understanding, not in terms of participation"; it will be clear that the Creator is not to blame for sin, and those souls themselves will naturally remain without any part in His uncreated blessedness.[14] Florovsky, in his exposition of Maximus' teaching, remarks that God will indeed return to sinners everything they had lost through sin, restoring their souls to the fullness of their natural powers and capabilities. They will "cognize" God and have a certain understanding of Him, but without participation in his blessings. Thus they will be constantly experiencing their lack of communion with Life, constantly realizing in all sorts of ways the terrible pointlessness of the spiritual path they took in rejecting God's love and making their own hell through the perverted movement of their gnomic will.'[15]

All this happens on the "eighth day".

'The eighth and first day, or rather the one ceaseless day, is the unmingled and all-radiant presence of God, which comes about after the cessation of things that are in motion; when in His entirety He comes to dwell, as is fitting, in the total [being] of those who by choice

13 Loudovikos (2010), p.82.

14 *Questions and Answers*, PG 90: 796A-C: "The Church recognizes three sorts of *apokatastasis* ('restoration'). One is the restoration of each being through the *logos* of virtue, when he is restored after fulfilling the *logos* of virtue which exists for that end. The second is the restoration of the entire nature to incorruption and immortality at the resurrection. The third, which Gregory of Nyssa misuses in his homilies, is the restoration of the soul's powers, which had succumbed to sin, to [the state in which] they were created. For as the whole [of human] nature at the resurrection will receive incorruption of the flesh in the time hoped for, even so, as the ages go by, the perverted powers of the soul should put off the memories of evil instilled into the soul. And when the soul has passed through all the ages and found no place to stop, it will come to God who has no end. And thus the soul will regain its powers in terms of understanding, though not in terms of participation in good things, and will be restored to its original state. And it will be shown that the Creator is not to blame for sin.

15 G. Florovsky, (1987), pp. 244-5: "In fulfilling the fates God will restore the full entirety of his creation not only in existence but also in eternal existence. But not in good-existence, for good-existence cannot be given without the demanding and accepting of love. God will give to sinners and return everything they lost through sin, restoring their souls in the fullness of their natural forces and capabilities. They will receive the capacity for spiritual knowledge and moral evaluation. They will cognize God. Perhaps they will even lose memory of sin and come to God in a certain understanding – *ti epignosei*. However, they will not receive communion with his blessings – *ou te methexei ton agathon*. Only the righteous are capable of savouring and enjoying. Only they receive communion with life, while people of evil will who have collapsed in their thoughts and desires are far from God, are devoid of life, and constantly decay and constantly die. They will not taste life, and will be tormented by belated repentance, by the consciousness of the senselessness of the path they took to the very end. This will be ineffable sorrow and sadness. According to St Maximus' notions, it is not God but the sinner himself who prepares his own torment and grief on judgement day." Let us not forget that here the Confessor is also trying to correct Gregory of Nyssa's theory of *apokatastasis*.

> have used their *logos* of being in accordance with nature, and grants them eternal well being through participation in Himself, since He alone properly speaking *is*, and is eternally, and enjoys well being. But to those who by their gnomic will have used their *logos* of being in a way contrary to nature He properly apportions woe-being instead of well-being, since they lack the capacity to receive well being, having set their faces against it.'[16]

It is thus obvious that without the personal synergetic direction of our natural will to God, in Christ, through the Spirit, it is impossible to participate indeed in divine life.

Concerning now the particular topic of this paper, it is obvious that it can be taken as an axiom that *so much transcendental or ecstatic will, that much ecstatic solipsism;* the primacy of intellect, which is the vehicle of, precisely, the alleged *transcendentality* of will, results practically to affirm individualism, precisely because it is the other parts of the soul that create communion. Moreover, this will does not listen so much to nature, it generally prefers transcendence than transformation (or believes that transcendence is the only way for transformation). In that case communion exists, but in a second step, it does not belong to the *first philosophy.*[17] But in this case the original sin has to do with domination, conflict, power; Augustine and Origen had their way to ecclesialize their lives, but the germ of the will to power is already there.[18]

On the other hand, natural will has to respond to the nature's demands for unification, incorruption and absolute meaningfulness, through divine participation. But this passes only through bridging the rifts of the fragmented nature (made by human ecstatic transcendental will) as Maximus has so clearly explained; this is precisely the course to *homoousion*, consubstantiality, transferred from the Trinitarian life in creation, through Christ, in the Church.[19] The true gnomic realization of the natural will is thus ultimately (and this is also the way of both directing it and verifying its true function) *the will to consubstantiality.*

With such an understanding of will, such as that of Augustine's and Origen's it is difficult not to ultimately understand Christian *ascesis* in a sort of negation of oneself. Tillich, who, in general, claimed himself an Augustinian, wrote about his mentor: 'Augustine always remained under the influence of Manichaeism. He left the group and fought against it, but his thinking and even more his feeling were coloured by its profound pessimism about reality. His doctrine of sin is probably not understandable apart from his Manichean period'. Tillich avers that the future bishop of Hippo left Manichaeism *not* for religious reasons, but because of astronomy, which revealed to him the order and beauty of this allegedly bad world. After a period of legitimate scepticism, he wanted certainty, and his 'liberation from scepticism in the philosophical realm was brought about by his Neo-Platonic period', since he 'used this philosophy as the basis for a new certainty, the immediate certainty of God. In Neo-platonism you have the immediacy of truth in the inner soul, and from this he got his new certainty of the divine'.[20] Augustine's spiritual history, likewise Origen's, (though the latter was more sensitive than Augustine concerning the issue of freedom – but, nonetheless, he also was a *spiritualist*) did not allow him to understand human essence apart from a profound identification of it with soul, as an independent self-existing entity, which simply uses the body. Even when he assigns plausibility to bodily existence, he remains, as we said above, deeply pessimistic concerning its reality. Thus, he operates with an *ecstatic* understanding of the will, while Maximus, for whom the truth of human existence lies in its *whole*, that is, soul and body in a becoming of achieving nature's fulfilment, employs a concept of *natural will*, which contains all natural potency and desire.

16 *Ambigua*, PG 91: 1392D.

17 Loudovikos (2006), pp.92-93; Loudovikos (2016) , pp.136-143, 161-177.

18 As I tried to show in Loudovikos (2019), pp. 42-64, 207-228.

19 Loudovikos (2016), pp.213-232.

20 Paul Tillich (1967), pp.107-108.

Bibliography

Daley, B. (2008): "Making a Human Will Divine: Augustine and Maximus on Christ and Human Salvation". In: Demacopoulos, G. and Papanikolaou, A. (eds): *Orthodox Readings of Augustine.* Crestwood, New York: St Vladimir's Seminary Press, pp. 101-126.

Florovsky, G. (1987): *Byzantine Fathers of the Sixth to Eighth Century, The Collected Works of Georges Florovsky*, Volume 9. Vaduz: Buchervertriebsanstalt.

Loudovikos, N. (2006): *Ορθοδοξία και Εκσυγχρονισμός: Βυζαντινή Εξατομίκευση, Κράτος και Ιστορία στην προοπτική του Ευρωπαϊκού μέλλοντος.* Athens: Armos.

Loudovikos, N. (2010): *A Eucharistic Ontology: Maximus the Confessor's Eschatological Ontology of Dialogical Reciprocity.* Boston: Holy Cross Sem. Press.

- (2016): *Church in the Making. An Apophatic Ecclesiology of Consubstantiality.* New York: St Vladimir's Seminary Press.
- (2019): *Analogical Identities:The Creation of the Christian Self. Beyond Spirituality and Mysticism in the Patristic Era.* Turhout: Brepols 2019.

Tillich P. (1967): *Systematic Theology* [vol. 3]. Chicago: University of Chicago Press.

PART II

Peripatetic Philosophy and Late Neoplatonism

Alexander of Aphrodisias on the first cause, divine power, the city and the household

Frans A.J. de Haas

Leiden University

Being a power from the gods, nature is capable of preserving the right order of movement according to a certain harmonious sequence, not in virtue of any reasoning process or thought *(noesis)*, but because it is from the gods.

ἡ φύσις … τῷ ἀπὸ θεῶν οὖσα δύναμις τὸ εὔτακτον τῆς κινήσεως σώζειν κατ᾽ ἀκολουθίαν τινὰ ἡρμοσμένην, μὴ κατὰ λογισμόν τινα καὶ νόησιν, ἀλλὰ τῷ ἀπ᾽ ἐκείνων εἶναι.

(Alex. *in Metaph.* 104.7-10)

Abstract

Alexander of Aphrodisias (c. 200 CE) was concerned to show that Peripatetic philosophy provided the most successful theory about the relation between the universe, and the First Cause that is responsible for the unity and order of the universe. In this paper I first describe the state of the discussion between Stoics, Platonists and Peripatetics on this issue. Then I examine how Alexander introduced a divine power, which he identified with the non-rational nature at work in each natural thing. This power resides in the outer sphere of the universe as an effect of its rational desire for the First Cause, and is transmitted all the way down to the nature of the elements in prime matter. Thus the First Cause is a form that is responsible for all forms; and an intellect that is responsible for all intelligibility and intellection in the universe. In this way Alexander made the most of Aristotelian principles, while rejecting the Platonic World Soul and Forms, as well as the Stoic all-pervading material God.

Alexander of Aphrodisias is a major source for theories concerning the order of nature. He attempted to put together a coherent Peripatetic theory of the universe which would do justice both to Aristotle's texts, and to all the questions Aristotle's text had raised before his time, with fellow Peripatetics and opponents alike. The question on which we shall focus here is the nature of the relationship between the First Cause, Aristotle's Unmoved Mover, and the rest of the universe. Since this issue has been the subject of an impressive amount of scholarship already, I will here limit myself to providing an outline of the various philosophical challenges Alexander was faced with. Then I shall highlight the main features of the way Alexander set out to meet those challenges, notably the introduction of a divine power. In particular I shall focus on how Alexander illustrated his novel account of cosmic order by means of adopting and adapting two familiar analogies, viz. the rule of the city, and the organization of the household. I conclude by assessing how and to what extent Alexander succeeded in providing a Peripatetic cosmology that made good on the questions of his

in: Mouzala, M.G. (ed.) 2025: *Nature and Human Nature in Ancient Greek Philosophy and Its Reception.* Leiden: Sidestone Press, pp. 61-74.

Peripatetic predecessors, and steered safely between the Stoic Scylla and the Platonic Charybdis while adopting some of the benefits of their respective philosophical positions.

Philosophical challenges: setting the stage

In Aristotle's works the order of the universe is explained by the interplay of four causal powers, summarized in the maxim 'nature is the cause of order in everything' (*Physics* VIII.1, 252a12). As is well-known, in *Phys.* VII-VIII Aristotle tries to reduce all change to circular motion, and circular motion to a first cause of motion which is completely unmoved, hence without potentiality, incorporeal, and eternal. But how can such a baffling cause be the starting-point of motion? In *Physics* VIII Aristotle does not say.

In *Metaph.* XII Aristotle starts by suggesting that whether the universe is a whole, or coheres by virtue of an ordered succession, substance plays the most prominent role in it.[1] In *Metaph.* XII.2-4 Aristotle reminds us of the physical model of underlying subject, form, and privation, supplemented by the distinction between potentiality and actuality, which both apply to all four kinds of change (viz. change in place, quantity, quality, and substance). In this analogical sense the principles are the same for everything, although they are different in each particular case.[2] Hence this model, Aristotle insists, also applies to eternal heavenly bodies that only change in place: they must have a matter for change in place,[3] as well as a cause of their change. What is the cause of their change?

As is well-known, *Metaph.* XII.6-9 develops a sustained argument for the existence of such a special kind of substance. A substance that is both eternal and not subject to any change fills a necessary spot next to substances that come to be and perish (in the sensible world), and eternal substances that are subject to motion (the heavenly bodies).[4] The *eternal* circular movement of the heavenly bodies cannot exist without a cause that eternally remains the same in actuality, while they are subject to motion. The cause of their motion must be external to them.[5] The activity that constitutes its being is the highest activity in Aristotle's universe: thinking. Since it is the highest substance it can only think about itself, for thinking something else would make it dependent on something lesser than itself. Thus the first cause is a thinking of thinking (νόησις νοήσεως).[6]

However, this self-contained first substance creates a major problem: *how* does it cause the eternal motion of the heavenly bodies? And how is it related to the rest of the universe, both supralunary and sublunary, which, Aristotle claims, depends on it?[7] Here Aristotle famously introduces the way in which an object of desire and an object of thought can cause motion: without themselves being moved in any way.[8] In *De anima* III.9-10 and *De motu animalium* Aristotle discussed in more detail how objects of desire (in all animals) and objects of thought (in human beings) cause the soul to initiate a cascade of physiological changes that issues in locomotion and other actions. These two kinds of object initiate motion as unmoved movers: final causes that may be real or apparent goods concerned with actions.

At the start of *De motu animalium* 6 Aristotle refers back to both his *De anima* and *Metaph.* XII, when he clearly sets apart the application of this theory to the movement of the outer sphere from other applications.[9] For objects of desire and thought in animals constitute limited goals that cause limited motions, whereas the movement of the outer sphere is unlimited because it is directed towards that which is eternally beautiful and truly and primarily good.[10] In short: the hierarchy of final causes at which motions are aimed is the explanation for this difference between the motions caused. Moreover, according to *MA* 1-2 self-movement in animals requires a point of rest inside the animal (e.g. a joint at which arms and legs bend for locomotion), as well as outside the animal (e.g. the earth against which a walker pushes himself forward). The movement of the universe as a whole can only be explained when it has a cause of motion outside itself (*MA* 3-4).[11] The model of desire and thought, then, requires that the heavenly bodies have souls with a desire towards the first principle.

This approach can be regarded as a further development of the theory that Aristotle's explored in *De caelo* II.[12] In *Cael.* II.1, 284a18-24, when assessing the 'mythical' views of his predecessors, Aristotle denies the existence of souls in heavenly bodies; but in *Cael.* II.12, he acknowledges that it would solve many problems if one would ascribe 'activity and life' to them (*praxis kai zōē*, 292a18-22). He explains the increasing number of different motions in the universe from the degree to which each member of the universe succeeds in reaching the first, or a more limited, goal.

The resulting picture is described in *Metaph.* XII.7:

> **T1** There is, then, something which is always moved with an unceasing motion, which is motion in a circle; and this is plain not in theory only but in fact.

1 Arist. *Metaph.* XII.1, 1069a19-21.

2 *Metaph.* XII.4-5. On *Metaph.* XII see e.g. Frede, and Charles (2000).

3 *Metaph.* XII.2, 1069b24-26 with *Metaph.* VIII.1, 1042b5-6.

4 *Metaph.* XII.6, 1071b3-11, cf. XII.1 1069a30-33, with the corresponding distinction into three types of study (πραγματεία) at *Phys.* II.7, 198a29-31.

5 *Metaph.* XII.6, 1071b19-22; 1072a9-18; XII.7, 1071a21-26.

6 *Metaph.* XII.7, 1072b14-30; 1073a3-13; XII.9, esp. 1074b34-35.

7 *Metaph.* XII.7, 1072b13-14, quoted below T1 (last sentence).

8 *Metaph.* XII.7, 1072a26-30.

9 *MA* 6, 700b4-11.

10 *MA* 6, 700b13-701a2.

11 For a detailed analysis of *MA* see Primavesi, and Corcilius (2018) and Rapp, and Primavesi (2020).

12 On the interpretative problems surrounding Aristotle's theory of heavenly bodies see esp. Bodnár (1997).

> Therefore the first heaven (*prōtos ouranos*) must be eternal. There is therefore also something which moves it. And since that which is moved and moves is intermediate, there is a mover which moves without being moved, being eternal, substance, and actuality. And the object of desire and the object of thought move in this way; they move without being moved.
>
> The primary objects of desire and of thought are the same. For the apparent good is the object of appetite, and the real good is the primary object of wish. But desire is consequent on opinion rather than opinion on desire; for the thinking is the starting-point. And thought is moved by the object of thought, and one side of the list of opposites is in itself the object of thought; and in this, substance is first, and in substance, that which is simple and exists actually. [...] But the good, also, and that which is in itself desirable are on this same side of the list; and the first in any class is always best, or analogous to the best. [...]
>
> But since there is something which moves while itself unmoved, existing actually, this can in no way be otherwise than as it is. For motion in space is the first of the kinds of change, and motion in a circle the first kind of spatial motion; and this the first mover sets in motion (*kinei*). The first mover, then, of necessity exists; and in so far as it is necessary, it exists in a good way (*kalōs*), and in this sense it is a first principle.
>
> For the necessary has all these senses – that which is necessary perforce because it is contrary to impulse, that without which the good is impossible, and that which cannot be otherwise but is *absolutely* necessary. On such a principle, then, depend the heaven (*ouranos*) and the world of nature (*phusis*).[13]

As moved mover, the eternal circular motion of the heavens requires an unmoved mover – such as objects of desire and thought are. This particular object of desire and thought has to be an eternal substance in actuality. The second paragraph provides a further specification that is necessary if we want to apply the general notion that all objects of desire and thought are unmoved movers, to the object of desire and thought that is the Unmoved Mover of the universe. Aristotle loosely refers to a list of opposites with positive and negative terms, which elsewhere he regards as a Pythagorean legacy,[14] and reduces to the opposites being and non-being.[15] He assumes that the members of the positive column are all objects of thought. Among beings, simple substance in actuality is first, among desirable objects that which is beautiful and desirable in itself is first. All firsts coincide in being the best, if only by analogy.

This is meant to entail that the Unmoved Mover has to be both the *primary* object of desire (which has to be an object of *rational* desire for a *real* good, whose eternity renders it absolutely *necessary* and the *primary* good without which no goodness exists),[16] and thereby the *primary* object of thought – which will be the reason why its thinking is directed at its own activity of thinking as well.[17] The hierarchies of objects of desire and thought converge in a single first principle. It is this principle which causes the circular motion of the heaven, always in actuality, which is the first among spatial motions, which in their turn are prior to all other motions. The first heaven is the moved mover that is (somehow) responsible for all other motions.[18]

This theory seems to imply that the first principle does not *directly* affect everything in the universe, but only by mediation of the heavenly bodies. Strictly speaking, the first principle might serve as direct object of rational desire *only* for the soul of the outer sphere, which then somehow transmits its movement to the other spheres. One type of transmission of motion is suggested in *Metaph.* XII.8 where Aristotle uses contemporary astronomy to provide the most likely explanation of the successive motions of the heavenly bodies. The changing position of the sun moving along the ecliptic causes the seasons, which cause processes of generation and corruption.[19] The heat of the sun also causes exhalations from water and earth, which cause further geological and meteorological phenomena.[20] But these processes seem rather haphazard and crude. Where does the precise order and diversity in all these processes come from?

Alternatively, each of the heavenly bodies independently desires the same first principle, but then the issue arises how to explain the differences between their heavenly trajectories. They are all made of the same ether, and if they all strive for the same final cause, why

13 *Metaph.* XII.7, 1072a21-32, 34-b1, b7-14, transl. Barnes (1991) with modifications (cf. note 18).

14 In *Metaph.* I.5, 986a22-31 Aristotle lists limit-unlimited, odd-even, one-manifold, right-left, male-female, at rest-in motion, straight-curved, light-dark, good-bad, and square-rectangular as a list of proposed principles of nature which he does not himself endorse, cf. *Metaph.* XIII.6, 1093b7-21.

15 Cf. *Metaph.* IV.2, 1004b27-1005a3; this is part of his argument to establish being-qua-being as the proper subject of first philosophy, to which our text can be compared as a further application.

16 If all three senses of 'necessary' apply to the Unmoved Mover, I am tempted to regard the first type, the necessity that opposes natural impulse, as an indication of how this theory of the Unmoved Mover supersedes the circular motion inherent in ether, by explaining more than just the kind of its motion.

17 *Metaph.* XII.9.

18 I pass over the difficulty that T1 starts by identifying the *first* heaven, i.e. the outer sphere, but seems to comprise (the spheres of) *all* heavenly bodies in its last sentence. The Barnes translation obscures this problem by translating 'heavens' in plural.

19 Cf. e.g. *Metaph.* XII.5, 1071a13-17; *GC* II.10, 336a32-b2, b17-19.

20 Cf. e.g. *Mete.* I.2, 339a21-32; I.4, 341b5-18.

do they move in different circles at different speeds? Do their differences depend on their individual natures, i.e. their souls, or perhaps on their distance from the first principle, or both? In view of Alexander's solution it is important to note in advance that the final causation of the first principle neither explains the existence of the heavenly bodies, nor the coming to be and perishing of sublunary substances and their natures – even though both heaven and nature depend on the first principle. More is needed to explain the order exhibited by the universe.

More explanation is exactly what Theophrastus' summoned the Peripatetics to provide through the incisive questions that fill his so-called *Metaphysics*.[21] In this area Theophrastus was to set the Peripatetic agenda, as he also did in the context of e.g. the ancient commentaries on *De anima* III.[22] A quick survey may show the penetrating nature and exhaustiveness of his questions, and at the same time suggest a possible motivation for Alexander's theory.

In Aristotle the sublunary realm is severed from the heavenly spheres by the fact that the latter consist of ether which does not interact with the four elements of the sublunary world; in addition, the whole edifice is crowned by a separate self-absorbed intellect. Theophrastus wonders why the universe does not fall apart because the intelligible and sensible are never unified (aporia 2 and 5). He speaks approvingly of the superior power (*dunamis*) of the first principle that lies in its nature of being an object of desire, but complains that it is rather the notion of desire (*ephesis*) on the part of the heavens that leaves much to be explained (aporia 6). What is the final cause of their seemingly opposed rotations? Do they each have a different unmoved mover, and if so how many are there (aporia 7)? Why do the heavenly bodies pursue motion rather than rest if the first principle they desire is at rest? If desire implies soul, is not that soul's thinking (*dianoia*) the first motion, and prior in rank to the rotation of the heavens because soul causes life and desire itself (aporia 8)?[23] Furthermore (aporia 9), why are only the rotations of the heavens explained by desire, and not also the changes in the sublunary world down to the centre? Is the first principle too weak to reach so far down (*pace* Homer), or is the sublunary world somehow unreceptive of its power, so that the changes in it come out as merely accidental?[24] Focusing on the heavenly bodies, one might ask whether their desire for the first principle is accidental or belongs to their essence (aporia 11). The last question Theophrastus raises for our topic deserves to be quoted in full because, I propose, it makes a suggestion that Alexander's theory fleshes out in more detail:[25]

> **T2** (Aporia 14.2) Again, it is difficult to ascribe to each [set of things] its [own] formal principles by a collective referral to a final cause in all [cases]-both in animals and in plants and even in the very bubble[26]-unless it happens that, by reason of the order and change of *others*, there come about all manner of shapes and varieties of atmospheric and terrestrial [things]; of which in particular some make the greatest paradigmatic [cause] to be the [things] relating to the seasons of the year, in which [seasons] there are generated alike animals and plants and fruits, with the sun being, as it were, the begetter.[27]

The multitude of formal principles is hard to refer to a final cause, Theophrastus suggests, unless cosmic variety arises from the order and change of other things, under the general influence of the seasons caused by the sun as general cause of generation and corruption. We shall see that Alexander will try to establish exactly what Theophrastus considers difficult: to refer the multitude of forms to the final cause, which thereby also assumes a role in establishing the order and changes of all things due to their individual nature.

It seems fair to say that the Stoic view of the universe was designed to avoid all of the aforementioned problems.

21 See Gutas (2010) for the Greek, Arabic, and Latin versions of this text, with translation and extensive commentary. Gutas prefers the title *On first principles* preserved in the Latin version. In the text I use his numbering of "aporiae".

22 For the role of Theophrastus' questions on intellect see De Haas (2020) 24 with n. 46.

23 For the reduction of the primary type of desire, rational wish, to thought see T1 above.

24 Note that *GC* II.10, 336a1-337a7 makes clear that the rotation of the heavenly bodies, esp. sun and moon, is the medium by which sublunary rectilinear motions, as well as the eternal cycle of generation and corruption of individuals of the species can be said to refer back to the first principle, there referred to as 'god' (336b32). 'Nature in all cases desires the better' (336b27-28) already suggests that desire may not be limited to the heavenly bodies. This passage also states that there is corruption (non-being) because not everything can always have being 'since they are too far removed from the principle'. We shall see this principle return in Alexander.

25 See below, p. 68-71.

26 As Gutas notes, this is probably a reference to the 'bubble' of air and vital heat that is the beginning of spontaneous generation according to Aristotle, cf. *GA* III.11, 762a21-25.

27 Theophr. *Metaph.* 7a19-b5 transl. Gutas.-The last sentence refers to Aristotelian doctrine, cf. *Metaph.* XII.5 1073a15-23: "But the distinction of actuality and potentiality applies differently to cases where the matter is not the same, in which cases the form also is not the same but different; e.g. the cause of man is the elements in man (viz. fire and earth as matter, and the peculiar form), and the external cause, whatever it is, e.g. the father, and besides these the sun and its oblique course, which are neither matter nor form nor privation nor of the same species with man, but moving causes." (transl. Barnes (1991)). Cf. note 19.

Their god, an active material principle, is in no way separate from the universe, but thoroughly pervades it. The cohesion or tension in bodies, the nature in plants, soul in animals, and rationality in humans are all manifestations of this same principle.[28] The complete unity of the resulting universe, which obeys the same principles down to the smallest detail, is a serious challenge to Peripatetic physics.

An influential earlier Peripatetic answer to Theophrastus and the Stoics exists in the pseudo-Aristotelian *De mundo* – which Alexander probably knew.[29] In the *De mundo*, we find a single power or nature pervading the universe in order to create and preserve its order, which is clearly set off against the substance (*ousia*) of the first principle: the principle's *substance* remains aloof as is befitting for a god and ruler, only its *power* pervades the universe.[30] Furthermore, this power controls the balance and agreement (*homologia*) of the four elements of the sublunary sphere,[31] and holds the universe together as a cohesive cause.[32] Despite this distinction, and despite the contributing role of the elements and other opposites that operate in the universe, god fully deserves the title of creator and preserver of the universe.[33] Surely this first principle is more involved with the universe than Aristotle (and therefore Alexander) would allow, but it makes for a strong alternative to Stoic philosophy.

A further interesting feature of *De mundo* is a series of analogies used to illustrate the author's cosmology, in which each analogy emends a deficiency in a previous one, or expands on it creating a cumulative effect.[34] Among them we find the lawgiver and military commander that have a long history in ancient philosophy.[35] From God as the lawgiver, the author of *De mundo* moves to his final image of God as the law:

> **T3** For [God], established in the immovable, moves all things with power and leads them around, where and how he wills, in different forms and natures, just as, for instance, the law of the city, being immovable in the souls of those who use it, administers all things in public life. For it is clear that in obedience to the law the chief magistrates go to their offices, the junior magistrates to the appropriate courts, and the councillors and members of the assembly to their respective meeting-places; one man walks to the town-hall to eat, another to the courts to defend himself, still another to prison to die. Ordained by law there are also public feasts and annual festivals, sacrifices to the gods, cults of heroes, libations to the deceased.[36]

This analogy affirms both the immovable and separate nature of the first principle, and the power by which he is present in the different officials and citizens that each make their contribution to the city according to the law engrained in them.

> **T4** So we must also think about the greater city, I mean about the cosmos: for god is an evenly balanced law to us, admitting no correction or change, but stronger, I think, and surer than those inscribed on the triangular tablets. When he leads in an unmoved and harmonious manner, the whole orderly arrangement of heaven and earth is administered, distributed to all things through their own seeds, and to plants and animals according to genus and species.[37]

The law present in nature causes the orderly arrangement of the universe, including the variety of seeds, plants, and animals, by means of their own principles or natures. In *De mundo* the analogies illustrate the position of the first principle, which comprises both its own nature and its power – in Alexander, as we shall see, the same analogies illustrate *not* the separate first principle, but the all-pervading divine power that the first principle has established in the outer heaven by being the object of its desire – to which we shall return below in more detail.

Meanwhile, Alexander does not only have to deal with this Peripatetic agenda. The Platonists were experiencing problems of their own, and sought to oppose Stoic materialism at the same time. The Platonic view of the order in the universe largely depends on the interpretation of Plato's *Timaeus*, but that dialogue had been a source of rival interpretations ever since it had been written. What

28 See e.g. Long, and Sedley (1987) section 46A-D, 47A and O, with Sellars (2006) ch. 4. Within the confines of this paper I can only skim the surface of Stoic (meta)physics.

29 See esp. Thom (2020), with Thom (2014) and Gregorić, and Karamanolis (2020). Moraux (1984) 35-38 has discussed the influence of Theophrastus on this work, albeit mainly on its meteorology. Genequand (2001) 6 and Fazzo (2002) 164-168, 184-186 infer from the parallels in Alexander's *On the principles of the universe, On providence* and *Quaestio* II.3 that Alexander knew *De mundo*; given that he changes its cosmology significantly (see below) I suspect he is treating the work as a Peripatetic precursor rather than as a genuine work of Aristotle.

30 *De mundo* 6, esp. 397b19-30, specifying that the region closest to god profits most from this power. Cf. *De mundo* 6, 398b21-27.

31 *De mundo* 6, 396b34-397a5.

32 *De mundo* 397b9, appropriating the Stoic term for the Peripatetic alternative.

33 God is begetter (γενέτωρ), cf. *De mundo* 6, 397b21, 399a31, as wel as its cause of preservation (σώτηρ, σωτηρία), cf. *De mundo* 5, 397a30-31; 6, 397b16-24, 398a4, 400a4-5.

34 For the nature and interconnection of the analogies in *De mundo* see esp. Betegh, and Gregorić (2014), further pursued in Betegh, and Gregorić (2020).

35 *De mundo* 6, 400b608. See Adamson (2016) for a recent survey of analogies connecting soul, household, city, and cosmos.

36 *De mundo* 6, 400b11-23 transl. Thom (2014).

37 *De mundo* 6, 400b27-34 transl. Thom (2014).

is the status of the Demiurge in relation to the model he used for his creation of the universe, the world of Forms? What is the status and role of the World Soul, both created by the Demiurge, and the immaterial source of orderly motion in the entire material universe? Is a different soul responsible for the disorderly motion that exists prior to the Demiurge's interventions?[38]

Against this background Atticus (fl. 176 CE), who held the chair of Platonism in Athens shortly prior to Alexander's appointment in the chair of Aristotelianism in the same city around 200 CE, launched a series of criticisms at Peripatetic philosophy that may well have made a Peripatetic reply even more urgent for Alexander.[39] In Fr. 8 Des Places Atticus complains that (1) Aristotle denies that nature is soul: everything on earth is organised by nature, but without proper explanation he assigns different causes to different things (fate for heavenly bodies; nature for sublunary things; intelligence, providence and soul for humans). Although this summary also seems to reflect later Peripatetic developments of Aristotle's philosophy, esp. providence, he is right that Aristotle denies the existence of a unifying world soul – and his complaints about unity echo Theophrastus. And while Aristotle's set of four causes and the potentiality/actuality distinction apply everywhere, Aristotle indeed insists on identifying different causes in each case.[40]

Atticus further complains (2) that 'if there is not a single animate power pervading all and binding everything and keeping it together, the universe could not be arranged in a reasonable or beautiful way.' He emphasizes the problem by means of an analogy of the universe as a well-organized city:

> **T5** It would be as short-sighted to hope that a city could ever come to be well arranged without a unifying principle as it is to think that one could advance an argument to preserve this universe, supremely beautiful as it obviously is, which did not bind it together and harmonise its parts by having them share in one common thing. Aristotle, then, said that there was something like this, which pervades everything as a principle of motion; but he would not allow that it is soul – even though Plato had shown that soul is the "principle and source" of motion for all moving things (*Phdr.* 245c). What ought to be work of rational, thinking soul, namely to "make nothing in vain", this Aristotle attributes to nature (e.g. *DA* 432b21).[41]

Atticus does not deny that Aristotle has 'something like this which pervades everything as a principle of motion' but he is right that it is not a soul. To this extent Atticus seems to echo Theophrastus' concerns, that all parts of the universe do not share in one common thing. At the same time we see that Atticus sets up Plato's World Soul for the same job that the Stoics assigned to their all-pervading first principle (which itself may well have been inspired by Plato).

To summarize, these are the most important challenges Alexander has to meet:[42]

1. make good and coherent sense of all relevant Aristotelian texts;
2. answer Theophrastus' concerns;
3. replace the Stoic all-pervading god with an Aristotelian principle or power;
4. answer the Platonic criticism of Aristotle by (e.g.) Atticus.

Alexander on the first cause

Alexander clearly identifies the Unmoved Mover of *Phys.* VIII with the God of *Metaph.* XII. In *Quaestio* I.1 he combines arguments from *Phys.* VIII and *Metaph.* XII.6-7 into an argument by analysis that serves to establish the nature of the first cause.[43] As we should expect, Alexander largely follows Aristotle. Alexander's first cause must also be single, eternal, unmoved, incorporeal, and pure actuality, if it is to cause the heavens to move with the only movement that is eternal and continuous: motion in a circle. The first cause is also the highest object of *desire*, because it is beautiful (*kalos*) to the highest degree among substances. And it is the highest

38 For a representative sample of issues concerning the World Soul in the later philosophical tradition see Boys-Stones (2017) chapter 8, and Helmig, and Marongiu (2020).

39 For the fragments of Atticus see Des Places (1977), esp. Fr. 8 apud Eus. *PE* 15.12.1-4, transl. Boys-Stones, fr. 11B, p. 336. In addition, Porphyry *On Principles and Matter* §§73-83 (edition Arzhanov (2021) 112-119) has preserved a concise summary of Atticus' own views on first principles. For Atticus as a motivation for Alexander see e.g. Sharples (1992) 94n307 (on *Quaest.* II.3 discussed below).

40 The text quoted in note 27 above nicely illustrates the tendency in Aristotle to find explanations specific to each case.

41 Transl. Boys-Stones (2017), p. 336, Text 11B.

42 Of course I do not claim to be exhaustive: I am sure Alexander was motivated by a larger set of interconnected issues, both in Peripatetic thought and in his philosophical environment. One important issue I have to leave out of consideration here is the introduction of providence in Aristotelian physics, in response to the Stoic and Platonic insistence on divine providence (see p. 71-72 below). In Alexander's thought the cosmology expounded in the main text of this paper *also* serves as the backbone of a Peripatetic version of providence down to the preservation of species. The main sources for Alexander's view of providence are Alex. *On providence* (with Fazzo, and Zonta (1999), Thillet (2003)), *Quaestio* I.25, II.19, II.21, *Princ.* 91, and an extended report on Alexander's conception of providence in Simpl. *in Phys.* II.3, 194b26ff, 310.25-311.38 Diels (translation in Fleet (1997) 67-69). I am grateful to Orna Harari for alerting me to this last text.

43 Cf. Sharples (1992) 16-19, Bodnár (1997), Fazzo (2008), Bodnár (2014), and De Haas (2024). See the magisterial article by David Twetten (2016) for a survey of the entire Greek and Arabic tradition on Aristotelian cosmology.

object of thought, and therefore the most intelligible thing. Nothing surprising so far.[44]

But in *Quaestio* I.1, and more elaborately in his *On the principles of the universe*, Alexander modifies Aristotle's argument in at least three highly significant ways:

1. Alexander argues that the first cause can only cause the best movement in *the best of bodies* (*ariston tōn sōmatōn*). The best of bodies is not only eternal but also ensouled (*empsychon*), because ensouled body is prior to inanimate body.[45] If it has a soul, this soul must be moved in accordance with impulse (*hormē*) and desire (*ephesis*) towards something in desire for which it is moved in its eternal movement.[46] Hence this divine body will be moved by thinking the first substance, and by desiring to become similar to it (*homoiōsis*).[47]

By introducing an ensouled divine body as the best of bodies necessarily moved by impulse and desire, Alexander addresses Theophrastus' concerns about the essential nature of the unflinching desire that is the necessary link between the first cause and the eternal superior motion it causes.[48] In addition, he prepares a proper seat for the divine power (*theia dunamis*) which, as we shall see, works downwards from the first divine body. Meanwhile, the soul of the divine body is still *not* self-moved (against Platonists), but moved by a specific rational desire for the first cause, which is prior to it.[49]

2. We have seen that the first cause is the first intelligible object, and intelligible to the highest degree. Alexander insists that the first intelligible properly speaking (*kuriōs*) is to be identified as *form* rather than matter, which is intelligible only by analogy or, 'as Plato says (*Tim.* 52b2), by "bastard reasoning"' (4.10-11). What kind of form is at stake here? Form in the category of substance ranks higher than form in other categories, and among forms in the category of substance the form that is by nature most simple and always in actuality ranks highest – this explains why it is most intelligible.[50] The first cause is also to be identified as form because it is the first object of desire: the most beautiful (*kalos*) is form rather than matter, and it is the most determinate in actuality, which again points to substantial *form*.[51]

The explicit identification of the first cause as the highest *substantial form* in both these ways not only confirms the Aristotelian convergence of the hierarchies of objects of thought and desire, but it will enable Alexander to relate the first cause to the existence of *forms* throughout the universe. For this purpose Alexander needs one more ingredient.

3. Enmattered forms become intelligible (or: objects of thought, *noēta*) when the mind separates them from that in which they are, and regards them as if they are simple. Such is the nature of the substance that moves all, i.e. separate, simple, and therefore most intelligible.[52]

This argument assumes the identification of the first cause and the famous active intellect of *De anima* III.5, 430a10-15 which Alexander describes in similar terms in his own *De anima*.[53]

In this context it becomes clear that the object with the highest intelligibility is also responsible for the intelligibility of everything intelligible. This is an instance of Alexander's so-called 'principle of causality of the maximum' which he most likely derived from Aristotle *Metaph.* II.1, 993b23-31.[54] In this disputed text, considered genuine by Alexander, Aristotle states that the highest instance of a mode of

44 Alex. *Princ.* 4-5, 24-54, 57-80, 94-103 argues for the same view. The work survives in different Arabic versions, one of which has been translated into English in Genequand (2001). My interpretation is based on Genequand's translation of Text A. In the footnotes below I register the main parallels between the concise *Quaestio* I.1 and the far more elaborate *On the principles of the universe*.

45 *Quaest.* I.1, 3.9-14; cf. *Princ.* 7-8, 94; *Quaest.* II.18.

46 *Quaest.* I.1, 3.14-4.1; cf. *Princ.* 5-14, and 76, where Alexander adds the specification that the relevant type of desire is not appetite or passion but will, or rational wish (*boulēsis*). The soul of the best of bodies is only rational, and it has no other desire than rational wish always aimed at the good that exists in god alone.

47 *Quaest.* I.1, 4.1-4. This brief mention of similarity (*homoiōsis*) leaves unsolved the unclarity about similarity (*mimēsis*) that Theophrastus indicated. In *Princ.* 21-23, 76-81 Alexander explicitly expands this impulse to all things in the universe, albeit with different results according to their specific natures. In *Princ.* 86 he explicitly discards the option that each heavenly body has its own unmoved mover: they all know and strive for the first cause.

48 *Princ.* 55, 76-78, 82 emphasize that the divine body imparts motion simultaneously to all things that follow it in virtue of its own essential motion, thus adding a further guarantee against Theophrastus' concerns. Cf. *Quaestio* II.19.

49 See also Alex. *Quaest.* II.2 and II.10, and the sustained argument against self-motion in *Princ.* 32-50.

50 *Quaest.* I.1, 4.9-15; cf. *Princ.* 100-102.

51 *Quaest.* I.1, 4.17-26; cf. *Princ.* 17-19, 92-96 where it is specified that whereas composite bodies have a motion that derives from their material constituents in addition to the motion that derives from their soul, which is their nature, in the simple divine bodies there is no such difference: their nature is their soul, and they have no other motion than the motion caused by their soul. The different motions of the incorporeal spheres are attributed to the differences between their individual souls. This seems to remove the natural motion of ether from the picture entirely.

52 *Quaest.* I.1, 4.15-17.

53 See e.g. Alex. *DA* 84.6-9, 85.14-19, 87.24-25 (knowing enmattered forms is regarding them as separate from their material conditions); 87.24-27 (forms that exist *per se* are *noēta* properly speaking); 89.16-19 (the First Cause has been shown to be an intellect properly speaking because a non-enmattered form is an intellect properly speaking). For these complex issues in Alexander and other commentators see e.g. Bergeron, and Dufour (2008) for Alex. *DA*; De Haas (2019), (2020), and (2023) with the extensive secondary literature listed there.

54 For this "principe de causalité du maximum" see the excellent analysis by Guyomarc'h (2015) 104-111. For another instance at Alex. *in Metaph.* 11.19-21 see De Haas (2021) 90, and T6 below.

being is the cause of, or somehow responsible for (*aitios*), all inferior degrees of that mode of being in everything else. For instance fire, as the hottest substance, is responsible for the heat in everything else; the highest eternal truth is responsible for the truth of all beings.

Alexander's account of the active intellect in his *DA* 88.26-89.11 is a most instructive application of this same principle:

> **T6** For in all cases, something that is a certain kind of thing properly speaking and to the highest degree is responsible (*aition*) for other things being that kind of thing as well. For what is visible to the highest degree – such as light – is responsible for other visible things being visible too. So too, what is primarily good to the highest degree is responsible for other goods being such, since other goods are distinguished by means of the contribution they make to it.
> It is reasonable, then, that what is intelligible (*noēton*) to the highest degree and by its own nature, is responsible for the thinking (*noēsis*) of other things too; and since it is this kind of thing, the active intellect would be [responsible for this]. For if there would not be something intelligible by nature, nothing else would be intelligible either, as stated above. For in all cases in which one thing is a certain kind of thing properly speaking, and another in a secondary sense, the one that is so in the secondary sense gets its being from the one that is so properly speaking. Furthermore, if the First Cause, which is responsible for the being of everything else as its origin and principle, is this kind of intellect, then it would also be productive (*poiētikos*) in such a way as to be responsible for the being of all things thought.[55]

Alexander first provides two additional examples of his principle: he credits light, being visible to the highest degree, with the responsibility for the visibility of everything else; and he credits the highest good with the responsibility for the goodness of everything else that is measured after its contribution to the highest good. Then he applies the principle to his understanding of the active intellect of *DA* III.5: the First Cause, which meets the criteria of Aristotle's active intellect, is not only the cause of the *being* of all other beings, but also for their being *objects of thought*.

It is hard not to be reminded of the comparison between the Good and the sun in Plato, *Rep.* VI, 506d-509d. Like the positive reference to Plato's *Timaeus* we saw earlier, this adumbration of Platonic insights on the part of Alexander may have had as one of its purposes to win Platonists over to the Peripatetic camp by providing a proper philosophical home for their most cherished doctrines – the converse of multiple Platonic attempts to align Aristotle with Platonic philosophy.[56]

In this way Alexander has managed to merge the first principles of Aristotelian physics, metaphysics, and philosophy of mind into one. The first cause is the first cause of all physical motion by being the most eligible object of both desire and thought for the soul of the divine body engaged in the most perfect spatial motion; as the highest being, a pure substantial form always in actuality, it is the first cause of all beings; and as the highest object of thought, it is the first cause of the intelligibility of all things thought. It now seems that – at least in formal terms – the connections between Aristotle's separate immaterial principle and the universe have been strengthened. But the question remains: if the first cause remains separate, how exactly does its influence manage to pervade the universe in all of these ways?

Alexander on divine power

For this purpose Alexander has developed his own characteristic notion of a divine power (*theia dunamis*), which can be regarded as his alternative for both the Stoic all-pervading material god, and the Platonic all-pervading immaterial World Soul. It constitutes both his most comprehensive reply to Theophrastus' query in T2, and a correction of the Peripatetic *De mundo*.[57]

For the divine power we have to turn to two further works of Alexander. Alexander's longest sustained argument on the first cause and its relation to the universe is found in his *On the principles of the cosmos*. Here I shall limit myself to one interesting feature of *On the principles* that we need for the purposes of this paper: the power of the divine bodies (127-128), and its illustrations (128-137).[58] In addition, the deliberations in *Quaestio* II.3 show how exactly the effect of the divine power may be conceived to reach down to the lowest physical level of the Peripatetic universe. In this context the insight that the first cause is the highest *form* will prove valuable again.

In *On the principles* 127-128 Alexander introduces the divine power in the following way:

55 Alex. *DA* 88.26-89.11 (my translation); cf. *Princ.* 97-126.

56 Here one example may suffice: Golitsis (2018) has shown how Simplicius, in his turn, criticizes Alexander for ignoring the intelligible world, and argues that according to Aristotle's *Physics* the first cause is also an efficient cause; see also Bodnár in this volume. A full survey of Alexander's use of Platonic doctrine is still a desideratum of scholarship.

57 Cf. Fazzo (2004).

58 Bodnár in this volume uses the same passages from *On the principles* and *Quaestio* II.3 in order to verify to what extent Simplicius' rendering of Alexander's philosophy is correct.

T7 (127) Since the First Mover is as we have described it, and the things moved by it without intermediary are also in that state,[59] there follows from the motion of these things the generation and change of the perishable bodies having matter, according to the power of those <heavenly bodies> reaching them according to <the former's> diversity, and according to the assimilation of those different things which we have mentioned, because of the change and diversity of their motion, as we said before.
(128) This nature and power are the cause of the unity and order of the world. In the same way as happens in one city having one ruler residing in it, not separate from it, we also say that a certain divine power[60] penetrates the whole world and holds its parts together. (129) Since the city is ruled by one authority only which is its leader or established law, so is the one world, since it is one body, continuous, eternal, imperishable, containing and encompassing all things, and comprehending them, and all things which are in it seek to be in contact with the thing which is unchangeable and aim at material union <among them> thanks to[61] that which rules and governs <the world> and preserves its arrangement and order by a power which penetrates all parts of it which deserve that it should penetrate them according to what <the ruler> thinks, not the people.[62]

Here nature as a whole is identified with the divine power located in the heavenly bodies, which regulates all generation and corruption in the sensible world. The power in the heavenly bodies differs according to the differences in their natures and movements – which also help explain the variety in the sensible world. The analogies of the ruler and the law of a city now clearly turn on a principle that is *present in*, not separate from, the whole, unlike Aristotle's first cause. The city has unity and order when it is ruled by a single authority 'resident in it' (whether as a single leader or the established law), 'not separate from it'. With the help of the same analogy in *De mundo* (T3) we may expand: the law regulates all the various goal-directed activities of the members of the citizens, and does so without being visible except by reason, effortless, without any help, and without any change in itself – assuming that the law is in the souls of the citizens, or rather the object of their thought.

This analogy also reminds us of Aristotle *Metaph.* XII.10, 1075a11-18 where Aristotle is deliberating how the good is present in the universe: as something separate, as the order, or both? The latter option is illustrated by an army: on the one hand there is the general, on the other the order, and the order exists because of the general (not vice versa); indeed the best authority is a single authority (1076a4). But a single authority does not rule out variety: despite the variety of species and their mutual interaction it is true to say that everything in the universe has been co-ordinated (*suntetaktai*) towards a single goal.[63]

In T7 Alexander presents the sensible world as one body, continuous, eternal, imperishable, containing and encompassing all things: as a whole it is a remarkable expression of the properties of the divine body as well as its first cause, to which all things in the universe strive. The letter of this description matches Stoic and Platonic descriptions of the coherence of the universe. This confirms our hypothesis that Alexander introduced the divine power not only to give the best possible interpretation of Aristotle, but also to present an alternative to the Stoic and Platonic cosmologies while preserving some of their virtues.

By means of the power which penetrates all parts of the universe from the first divine body downwards, the first cause can be held responsible for the arrangement and order of the world and their preservation without forfeiting its separate position. Alexander differs from the author of *De mundo* in that for him the divine power is not a power *of* the first cause, but of the divine body: it is enshrined in its essential circular motion that issues from the desire of the divine soul for the first cause.

Princ. 127 repeatedly refers back to earlier chapters in which Alexander has explained in more detail how the variety exhibited in both the supralunary and sensible worlds is to be explained by two complementary principles:

1. differences in their respective natures: these are set in a fixed hierarchy of nobility, but also reflect their providential purpose in the universe, and even their knowledge of the world of generation and corruption;[64] in addition there is
2. the distance from the first cause, which results in different ways in which subsequent natures are capable of receiving the effects of divine power, in other words: the different levels of perfection they can achieve by their desire for the first cause.[65]

The first point is repeated in *Princ.* 127: each heavenly body moving according to its own nature (= soul) has a different effect on the sublunary world. For instance, only the sun, moving along the ecliptic, causes the seasons.

59 I.e. have an eternal happy life, *Princ.* 126.
60 See Genequand (2017) 128 for taking 'spiritual' in the sense of 'immaterial' or 'divine' in this context.
61 Here I follow the revised (French) translation in Genequand (2017) 90, with p. 141 ad loc.
62 *Princ.* 127-129 transl. Genequand 2001.
63 Cf. the mention of the commander of a military camp at *De mundo* 400b8.
64 *Princ.* 91-96 with 56, 78, 85.
65 *Princ.* 21-22, 78. For the distance from the first cause as an explanation of variety cf. Arist. *GC* II.10, 336b25-337a7.

For the notion that individual natures constitute a different effect of the same power, we may compare Aristotle *De motu animalium* 10, 703a29-b2. There Aristotle supports a different point, viz. the position of the soul in the heart, by an analogy with the monarch in a city: once order has been established the king does not have to be involved in everything all the time, but can reside in a single place. The whole body is alive because it has grown onto the soul, not because soul is present throughout the body. Despite the different context, it is interesting to see that Aristotle holds nature in general (703a35) and the natural constitution of each of the bodily parts (703b2) responsible for this. This comes close to what Alexander does here: every part of the whole expresses the order of nature: it does what it needs to do for the benefit of the whole due to its own nature.

The relevance of (2) the distance from the first cause, is further illustrated in *On the principles* by means of an analogy with the household. In Aristotle *Metaph.* XII.10 a comparison with a household followed the analogy with the army referred to above.[66] In Aristotle the variety in the universe is compared to the position of free men, slaves, and domestic animals in a household. Free men contribute most to the common cause; by consequence, they have less freedom to do what they want. Slaves and domestic animals contribute less to the common cause, which results in more freedom to do whatever they like. By way of explanation Aristotle states: 'Such a principle is the nature of each' (1075a22-23). Once more, this analogy connects the explanation of different contributions to the whole by means of the nature of each.[67] Here is how Alexander inserts the household analogy in his own cosmology:

> **T8** (133) Just as all the parts of the house aim at one and the same thing, viz. that which will bring it about and fit it together so that it becomes one, so is the state of free men: they do all that they do, or most of it, according to an arrangement and an order, and their aim in all that they do is the preservation of the household, since there is no way for them to live as free men in opposition to that. (134) But the slaves and suchlike have only a feeble share in this order and disposition which have been established in the interest of the whole; and because of this feeble share they also endure, since they are a part of the house. Most acts issuing from this class are merely by chance and spontaneity. For the nature proper to it, which is in all its parts principle and cause of its being, does not receive anything of importance in the way of good organization and order.[68]

Alexander's text follows his Aristotelian model closely. The differences in nature, however, are attributed to the different share that free men and slaves have in the general order established in the interest of the whole. Because of this, their nature does not receive 'anything of importance in the way of good organization and order'. When Alexander applies both analogies to the universe we get:

> **T9** (135) The state of the world is similar to that of the city or the house: among the things which are in it, the nature proper to them has caused some of them to happen always according to organization and order, because they are not susceptible to any kind of disturbance, I mean lack of order; others are in this state most of the time; others still have a feeble share in this state, I mean the state of organization and order. (136) By this kind of organization and government, the universe remains eternal and imperishable: part of it is such in number, and part of it is in this state in species because of the continuous motion, ordered according to its diversity and variety, of which we have said that eternity belongs to it in number.[69]

There is a fixed distribution and hierarchy of natures: some are eternal in number, viz. each individually, and allow no disturbance (the heavens); some are stable most of the time (perishable substances), but have eternity only in species – thanks to the continuous motion of the heavens; some share even less organisation and order. Nevertheless everything contributes to the whole – or at least does not jeopardize it.

> **T10** For all things existing by nature have in the very nature appropriate to them an impulse towards the thing which is the First Cause and better than all things, since nature and all things existing by it do what they do according to the nature proper to them out of desire to imitate that thing from which they were generated primarily.[70]

In this section of *On the principles* Alexander states in the clearest possible terms that *all things existing by nature* have an impulse directed towards the first cause. For whatever they do according to the nature proper to them, they do out of desire to imitate the first cause. So this is not

66 See above p. 69.
67 As moved movers these natures can be regarded as instrumental causes, cf. Alex. ap. Simpl. 315.12-18, 317.20-28 (see further Bodnár in this volume).
68 *Princ.* 133-134, transl. Genequand (2001). Cf. *Princ.* 80-81.
69 *Princ.* 135-136, transl. Genequand (2001).
70 *Princ.* 21 with commentary in Genequand (2017) 110-111 ad loc.

only true for the natures (= souls) of the heavenly bodies, but also for everything else that has a nature.

However, one problem is still out. In T7 (129) Alexander emphasizes that it is the 'ruler, not the people' who somehow decides what mode of reception of divine power each nature has. In T7-9 the hierarchy of natures appears as a given: because each thing has a specific share of order, it is capable of specific, limited contributions to the order of the whole. In T10 everything acts in accordance with its nature out of desire for the first cause. But *how* does the divine power issuing from the heavenly bodies determine the extent to which perishable beings receive the divine power? The problem becomes more acute in light of the metaphysical speculations recorded above: if the first cause is the first being, the first good and the first intelligible object, and as such somehow responsible for all being, goodness and intelligibility in all lesser beings, how does the divine power achieve this?

Divine power in *Quaest.* II.3: how the final cause causes forms

This is the question that led to Alexander's famous *Quaestio* II.3 on the divine power.[71] The problem it puts on the table is: 'What is the power that comes to be, from the movement of the divine body, for the body adjacent to it which is mortal and subject to coming-to-be?' (47.28-29) So the question zooms in on the relation between the heavens and the sublunary world, which was Theophrastus' second aporia:[72] how does the divine power that issues from the heavens act on the sublunary world? Alexander explores two possible solutions: (1) either the divine power is a nature *different from* the nature of each of the natural bodies, i.e. their principle of motion and rest;[73] or (2) the divine power *comes to be* the nature of the simple bodies.[74]

The first option (1) quickly runs into difficulties (48.1-22). Since each body is either a simple or compound body in actuality, what does the nature that is the divine power *add* to such an already existing nature? What is transmitted from fire, which the divine power affects first, down to the other elements and their mixtures? On this view, the four elements already have the natural movement towards their proper place. In the case of compound bodies it would contribute nothing to their being inanimate, or to their having a soul of some kind, being a human or a plant. Worst of all: what is left of providence, which supposes that the divine power is responsible precisely for, e.g., humans having rational souls and all the benefits that come with it.[75]

If we stick with this approach (1) nonetheless (48.22-49.4), and the divine power only adds a nature, we best assume that the divine power adds itself from the outside *only* to the four elements – these at least show no sign of having a soul or anything divine in them *by themselves*. So let each of the four elements receive a share of the divine power that is proportional to their proximity to the divine body: fire most, then air, then water, and earth least of all. All composites that come to be as mixtures of the elements will then have the divine power 'sown' into them in proportion with the elements that constitute them. This would explain how, in addition to the natural inclination that they also derive from their mixture of elements, they acquire a further psychic motion, and a kind of soul proportionate to the divine power added to the elements. More earth leads to a less perfect soul, more fire leads to a more perfect soul.[76] There would be one exception: this only works in the case of genuine mixtures,[77] not in cases of mere composition and juxtaposition of the simple bodies: in those cases the divine body does not add another nature (49.4-28).

In the characteristic style of many of the *Quaestiones*, Alexander provides no words of assessment or transition to the next option, so at this point we have to guess whether it is the incompatibility with providence, or something else that renders an alternative option necessary.

Anyway, Alexander continues to discuss the second option (49.28-50.27). What if the divine power is itself the cause of the difference between the elements and their coming to be, by itself *becoming their form and nature*? In this case we assume that prime matter (which by itself has neither form nor shape) is given form and shape by the power that comes to be in it from the divine bodies. Now the rule of proximity to the divine body directly explains that fire is hot and dry as the first affections that the sublunary world receives from the divine bodies. The divine power also constitutes the nature of the elements themselves, not only that of their mixtures. Generation and corruption of the elements comes to be when cold and/or wet are coupled with hot and/or dry as a result of different relations, viz. changing proximity,

71 See Moraux (1967), Sharples (1992) 93-98, Fazzo, and Zonta. (1999) 195-219, and especially Fazzo (2002) 175-212.

72 See above p. 64.

73 *Quaest.* II.3, 47.31-49.27. Fazzo (2002) 184-187 highlights the parallels with *De mundo* 6.

74 *Quaest.* II.3, 49.28-50.27.

75 Cf. *Mant.* §23, 172.17-173.3.

76 Although the text at *Quaest.* II.3, 48.27-49.4 is not crystal clear in this respect, I take it to mean *not* that the divine power is added to each of their natures at each instance that a mixture comes to be, but rather that on top of the contribution of the usual properties of an element to their mixture, they receive a measure of that element's share in divine power as well. This is 'sown' into the mixture with the element as much as it was 'sown' into the element in the first place. Cf. *Quaest.* II.3, 49.14-18: the divine power uses the simple natural bodies as material for the coming-to-be of bodies that are more perfect and animate.-For this notion in Aristotle cf. *GA* II.1, 732b31-733b16.

77 For Alexander's theory of mixture see esp. Alex. *Mixt.* XIII-XV, with Guyomarc'h, and De Haas (2023).

between the e.g. the sun and the moon, and the sublunary world. By consequence, mixtures of the four elements will be compounded and more perfect than each of the elements, because they share in several elements and their powers. Moreover, *their* form and perfection becomes different precisely in accordance with the proportion of the elements that contribute to their mixture. Closer to the divine motion = rare and more active = more perfect form; further away from the divine motion = denser and more passive = less perfect form. On this note *Quaestio* II.3 ends.

Again, Alexander does not assess option (2), nor does he conclude *Quaestio* II.3 with anything resembling a conclusion. However, scholars have rightly noted that option (2) has much in common with the description of the coming to be of complex forms and souls in Alexander's *De anima*, and the description of the role of divine power in *On providence*. Although *De anima* is often read in isolation as a strictly materialist account of the generation of soul and form, Fazzo was right to emphasize that this is only half the story.[78] *On providence* and *Quaestio* II.3 insist on the role of divine power, which renders Alexander's cosmology a genuine rival of Stoic and Platonist theories without coinciding with either. In all of this we need to keep in mind that *Quaestio* II.3 does not give us a story of creation: the universe is eternal, so this theory expresses causal dependence and hierarchy rather than stages in a creation process.

This cosmology is both top-down and bottom-up in a remarkable way. The divine power 'arrives' in sensible nature top down, from the divine body, and 'creates' the elements in the order of their natural places in the universe from the top down (fire, air, water, earth); the divine power is also stronger in the elements closest to the divine; and providence reaches down until the level of the species. At the same time it 'creates' the universe bottom up, by in-form-ing prime matter with the basic qualities that constitute the four elements, which then 'build up' the forms of higher compounds and animate substances to which providence applies.

From our examination it should be clear that we need option (2) *also* to understand how the first cause, by means of the divine power it has sparked, is responsible for the *forms* of the elements – and through them, for all higher forms including the variety of souls. Only in this way Alexander has the theory to explain how the first cause *qua* form can be held responsible for the being, goodness, and intelligibility of all lesser beings. Indeed, the hierarchy and order of nature, including the desire for the first cause itself, come to the universe in accordance with the nature of each thing. We now know that each nature and soul *is* the divine power. Each form arises in accordance with the natural interaction that occurs between all things, both eternal and perishable, again in accordance with their nature that is the divine power. It is in this way that the first cause is responsible for all forms that constitute the natural order in Alexander's universe.

This bold theory has further benefits for our understanding of the polemical purposes of Alexander's corpus. For instance, it explains how, against Platonists and Stoics alike, Alexander can hold both that nature is a demiurge, even a divine art, *and* an irrational power, not divine because it uses a divine model, or divine reasoning, but because it comes from the gods. Without reason nature cannot contemplate a model, let alone execute a divine plan.[79] Instead, the first cause as intellect and highest object of thought remains a separate first final cause, which does not meddle with the details of the universe, but is nevertheless responsible for the existence and intelligibility of everything in the universe, through the forms it causes by means of the divine power, among which we find the potential intellect that allows humans to understand.[80] Against Atticus Alexander can affirm that all forms, hence all natures and souls, are the effects of a single first cause – but continue to deny with Aristotle both that nature is a (world) soul, and that all motion derives from souls. To the Stoics Alexander can offer a single divine power that permeates the entire universe from the outer sphere down to prime matter, which at the same time underlies (his own version of) providence – without turning the first cause into an efficient cause. Finally, he can reassure Theophrastus: the unity and order of the cosmos is safe. The very variety and differentiation that seemed to threaten it turn out to be the expression of its first final cause along an unbroken chain of natures with each an essential desire towards their single cause.

*****

78 Fazzo (2002) 179.

79 Cf. Alex. *in APr* 3.17-21; *in Metaph.* I.9, 103.45-104.14; *Prov.* 151.23-153.20, and Alex. ap. Simpl. *in Phys.* II.3, 310.25-311.38.

80 Cf. the grand summary of the role of the agent intellect in the universe, including criticism of the Stoic God, in *Mant.* §2, 113.4-24.

Bibliography

Adamson, P. (2016): "State of Nature: Human and Cosmic Rulership in Ancient Philosophy". In: Höfele, A. and Kellner, B. (eds): *Menschennatur und politische Ordnung*. Paderborn: Wilhelm Fink, pp. 79-94.

Arzhanov, Y. (2021): *Porphyry, On Principles and Matter. A Syriac Version of a Lost Greek Text with an English Translation, Introduction, and Glossaries. Scientia Graeco-Arabica*, edited by Marwan Rashed, vol. 34. Berlin-Boston: De Gruyter.

Bergeron, M., and Dufour, R. (2008): *Alexander Aphrodisiensis. De l'âme. Texte grec introduit, traduit et annoté*. Paris: Vrin.

Betegh, G. and Gregorić, P. (2020): "God's Relation to the Cosmos (Chapter 6)". In: Gregorić, P. and Karamanolis, G.: *Pseudo-Aristotle: "De Mundo" ("On the Cosmos"): A Commentary*. Cambridge-New York: Cambridge University Press, pp. 176-212.

Betegh, G. and Gregorić, P. (2014): "Multiple Analogy in Ps.-Aristotle *De mundo* 6". *Classical Quarterly* 64, No. 2: pp. 574-591.

Bodnár, I. (1997): "Movers and Elemental Motions in Aristotle". *Oxford Studies in Ancient Philosophy* 15: pp. 81-118.

Bodnár, I.M. (2014): "Alexander's Unmoved Mover". In: Cerami, C. (ed.): *Nature et sagesse. Les rapports entre physique et métaphysique dans la tradition aristotélicienne. Recueil de textes en hommage à Pierre Pellegrin*. Leuven: Peeters, pp. 387-416.

Bodnár, I.M. (1997): "Alexander of Aphrodisias on Celestial Motions". *Phronesis* 42, No 2: pp. 190-205.

Boys-Stones, G. (2017): *Platonist Philosophy 80 BC to AD 250. An Introduction and Collection of Sources in Translation*. Cambridge: Cambridge University Press.

De Haas, F.A.J. (2020): "Aristotle and Alexander of Aphrodisias on Active Intellectual Cognition". In: Decaix, V. and Mora Márquez, A.M. (eds.): *Active Cognition. Challenges to an Aristotelian Tradition*. Studies in the History of Philosophy of Mind. Edited by Lagerlund, H. and Yrjönsuuri, M., vol. 23. Dordrecht: Springer, pp. 13-36.

De Haas, F.A.J. (2021): "Deduction and Common Notions in Alexander's Commentary on Aristotle's *Metaphysics* A 1-2". *History of Philosophy & Logical Analysis* 24: pp. 71-102.

De Haas, F.A.J. (2019): "Intellect in Alexander of Aphrodisias and John Philoponus: divine, human or both?". In: Sisko, J.E. (ed.): *Philosophy of Mind in Antiquity*. The History of the Philosophy of Mind. Edited by Copenhaver, R. and Shields, Ch., vol. 1. London-New York: Routledge, pp. 299-316.

De Haas, F.A.J. (2023): "Alexander of Aphrodisias on the Ancient Debate on Hylomorphism and the Development of Intellect". In: Charles, D. (ed.): *The History of Hylomorphism. From Aristotle to Descartes*. Oxford: Oxford University Press, pp. 174-196.

De Haas, F.A.J. (2024): "Alexander of Aphrodisias on Analysis to the First Principle". *Studia graeco-arabica* 14: pp. 59-68. doi:10.12871/97912560807006

Des Places, É. (1977): *Atticus Fragments*. Paris: Les Belles Lettres.

Fazzo, S. (2002): *Aporia e sistema. La materia, la forma, il divino nelle Quaestiones di Alessandro di Afrodisia*. Pisa: Edizioni Ets.

Fazzo, S. (2004): "Sur la composition du traité dit *de motu animalium:* contribution à l'analyse de la théorie aristotélicienne du premier moteur". In: Laks, A. & Rashed, M. (Eds.): *Aristote et le mouvement des animaux. Dix études sur le De Motu Animalium*. Presses universitaires du Septentrion, pp. 203-229.

Fazzo, S. (2008): "L'exégèse du livre *Lambda* de la *Métaphysique* d'Aristote dans le *De principiis* et dans la *Quaestio* I.1 d'Alexandre d'Aphrodise". *Laval théologique et philosophique* 6, No 3: pp. 607-626.

Fazzo, S. and Zonta M. (1999): *Alessandro di Afrodisia. La Provvidenza – Questioni sulla provvidenza*. Milano: Biblioteca Universale Rizzoli.

Fleet, B. (1997): *Simplicius: On Aristotle's "Physics 2"*. Ithaca: Cornell University Press.

Frede, M., and Charles, D. eds. (2000): *Aristotle's Metaphysics Lambda, Symposium Aristotelicum*. Oxford.

Genequand, C. (2001): *Alexander of Aphrodisias on the Cosmos. Islamic Philosophy, Theology and Science. Texts and Studies*. Edited by Daiber, H. and Pingree, D., vol. 44. Leiden-Boston-Köln: Brill.

Genequand, C. (2017): *Alexandre d'Aphrodise. Les Principes du tout selon la doctrine d'Aristote. Introduction, texte arabe, traduction et commentaire*. Paris: Librairie Philosophique J. Vrin.

Golitsis, P. (2018): "Alexandre d'Aphrodise, Simplicius, et la cause efficiente de l'univers". In : Balansard, A. and Jaulin, A. (Eds.): *Alexandre d'Aphrodise et la métaphysique aristotélicienne*. Aristote. Traductions et Études. Edited by Destrée, P. Leuven: Peeters, pp. 217-235.

Gregorić, P. and Karamanolis, G. eds. (2020): *Pseudo-Aristotle: "De Mundo" ("On the Cosmos"): A Commentary*. Cambridge-New York: Cambridge University Press.

Gutas, D. (2010): *Theophrastus on First Principles (known as his Metaphysics). Philosophia Antiqua*, vol. 119. Edited by Algra, K.A., De Haas, F.A.J., Mansfeld, J., Rowe, C.J., Runia, D.T. and Wildberg, Ch. Leiden-Boston: Brill.

Guyomarc'h, G. (2015): *L'unité de la métaphysique selon Alexandre d'Aphrodise. Textes et Traditions*. Edited by Goulet-Cazé, M.-O., Goulet, R. and Hoffmann, P. vol. 27. Paris: Librairie Philosophique J. Vrin.

Guyomarc'h, G. and De Haas, F.A.J. eds. (2023): *Studies on Alexander of Aphrodisias' On Mixture and Growth. Philosophia Antiqua*, vol. 170. Edited by De Haas, F.A.J. Leiden-Boston: Brill.

Helmig, C. and Marongiu, L. eds. (2020): *World Soul – Anima Mundi. On the Origins and Fortunes of a Fundamental Idea. Topics in Ancient Philosophy / Themen der antiken Philosophie*. Vol. 8. Edited by Jansen, L., Jedan, C. and Rapp, C. Berlin-Boston: De Gruyter.

Long, A. A., and Sedley, D.N. (1987): *The Hellenistic Philosophers. Volume 1: translations of the principal sources, with philosophical commentary*. Vol. 1. 2 vols. Cambridge: Cambridge University Press.

Moraux, P. (1967): "Alexander von Aphrodisias Quaest. 2,3". *Hermes* 95, No. 2: pp.159-169.

Moraux, P. (1984): *Der Aristotelismus bei den Griechen. Von Andronikos bis Alexander von Aphrodisias. Der Aristotelismus im I. und II. Jahrhundert n.Chr.* Vol. II. *Peripatoi. Philologisch-historische Studien zum Aristotelismus*, vol. 7. Edited by Moraux, P. Berlin-New York: Walter de Gruyter Verlag.

Primavesi, O. and Corcilius, K. (2018): *Aristoteles De motu animalium. Über die Bewegung der Lebewesen*. Edited by Primavesi, O. and Corcilius, K. Hamburg: Felix Meiner Verlag.

Rapp, C. and Primavesi, O. eds. (2020): *Aristotle's De motu animalium (Symposium Aristotelicum)*. Oxford: Oxford University Press.

Sellars, J. (2006): *Stoicism. Ancient Philosophies*. Chesham: Acumen.

Thillet, P. (2003): *Alexandre d'Aphrodise. Traité de la providence (Περὶ προνοίας). Version arabe de Abū Bišr Mattä ibn Yūnus*. Lagrasse: Verdier.

Thom, J.C. (2014): *Cosmic Order and Divine Power: Pseudo-Aristotle, On the Cosmos*. Scripta Antiquitatis Posterioris ad Ethicam REligionemque Pertinentia (SAPERE) XXIII. Tübingen: Mohr Siebeck.

Thom, J.C. (2020): "The power of god in Pseudo-Aristotle's *De mundo*: An alternative approach". In: Helmig, C. and Marongiu, L. (Eds.): *World Soul – Anima Mundi. On the Origins and Fortunes of a Fundamental Idea*. Topics in Ancient Philosophy / Themen der antiken Philosophie. Edited by Jansen, L., Jedan, C. and Rapp, C. Vol. 8. Berlin-Boston: De Gruyter, pp. 135-152.

Twetten, D. (2016): "Aristotelian Cosmology and Causality in Classical Arabic Philosophy and Its Greek Background". In: Janos, D. (ed.): *Ideas in Motion in Baghdad and Beyond. Philosophical and Theological Exchanges between Christians and Muslims in the Third/Ninth and Fourth/Tenth Centuries*. Islamic History and Civilization. Studies and Texts. Edited by Biesterfeldt, H., Günther, S. and Kadi, W. Vol. 124. Leiden-Boston: Brill, pp. 312-433.

Nature in Alexander of Aphrodisias' *Commentary on Book II of the Physics*

István Bodnár

Eötvös University (ELTE), Budapest
Central European University (CEU), Vienna

Abstract
This contribution pieces together Alexander of Aphrodisias' account of nature on the basis of the fragments from and testimonia about his commentary on Aristotle's *Physics* in Simplicius' *Commentary on Aristotle's Physics,* also taking into account some of his shorter works and quaestiones. Key issues of the account are what causal roles can be assigned to nature, in what sense talk about the nature of the world is admissible by Alexander's lights, and ultimately how the natural motion of the celestial bodies is caused by the Prime Mover of the universe.

1. Nature and productive and instrumental causes
The concept of nature – the inner principle of motion and rest, as established in the first chapter of book II of the *Physics* – is central to Aristotle's investigations in natural philosophy. One can easily slip into thinking of a principle of motion, an item that is responsible for at least some of the motions – the natural motions – as corresponding in Alexander's parlance to an efficient or productive cause,[1] which Aristotle refers to with the phrase ὅθεν ἡ ἀρχὴ τῆς μεταβολῆς, or even as ὅθεν ἡ ἀρχὴ τῆς μεταβολῆς ἡ πρώτη.[2] Aristotle's discussion of the motion of (sublunary) elements in *Physics* VIII.4 shows that such an identification of nature and moving cause would be premature – the nature of elements on inspection turns out to be a passive principle of motion.[3] We shall see that Alexander's take on the status of nature is even more restrictive. We have direct evidence for this in Alexander's *Commentary on Book Δ of the* Metaphysics, and also in the reports about and quotes from Alexander's *Commentary on the* Physics in Simplicius' *Commentary on the* Physics, especially in the course of the testimonies and quotes from book II. The occasion for this duplication of the evidence is provided by the fact that Aristotle's discussion of *Physics* II.3, about the different causes, is repeated *verbatim*

1 The term Alexander uses is ποιητικὸν αἴτιον. In what follows I will translate the term and its cognates consequently as 'productive cause', 'to produce' etc.
2 See e.g. *Physics* 194b29 f.
3 *Physics* VIII.4 254b12 – 17, b24 – 30 and then 255b29 – 31.

in: Mouzala, M.G. (ed.) 2025: *Nature and Human Nature in Ancient Greek Philosophy and Its Reception.* Leiden: Sidestone Press, pp. 75-90.

in *Metaphysics* Δ.2, the entry on cause (αἴτιον), in his so called philosophical lexicon.[4] Alexander remarks on this repetition, and says that owing to this the interpretation of the chapter in the *Physics* needs to be transferred to the commentary on the *Metaphysics* at this place.[5]

The comment on the productive cause starts at 349, 28. First Alexander turns to explaining the particular formulation Aristotle uses at 1013ᵃ28 f. (= *Phys.* 194ᵇ29 f.).[6] The productive cause can be responsible not only for the motion of an entity, but also for making it stop and also for its rest. Furthermore, the term μεταβολή, and not κίνησις is used so that causes of substantial generation and perishing should also be included in the scope of this type of cause. As a next step Alexander remarks on the specification that this cause has to be where the *first* principle of motion or rest is from:

> **T1** The specification that it is first is added, because this is productive cause to the utmost. For what is immanent in the entity that comes into being and produces that way what comes in succession has its cause from what produced it. Nor do the instruments have from themselves that they cause motion. The first is the cause also of these, and it is outside of [i.e. not immanent in] the item that comes into being.[7] (Alex. *In Meta.* 349, 33 – 37)

Although the word 'nature' is not mentioned here, it is beyond doubt that the phrase 'what is immanent in the entity that comes into being and produces that way what comes in succession' should refer to the nature of the entity in question.[8] And hence it is clear that Alexander at the same time restricts the claim that nature could be a productive cause – it cannot be the one that is productive to the outmost – and also allows for nature to be a dependent or derivative productive cause. Due to the causal efficacy of the ultimate productive cause, natures are also endowed with this dependent or derivative productive causal power of their own.

The first half of this claim – that nature is not a productive cause in its own right – is borne out by Alexander's comments on *Metaphysics* Δ.1, the chapter on principle (ἀρχή). Aristotle in that chapter first sets out several different ways of how, on the basis of what considerations things can be principles. Then he remarks that causes are also said in the exact same ways as the ones listed, because causes are principles. This remark is followed by a general claim about principles – that they have to be primary – and then by a distinction about two kinds of principles: some of them are immanent, the others are non-immanent. After all this, Aristotle gives a terse list, of six items – nature, element, thought, decision, substance and that for the sake of which – for principles (Arist. *Meta.* 1013ᵃ19 – 21).[9] Of these nature and element are clearly meant to be immanent principles, in contrast to thought, decision and for the sake of which.[10] Nature, as Bonitz and Ross suggest could just refer to whatever is the internal principle of motion and rest for the entity in question.[11] This, however, is not how Alexander understands Aristotle's list here. His interpretation rests on his understanding of Aristotle's requirement that principles have to be primary (Arist. *Meta.* 1013ᵃ17-19).[12] Accordingly, only a singular type of nature can be strictly speaking an internal principle. As he writes in his comments on Δ.1:

> **T2** Having said that of principles some are immanent to what they are principles of, while others are outside of them, because of this – meaning because some are such, and others are not such – nature and element are principles, for these are principles as being immanent [in the entity that they are principles of]. For it [the entity that they are the principles of] comes into being from these primary immanent items. Here he calls 'nature' the matter, and 'element' the proximate matter, which is already some body in actuality.[13] (Alex. *In Meta.* 347, 7-12)

---

4 Note that Alexander uses a more restrictive characterization. According to this *Metaphysics* Δ contains a systematic discussion of those πολλαχῶς λεγόμενα which are relevant for first philosophy. (Alex. *In Meta.* 344 f.)

5 Alex. *In Meta.* 348, 22 – 24. As we shall see, this 'transferal' is not a verbatim repetition on Alexander's part.

6 ἔτι ὅθεν ἡ ἀρχὴ τῆς μεταβολῆς ἡ πρώτη ἢ τῆς ἠρεμήσεως

7 τὸ δὲ πρῶτον πρόσκειται, ὅτι τοῦτο μάλιστα ποιητικὸν αἴτιον· τὸ γὰρ ἐνυπάρχον τῷ γιγνομένῳ καὶ οὕτως ποιοῦν τὰ ἐφεξῆς παρὰ τοῦ ποιήσαντος αὐτὸ τὴν αἰτίαν ἔχει· καὶ τὰ ὄργανα δὲ οὐκ ἐξ αὐτῶν τὸ κινεῖν ἔχει· τὸ δὲ πρῶτον καὶ τούτοις αἴτιον καὶ ἐκτὸς τοῦ γινομένου.

8 Alexander, as we shall see, will insert an intermediate step here. The causally relevant internal factor is first identified by him as the form of the entity (see especially **T3** below), and it is through this that it will take on the role of the nature of the entity in question. As Orna Harari suggests to me in this Alexander may well have been influenced by the doctrine of the cohesive cause of the Stoics.

9 τούτων δὲ αἱ μὲν ἐνυπάρχουσαί εἰσιν αἱ δὲ ἐκτός. διο ἥ τε φύσις ἀρχὴ καὶ τὸ στοιχεῖον καὶ ἡ διάνοια καὶ ἡ προαίρεσις καὶ οὐσία καὶ τὸ οὗ ἕνεκα·

10 About substance see the paragraph at n. 15 below.

11 See Bonitz (1849), p. 220 and, with some slight variation, Ross (1953), vol. I, p. 291.

12 πασῶν μὲν οὖν κοινὸν τῶν ἀρχῶν τὸ πρῶτον εἶναι ὅθεν ἢ ἔστιν ἢ γίγνεται ἢ γιγνώσκεται·

13 εἰπὼν τῶν ἀρχῶν τὰς μὲν ἐνυπάρχειν τούτοις ὧν εἰσιν ἀρχαί, τὰς δὲ ἐκτὸς εἶναι, διὰ τοῦτο, φησί, τὸ τὰς μὲν οὕτως ἔχειν τὰς δὲ οὐχ οὕτως, ἥ τε φύσις ἐστὶν ἀρχὴ καὶ τὸ στοιχεῖον· ἀρχαὶ γὰρ ταῦτα ὡς ἐνυπάρχοντα· ἐκ τούτων γὰρ πρώτων γίγνεται ἐνυπαρχόντων. φύσιν δὲ νῦν τὴν ὕλην ἂν λέγοι, στοιχεῖον δὲ τὴν προσεχῆ ὕλην, ἥτις ἤδη ἐνεργείᾳ τί ἐστι σῶμα.

Here, then, Alexander attributes to Aristotle a very restricted understanding of what nature can be an immanent principle: only prime matter can fit the bill.[14] Elements – which by Alexander lights are complexes of form and prime matter, and thereby are 'already some body in actuality' – are also principles of the bodies to which they are immanent: they are primary, because they form the lowest rung of actual corporeal existence in all the other bodies.

Nevertheless, this does not rule out that there can also be formal principles, they, however, cannot be internal principles. In the closely following discussion Alexander submits that when Aristotle includes substance (οὐσία) on this list of principles, what he means is the "principle according to form" (ἡ κατὰ τὸ εἶδος ἀρχή, Alex. *In Meta.* 347, 16). Such a principle when it exists before the entity whose principle it is, is not internal to it, hence it is not an immanent principle.[15]

The other side of the coin is Alexander's claim about nature in the discussion of *Physics* II. Although, as we have seen, Alexander remarked that he needs to transfer the interpretation of *Physics* II.3 to the commentary on *Metaphysics* Δ.2, it is clear from Simplicius' quotes from and summaries of Alexander's position in his commentary on the *Physics* that Alexander's commentary of the *Physics* was way more elaborate. First there is the testimony about Alexander's take on *Phys.* 194^b29-32 (the exact same lines as *Meta.* 1013^a29-32). It is along the same lines as what we find in passage **T1** from the *Metaphysics* commentary, additionally foregrounding that such nature[16] can be granted only dependent or derivative productive causal power:

> **T3** And one should keep in mind that here Alexander concedes that nature is not a productive cause in the principal sense, but rather a formal cause (ειδικόν), because it is not the first one among the productive causes. The instruments, too, seem to become causes of motion, but nor are these productive causes in the principal sense, because they [do not move] in a primary way, but move by being moved. One should also keep in mind that Alexander agrees that the instrument is also a cause in a way – even though not a productive cause in a principal sense, but it is exactly this: an instrumental cause.[17] (Simpl. *In Phys.* 315, 12-18)

What we learn in addition to the summary in the commentary on *Metaphysics* Δ.2 is that all these dependent or derivative productive causes can be taken as causes of motion, and even as productive causes. Moreover, the few lines about the causal status of instruments in the commentary of the *Metaphysics* guarantee that Simplicius' summary statement about Alexander's take on instrumental causes cannot be just Simplicius' addition. The exact terminology may remain in doubt, but the single clause in Alexander's commentary on the *Metaphysics* about instruments, that they cause motion, supports Simplicius' claim that by Alexander's lights instruments, although not productive causes in a principal sense, are nevertheless in some way productive causes (ποιητικὰ αἴτια).[18]

2. Nature and intellect as causes

One might think that all these considerations give rise to a sliding scale of derivative productive causes, each of them dependent on the non-immanent productive cause that is such in the proper, full sense of the term. What has to be recognized nevertheless is that among these different dependent or derivative productive causes nature has a special status. This is because it is not just a productive cause to a lesser degree. It is, as Alexander puts it, rather

---

14 Bonitz (1849), p. 220 and Ross (1953), vol. I, p. 291 take Alexander's identification of nature with matter in a generalizing fashion, among other instances of matter also including the elements. Instead, I suggest that we should take these two candidates as separate items, in an exclusive fashion for several reasons. First of all, most of the instances of matter may not qualify as primary: they are posterior to the elements which constitute them. Moreover, if matter *tout court* is a principle of a composite entity, it remains problematic why its correlative form does not qualify as a principle. (Actually, this could be one of the reasons why Bonitz and Ross submitted that nature could refer to both material and formal natures as principles.) And finally, if matter in general is a principle, the last clause about element, that it is already some body in actuality would not be pellucid, it would not serve as a contrast between the immediately preceding candidate. Note also that by Alexander's lights prime matter is matter in the principal sense (κυρίως), see Alex. *De anima* p. 7, 14 – 17, the first lines of **T6** below (this first matter is the substrate of the **first bodies**, which are the elements) and *Quaestio* II.24 p. 75, 6 and 8.

15 "The form, too, similarly [to the final cause] when it is a principle as preexisting and preconceived, is not immanent [to the entity whose principle it is]" (Alex. *In Meta.* 347, 26 f.: ὁμοίως δὲ καὶ τὸ εἶδος, ὅτε ἐστὶν ὡς προϋπάρχον τε καὶ προεπινοούμενον ἀρχή, οὐκ ἐνυπάρχει).

16 The contrast I intend here is between this looser understanding of nature, and the one Alexander ascribes to Aristotle in **T2**, about nature which is also a principle. This nature – prime matter – Is a principle in the strict sense of the word, but it can have no claim on being a productive cause whatsoever.

17 καὶ δεῖ μεμνῆσθαι, ὅτι ἐνταῦθα ὁ Ἀλέξανδρος ὁμολογεῖ μὴ εἶναι κυρίως ποιητικὸν αἴτιον τὴν φύσιν, ἀλλ' είδικὸν μᾶλλον διὰ τὸ μὴ εἶναι πρῶτον ἐν τοῖς ποιητικοῖς. καὶ τὰ ὄργανα δὲ δοκεῖ κινήσεως αἴτια γίνεσθαι, ἀλλ' οὐδὲ ταῦτα κυρίως ποιητικά ἐστιν, ὅτι μὴ πρώτως ἀλλὰ κινούμενα κινεῖ. καὶ τούτου δὲ χρὴ μεμνῆσθαι, ὅτι συγχωρεῖ ὁ Ἀλέξανδρος καὶ τὸ ὄργανον αἴτιόν πως εἶναι· εἰ καὶ μὴ κυρίως ποιητικόν, ἀλλ' αὐτὸ τοῦτο ὀργανικόν.

18 Simpl. *In Phys.* 316, 9.

a formal cause. Or, to put it differently, it is a formal cause which also has efficacy as a productive cause.[19] This is not so with the other dependent productive causes. Unlike them, nature is a metaphysical component of the item whose nature it is, it is what makes the (natural) thing the entity it is.[20]

T4 Each of the beings is what it is when it is in actuality; therefore things that are by nature too are by nature when they are in actuality. But everything is in actuality when it has its form, and things that are by nature are by nature when they have their form. But that thing by whose presence things that are by nature are by nature – this thing is their nature. Things that are by nature are by nature by the presence of their form. Therefore, their form is nature.[21] (Simpl. *In Phys.* 277, 31 – 278, 3)

This nature, this form responsible for what the entity is, understandably will be causally responsible for all the changes that flow from what this entity is. Or to put it otherwise: the essential changes of this entity. Simplicius reports that Alexander allows for different classes of such natural motions for different entities: only locomotion for the elements, all the three types of changes – quantitative and qualitative changes and locomotion – for the animals, and both quantitative and qualitative changes, but not locomotion for the plants.[22] This might suggest a *scala naturae*, from the rather meager scope of natural tendencies of the elements all the way to the vastly variegated affordances for natural motions the animals have. But simplicity need not be ranked below complexity. Indeed, as Simplicius reports nature is present in a principal way in the elements:

T5 "For – he [i.e. Alexander] says – it should be noted that Aristotle included also the soul in the definition of nature, if indeed the soul according to him [i.e. according to Aristotle] is the actuality of a natural body having organs, but nature in a principal way and primarily is in the simple bodies, and not in the ones having organs."[23] (Simpl. *In Phys.* 268, 18-21)

This characterization is in conformity with the way Alexander contrasts the nature of elements to the nature of more complex entities like living beings in his *De anima*. On the one hand, there is the nature and the natural motion of the elements:

T6 Of the natural bodies, whose underlying subject is simple – this [underlier] is matter in the principal sense, which underlies the simple and first bodies that are elements of the other bodies – their form and nature is also simple. Because of this, their nature is the cause of one simple motion. For if nature is an origin of motion, then a simple nature is the origin of a simple motion, and the simple [motion] is also one in the primary sense.[24] (Alexander *De anima* 7, 14 – 20, tr. Caston 2012, somewhat modified)

Compound bodies, on the other hand, have more complex forms, which rest on the capacities provided by the forms of the different components of what underlies them:

T7 The item, then, which has many differing forms as its underlying subjects, with [their] matter,[25] has a nature and form that is of necessity more complex and more complete, since each nature in the bodies underlying [this nature] makes a contribution to the form that stands over them all and is common to them.

---

19 This can be contrasted to forms of artifacts, which on their own lack this kind of causal efficacy.

20 Note that this applies differently to the matter of natural entities and to that of artificial objects. The material component of natural entities is potentially that natural entity. Accordingly, Alexander submits that "matter, too, is nature, although less so than form." (Simpl. *In Phys.* 278, 5) In the case of artifacts provided their matter has nature properly speaking, like in the case of the bed in Antiphon's thought experiment (see the pointer at *Phys.* II.1 193^{a}8), it is productive of something different from this artifact: it can only sprout a sapling, and is unable to generate further beds.

21 ἕκαστον τῶν ὄντων τότε ἐστὶν ὅ ἐστιν, ὅταν ἐντελεχείᾳ ᾖ· ὥστε καὶ τὰ φύσει φύσει ἐστίν, ὅταν ᾖ ἐντελεχείᾳ· ἐντελεχείᾳ δέ ἐστι πᾶν ὅταν τὸ εἶδος ἔχῃ καὶ τὰ φύσει ἄρα φύσει ἐστίν, ὅταν τὸ εἶδος ἔχῃ· ἀλλὰ μὴν οὗ παρουσίᾳ τὰ φύσει φύσει ἐστὶ τοῦτό ἐστι φύσις, τῇ δὲ τοῦ εἴδους παρουσίᾳ τὰ φύσει φύσει ἐστί· τὸ εἶδος ἄρα φύσις.

22 Simpl. *in Phys.* 265,1-6. Simplicius reports on Alexander's position only to criticize it – but details of his criticism are not relevant here.

23 "σημειωτέον γάρ, φησίν, ὅτι καὶ τὴν ψυχὴν περιείληφε τῷ τῆς φύσεως λόγῳ, εἴπερ ἡ μὲν ψυχὴ κατ' αὐτὸν ἐντελέχειά ἐστιν σώματος φυσικοῦ ὀργανικοῦ, ἡ δὲ φύσις κυρίως καὶ πρώτως ἐν τοῖς ἁπλοῖς ἐστι σώμασι καὶ οὐ τοῖς ὀργανικοῖς."

24 οἷς μὲν οὖν φυσικοῖς σώμασιν ἁπλοῦν τὸ ὑποκείμενον (ἔστι δὲ τοῦτο ἡ κυρίως ὕλη, ἥτις ὑπόκειται τοῖς ἁπλοῖς τε καὶ πρώτοις σώμασιν, ἃ στοιχεῖα τῶν ἄλλων ἐστὶ σωμάτων), τούτων ἁπλοῦν καὶ τὸ εἶδος καὶ ἡ φύσις. διὸ καὶ μιᾶς τε καὶ ἁπλῆς κινήσεως τούτοις ἡ φύσις αἰτία. εἰ γὰρ ἡ φύσις ἀρχὴ κινήσεως, εἴη ἂν καὶ ἡ ἁπλῆ φύσις ἁπλῆς ἀρχὴ κινήσεως. ἡ δὲ ἁπλῆ καὶ κυρίως μία.

25 I take it that this stresses that the forms in question are enmattered forms. Needless to say, these enmattered forms will be the forms of the distinct components of the matter of the compound entity.

For this sort of form is in a way a form of forms and a kind of completion of completions.[26] (Alex. *De anima* 8, 8 – 13, tr. Caston 2012, somewhat modified)

These considerations hold already at the level of the nature and form of homogeneous mixtures, not yet articulated into functional part or organs: they, too, contain the capacities of their ingredients at a second remove (δευτέρως), and the way their form rests on these allows that their nature and form can be immensely complex.[27] Similarly, the capacities of the form and nature of living beings of different complexity rest on the capacities provided by the underlying entities in them – from the elements and their compounds all the way to their organs.

T8 So in things whose underlying subject is not even a body,[28] the form is simpler too; whereas in things whose underlying subject is a body, and a compound one at that, with different parts useful for different activities, their form is conjoined with many powers, since it is a form and completion of a complex and organic body. For just this reason, then, the soul is a form[29] of this sort of body. [...][30] (Alex. *De anima* 10, 26 – 11, 2, tr. Caston 2012, somewhat modified)

In this *scala naturae* more complex natural bodies have more complex, more complete natures. But their completeness arises from the lower-level natures of their material components – all the way down to the nature of the fundamental and simple items, the nature of the elements.

These considerations also have a reverse side. Unlike other natures that rest on the capacities and operations of yet other embedded natures, these fundamental and simple natures are principally and primarily the natures that they are. They are fully self-contained, not even their substrate – prime matter, an entity without any form or nature of its own – can provide some capacity or operation of its own to support their operation.[31]

This fundamental nature of the elements can be responsible not only for the generation of the more complex entities, which contain them: mixtures, like blood, flesh or bone, and then the living beings that are composed of these tissues. The nature of the element – Its form – can also be responsible for the generation of other elementary masses of the very same species or genus. This is analogous to the reproduction of mortal living beings, in the process of which their form – their soul – replicates itself in the form of their offspring, which is an animal of the same species. In the case of animals, it is also possible that the offspring is not of the same kind as either parent animal is, but it belongs to the same genus. In the case of the nature of the elements the analogous cases are when one element is the cause of the generation of a different element, like cases where fire, the element with the greatest productive efficiency, is responsible for the generation of other elements. And finally and just as importantly, there is also a third case, that the motion of the celestial bodies, and most specifically of the sun is responsible for the generation of heat in the topmost region of the sublunary universe. The options are charted succinctly, in general terms as follows:

T9 "Generally[32] – says Alexander – what comes to be by nature seems to come to be by a thing that is the same either in species, or in genus, or in general by [a thing in] actuality. Things that come to be by the sun come to be as by [a thing in] actuality. For they are heated or cooled by its activity.[33] (Simpl. *In Phys.* 307, 3 – 6)

This is crucially important in the case of the elements. They constitute the fundamental layer of physical reality. Their nature plays a supporting role in the operations of all the other natural entities. As with all natures, theirs also are rather formal causes than productive ones. The role of productive cause is played by what generated them. These productive causes can be within the sublunary physical

26 ᾧ δὴ πλείω καὶ διαφέροντα εἴδη τὰ μετὰ τῆς ὕλης ὑποκείμενα, ἐξ ἀνάγκης τούτου καὶ ἡ φύσις καὶ τὸ εἶδος ποικιλώτερόν τε καὶ τελειότερον, ἑκάστης φύσεως τῶν ἐν τοῖς ὑποκειμένοις αὐτῇ σώμασιν συντελούσης τι πρὸς τὸ ἐπὶ πᾶσιν κοινὸν εἶδος αὐτοῖς. εἶδος γάρ πως εἰδῶν γίνεται τὸ τοιοῦτον εἶδος καὶ τελειότης τις τελειοτήτων.

27 Alex. *De anima* 8, 22 – 25.

28 By Alexander's lights the underlying entity of the elements is prime matter, which is not a body in its own right, since in his view bodies are composites of matter and form. Note that we have seen the same contrast operative at the end of **T2** above, and see also **T6**.

29 Note that Alexander in the following lines, at 11, 5 – 7 speaks about soul as the form and nature of such a body.

30 οἷς μὲν οὖν τὴν ἀρχὴν τὸ ὑποκείμενον οὐδέπω σῶμα, τούτων καὶ τὸ εἶδος ἁπλούστερον· οἷς δὲ τὸ ὑποκείμενον σῶμά τε καὶ τοῦτο σύνθετον καὶ ἔχον μέρη διάφορα, ὡς ἄλλο πρὸς ἄλλην ἐνέργειαν εἶναι χρήσιμον, τούτων δὲ καὶ τὸ εἶδος μετὰ δυνάμεων πλειόνων, ἅτε ὂν εἶδος καὶ τελειότης ὀργανικοῦ τε καὶ ποικίλου σώματος· διὸ τοῦ τοιούτου σώματος εἶδος ἤδη ἡ ψυχή. [...]

31 Its contribution is that only with this underlier can they form a body (see also the contrast at the end of **T2** above) and are able to transform into each other.

32 The claim is formulated this way, apparently because it is the generalization of Aristotle's claim that is commented upon, that "A human begets a human, and the sun [also does]." (194b13, ἄνθρωπος γὰρ ἄνθρωπον γεννᾷ καὶ ἥλιος)

33 "καθόλου δέ, φησὶν ὁ Ἀλέξανδρος, τὸ γινόμενον φύσει δοκεῖ αὐτὸ ὑπὸ τοῦ αὐτοῦ γίνεσθαι ἢ εἴδει ἢ γένει ἢ ὅλως ὑπὸ ἐνεργείας. ὑπὸ ἡλίου γοῦν οὕτως τὰ γινόμενα γίνεται ὡς ὑπὸ ἐνεργείας· θερμαινόμενα γὰρ καὶ ψυχόμενα ὑπὸ τῆς ἐνεργείας τῆς ἐκείνου. (Note that I resorted to translating the occurrence of ἐνέργεια in the last clause as 'activity'. This activity is tied to the actuality and essence of the sun itself.)

realm. But the causal operation of celestial revolutions, chief among them the revolutions of the sun play an indispensable part. So indispensable indeed that the claim of Aristotle which is commented on, about the generation of a human being by their father immediately adds that such a generation is also a case of a causal process for which the sun is responsible.[34]

Simplicius' immediately following report sets Alexander's comment in a larger context, suggesting that according to Alexander any natural generation can always be traced back to the generative influence of the celestial realm over the sublunary world:

> **T10** Alexander remarks also on the basis of what is said here that according to Aristotle the generation of the things here [i.e. in our sublunary world] is connected to the divine body, and is not separated from it.[35] (Simpl. *In Phys.* 307, 9 – 12)

Alexander's comment, as Simplicius attests, is an interpretation of Aristotle's claim that "a human – and the sun – begets a human."[36] Causal chains starting from the causal influence of the celestial body satisfy the requirement that their productive cause has to be external and separated from its effect. Moreover, this fully external productive cause is emphatically not of the same kind, or of the same form as the entities produced by it. This is in stark contrast to the nature of the sublunary entities generated by the (productive) causal influence of something of the same kind. In the case of causation from the celestial domain there is no way that such a cause and its effect could in any way be of the same form, or of the same nature. On the other hand the fact that this causal activity is at the head also of each and every sublunary causal chain definitely restricts the claim of the other members of these causal chains for being full blown productive causes in their own right. These two considerations then chime in well with Alexander's earlier remark in **T3**, that nature is not a productive cause in the principal sense, but rather a formal cause.

The same claim is reiterated, in a slightly different form as follows:

> **T11** Since those natural things that are generated and perish are generated proximately by the eternal bodies performing a circular motion – "for a human – and the sun – begets a human" –, it is clear that that which produces in the principal sense does not produce by being the immediate neighbor of the things that are generated and perish, but [does so] through the intermediary of the eternal things. This way the instrumental cause came to light, the one that is moved by some other thing, and moves something else. This can be observed clearly in artistic production, for the odze is an auxiliary cause, as it moves by being moved.
>
> Nature is also such – both the whole nature and the partial one –, as Alexander also concedes, rightly objecting that the productive cause in the principal sense has to be separate and detached.[37] (Simpl. *In Phys.* 317, 20 – 28)

The most important difference between this formulation and the previous one is that here there is reference to a productive cause beyond the activity of the celestial bodies. The productive causal activity of this primary cause, according to this line of argument, will apparently restrict whatever natural activity there is in the universe – be that celestial or sublunary – to the status of an instrumental cause. Note that this claim need not be in conflict with the one in the previous passage. There the claim was that nature – apparently any of the sublunary natures – does not have full productive causal status because its operation rests on the causal influence that the celestial domain exerts over the sublunary one. In a way one could claim that **T11** provides a crucial further element of the scheme, and also gives the proper terminology for describing the operation of nature, that it is an instrumental cause,

34 One should keep in mind that Aristotle does not make the fantastic claim that the sun could be directly responsible, in an act of spontaneous generation, for the coming to be of a human being. Such cases of spontaneous generation do occur, and they involve thermic phenomena, for which the sun is causally responsible. But they generate only low-level living beings, that are not capable of sexual reproduction. For a detailed discussion see Lennox (2001).

35 σημειοῦται δὲ ὁ Ἀλέξανδρος καὶ ἐκ τῶν ἐνταῦθα λεγομένων, ὅτι κατὰ Ἀριστοτέλην συνῆπται τῷ θείῳ σώματι ἡ τῶν ἐνταῦθα γένεσις καὶ οὐκ ἀπήρτηται ἀπ' αὐτοῦ.

36 ἄνθρωπος γὰρ ἄνθρωπον γεννᾷ καὶ ἥλιος (194b13), cf. also *Metaphysics* Λ.5, where Aristotle after listing the material, formal and immediate moving or productive causes of a human – the elements of which the human being is composed, the human form belonging to this particular individual and the father respectively – adds "and besides these, the sun and its slanted circle, which are neither matter, nor form, nor privation, not of the same kind [or: nor having the same form], but movers." (1071a15-17)

37 ἐπεὶ δὲ τὰ γινόμενα καὶ φθειρόμενα τῶν φυσικῶν προσεχῶς ὑπὸ τῶν ἀιδίων καὶ κυκλοφορητικῶν γίνεται ("ἄνθρωπος γὰρ ἄνθρωπον γεννᾷ καὶ ἥλιος"), δῆλον ὅτι τὸ κυρίως ποιοῦν οὐκ ἀμέσως πελάζον τοῖς γινομένοις καὶ φθειρομένοις ποιεῖ, ἀλλὰ διὰ μέσων τῶν ἀιδίων. καὶ οὕτως ἡμῖν ἀνεφάνη τὸ ὀργανικὸν αἴτιον, ὅπερ ἐστὶ κινούμενον μὲν ὑπ' ἄλλου, κινοῦν δὲ ἕτερον. καὶ σαφῶς ἐπὶ τῆς τεχνικῆς ποιήσεως ὁρᾶται· τὸ γὰρ σκέπαρνον συναίτιόν ἐστιν, διότι κινούμενον κινεῖ. τοιαύτη δὲ καὶ ἡ φύσις ἥ τε ὅλη καὶ ἡ μερική, ὡς καὶ Ἀλέξανδρος ὁμολογεῖ καλῶς ἐπιστήσας, ὅτι τὸ κυρίως ποιητικὸν αἴτιον χωριστὸν εἶναι χρὴ καὶ ἐξῃρημένον.

literally like an odze, an extremely powerful instrument in the hands of craftsmen, operated by their craft.[38]

The other difference between the two passages is that this second passage formulates the claim about nature in specifically technical terms. Both the whole nature and the partial nature – I take it this means that partial nature as such, or otherwise put, all the partial natures there are – are only instrumental causes, operating on the causal impact of the prime productive cause. What would need to be ascertained about this latter claim is to what extent this aligns with any of the ways of Alexander's understanding of nature. Most interestingly, one can argue both for and against such an alignment. One obvious point of departure here could be Alexander's comment on *Metaphysics* Δ, the chapter on nature.[39] There Alexander quotes Aristotle's summary statement approvingly that "among the ones that have been said the first nature and the one that is called [nature] in a principal way is the substance of the things that have the principle of their motion in themselves in so far as they are these things," and adds that through this statement Aristotle asserts that "nature in the principal sense is the enmattered form, from which the principle of motion is for the composite [i.e. matter and form] entity."[40]

These considerations suggest that talk about the nature of an entity in the primary sense will be connected to the form of this entity. Accordingly, in order to talk about the internal source of motion and rest of the whole of corporeal existence (or of the whole of sublunary corporeal existence) would require that these constitute a single entity with the form of its own. This may constitute a rather high bar. Indeed, by Alexander's lights the whole world does not possess a single nature of its own. Nevertheless, as far as the way of unpacking the claim in Simplicius' lines is concerned, there is a fair number of occurrences of the expression 'the whole nature' in Aristotle.[41] Without going into detail about each of these occurrences it is safe to claim that 'the whole nature' need not refer to an internal principle of motion and rest in these passages. Instead, it lumps together all entities – not necessarily all the entities there are, the collection can be somewhat selective, and differently so in different contexts. Importantly, there is no need to sort out on what basis the particular kind of entities are lumped together in these different contexts. What is relevant at this point is that this usage refers to substances and is not about their internal principle(s).[42]

This should mean that if we take the expression 'whole nature' as one that was employed by Alexander along the lines of its occurrences in Aristotle, the claim in the last clause of **T11** will be problematic. What could be established in terms of such a 'whole nature' as an aggregate is that this entity cannot operate independently of the causal influence of the prime productive cause. It might be possible to cash out the consequences of this claim in a way that one can make assertions about something which can be meaningfully referred to as the item responsible for the type of unity this aggregate has. But Simplicius' hasty remark does not provide us with the requisite details what such an item could be, and what mode of operation should be assigned to it. And we should also keep in mind that it is possible that in these lines Simplicius speaks in his own voice, summoning Alexander's authority only in the very last words of the sentence, where he contrasts the full force of (productive) causality of the entity at the head of the causal chains, to the causal status of nature.

Nevertheless, with all due reservations about the actual formulation Simplicius uses, one must admit that the contrast between the natures of individual entities ("particular natures") and some divine power permeating the whole, which on occasion can be also called nature (something like the "whole nature" in Simplicius' formulation), is present in several works of Alexander. One of these is *On the principles of the universe* (*De principiis*), extant in Arabic translation. There the causal influence of the motions of the eternal, celestial bodies is conjoined with a 'certain spiritual power' causally responsible for the generation and change of the perishable bodies:

T12 (127) Since the First Mover is as we have described it, and the things moved by it without intermediary are also in that state,[43] there follows from the

38 The craft is separate and detached from the instrument – but not from the craftsman operating it. This will be importantly different from the case discussed in section 3 below.

39 An important *caveat*: Alexander need not restrict himself to the list of meanings enumerated in this chapter. Nevertheless, in the case of an item which does not match one of these meanings we should require that there is a way to connect it to one of these, and ultimately to the core meaning of the term.

40 Aristotle, *Metaphysics* Δ.4 1015a13 – 15 and Alexander *In Meta.* 360, 1-3 and 4-5.

41 One can also add to these the occurrence of the phrase 'the nature of the whole' at e.g. *De caelo* I.2 268b11-13, where the issue is whether the nature of the whole is finite or infinite, and so "'the context [...] leaves no doubt that this is purely a question about dimensions" (Sedley 2000, p. 329), that is to say, dimensions of a corporeal entity, comprising all the bodies that there are.

42 Note that Aristotle lists this usage of 'nature' in *Metaphysics* Δ.4, the chapter on φύσις: "And from this sense of 'nature' [i.e. from the sense in which the substance of an entity is its nature] every substance in general is in fact, by an extension of meaning, called a 'nature', because the nature [of a thing] is one kind of substance." (1015a11-13, tr. Ross)

43 I.e. in a life of supreme excellence and of supreme bliss, of entities eternally (or presumably in the case of the heavens, always) accomplishing excellent things without obstacle or hindrance (126, following in the latter part of this sentence Genequand's later French translation, Genequandt 2017, p. 90).

motion of these things [i.e. of the heavenly bodies] the generation and change of the perishable bodies having matter, **according to the power of those [the heavenly bodies]** reaching them **according to [the former's] diversity**, and **according to the assimilation of those different things which we have mentioned**, because of the change and diversity of their motion, as we said before.

(128) **This nature and power** are the cause of the unity and order of the world. In the same way as happens in one city having one ruler residing in it, not separate from it, we also say that **a certain spiritual power** penetrates the whole world and holds its parts together.

(129) Since the city is ruled by one authority only, which is its leader or established law, so is the **one world**, since it is one body, continuous, eternal, imperishable, containing and encompassing all things, and comprehending them, and all things which are in it **seek to be in contact** with the thing which is unchangeable and **aim at the material union** granted by[44] that which rules and governs [the world] and preserves its arrangement and order by a spiritual power which penetrates all parts of it which deserve that it should penetrate them according to what [the ruler] thinks, not the people.[45]

[...]

(132) For since **the nature penetrating all parts of the world** is a divine power, it follows and turns to the most excellent being; therefore, all things which share in it do so **according to the state and position of each one of them in relation to it**.

[...]

(135) The state of the world is similar to that of the city or the house: among the things which are in it, **the nature proper to them** has caused some of them to happen always according to organization and order, because they are not susceptible to any kind of disturbance, ...; others still have a feeble share in this state, I mean the state of organization and order.[46]

According to the scheme presented in these paragraphs everything in the world – celestial bodies and sublunary beings alike – "seeks to be in contact with the thing which is unchangeable." The goal of this aspiration is some sort of "material union" these corporeal entities have. This material union then should be what integrates the individual entities beyond being the entities that they are into their environment, and also into the corporeal world at large.

What is important for us, as far as Simplicius' testimony is concerned, is the contrast between the spiritual power penetrating the whole world (128), the nature penetrating all parts of the world, which is a divine power (132) on the one hand, and the nature proper to the things which are in the world (135) on the other. The source of this spiritual power, of this nature penetrating all parts of the world is ultimately the First Mover. But as far as the sublunary world is concerned, the activity of the celestial bodies plays an indispensable role in communicating the spiritual power to the sublunary sphere: "... the generation and change of the perishable bodies having matter [follows], according to the power of those [the heavenly bodies] reaching them according to [the perishable bodies'] diversity." (127)

This actually might come quite close to Simplicius' testimony, who stresses the contrast on the one hand between the ultimate productive causal instance and the status of the 'whole nature' as instrumental cause, under the sway of the ultimate productive cause, and on the other that between this 'whole nature' and the particular natures, which are also relegated to the status of instrumental causes. In the presentation of the *De principiis* this is matched by two contrasts: on the one hand the one between the Prime Mover, the ultimate source of the spiritual power penetrating the whole world (128) and of the nature penetrating all the parts of the world (132), and then this spiritual power, or nature itself, which follows and turns to that most excellent being, and on the other hand the one between this spiritual power or nature present all way through in the one world, which is "one body, continuous, eternal, imperishable, containing and encompassing all things, and comprehending them" (129) and the nature proper to the things which are in it. (135)

Moreover, the more detailed account in the *De principiis* besides emphasizing the unity of the corporeal world effected by this spiritual power or nature also mentions the

44 I am following here Genequand (2017), p. 90, which has *grâce à ce qui le régit etc.* The earlier English translation has "since it [the one world] is one body, continuous, eternal, imperishable, containing and encompassing all things, and comprehending them, all things which are in it seek to be in contact with the thing which is unchangeable and aim at the material union **with** that which rules and governs [the world]." As the statement is about all the corporeal existents in the world, there is just no way to avoid the impossible claim that all the different corporeal beings aim at the *material* union with the *incorporeal* Prime Mover. This is also admitted by Genequand in a note to this paragraph, where he formulates some different considerations how one could avoid this problematic claim. (Genequand 2001, p. 165)

45 In the French translation: *selon ce qu'il pense lui et non les gens.* (Genequand 2017, p. 90) In accordance with this, the next paragraph in the French translation talks about animals being penetrated by the divine power – excluding, however, the imaginary ones.

46 Genequand (2001), pp. 113 – 117, with minor changes drawn from Genequand (2017), as indicated in the preceding footnotes above.

articulation of this world into two large regions of vastly different status: the celestial bodies moved directly by the First Mover, and the perishable bodies, whose generation and change are under the causal sway of the motion of the celestial bodies. (127) This actually corresponds to the first part of Simplicius' testimony in **T11** above, with its emphasis that the causal influence of the productive cause in the principal sense reaches the realm of generated and perishable bodies through the intermediary of the eternal things. The claim that sublunary causal chains go all the way back to causal triggers from the celestial domain has been asserted in **T10**. What the account of the *De principiis* and the first half of Simplicius' testimony here adds to that is that instead of the distributive, sort of piecemeal claim we have a formulation that looks at the larger regions of the universe as unified domains.

This also might suggest that although Simplicius mentions Alexander only at the very end of this testimony, some salient elements of the first part may also be connected to Alexander's commentary. All this may be further substantiated through Alexander's *Quaestio* II.3, "What the power is that comes to be, from the movement of the divine body, in the body adjacent to it which is mortal and subject to coming-to-be."

The very first thing to notice about this *quaestio* is that here the source of the power reaching the sublunary world, as set by the *quaestio* itself, is identified as the movement of the divine body. Whether that rests on the causal influence of a further, super-celestial entity, is not addressed in this particular discussion. The *quaestio* broaches different proposals for the manifestation of this power issuing from the celestial domain. In one of the solutions proposed the divine power is identified with a second nature (p. 49, 15), which is added to natural mixtures and blends as psychic motion – , or rather, as a source of psychic motion (p. 49, 1 – 4) – , over and above the baseline elemental natures of their ingredients. This second nature is then indispensable for the emergence of living, ensouled entities out of the elements. On the basis of the elemental natures they have, they could not possibly form such more perfect and animate bodies.

This proposal is then contrasted to a different one, according to which the divine power is the cause of the difference between the simple bodies, so that it comes to be their nature and form. (p. 49, 28 – 30, with Moraux' emendation[47]). As part of this activity, producing – or even becoming – the forms of simple bodies in prime matter, the activity of this divine power is continuously exerted, and keeps on producing different elements in the sublunary realm,

> **T13** [these elements] being given form in different ways according to the different relation of [the divine bodies] to things here [on earth][48] at different times which results from [their] movement on a circle of this sort. (*Quaestio* II. 3 p. 50, 5 – 8, tr. Sharples 1992)

As a result, the divine power will be responsible for the dynamic processes between these elements, and also for the emergence of the mixtures and blends composed of them:

> **T14** ... the [bodies] that come to be from the mixture and blending of these, since they have a share in more powers and different bodies, already come to be compounded and more perfect, and their perfection and form comes to be different according to the difference in the mixture of the bodies spoken of initially. (*Quaestio* II. 3 p. 50, 17 – 21, tr. Sharples 1992)

This proposal gives rise to a quite delicate and nuanced distinction between the divine power itself and the different natures of the different entities. The different elemental natures *are* this divine power itself. But the continuous activity of the divine power is responsible for the emergence of ever new pockets of these elements, which then leads to the emergence of different patterns and configurations of these elements. The interaction of the divine power with the configurations in the sublunary world will give rise to complexes of ever greater perfection. As these patterns and configurations could not possibly have arisen without the causal impact of this divine power, each of them is a manifestation of the creative opulence of the divine power.[49] They nevertheless remain the local manifestations of this creative power, so on this account too, one can draw a fine line between the particular natures and the overarching divine power, which is responsible for their generation and interactions.

The passages of *De principiis* I have quoted above and *quaestio* II.3 then jointly corroborate what is included in Simplicius' testimony above, irrespective of the particular terminology Simplicius uses for introducing the contrast between the 'whole nature' and particular natures.

What remains to be ascertained about this testimony is whether the distribution of causal labor as charted by

47 For Moraux' emendation see Sharples (1992), p. 124.

48 [on earth] is added by Sharples. Note that it has to be taken in a looser sense, as this region expands all the way to the celestial spheres.

49 One needs to keep in mind that the creative opportunities of this divine power are severely limited. Even under the continuous influence of this divine power sublunary material existence can house only the complexes that we encounter in the world. No further development is possible, least of all an open-ended evolution of different complex entities. An additional constraint is that this divine power is operative as the nature of these entities, and sublunary nature does not operate with exceptionless regularity, its effects are only for the most part.

Simplicius, where a transcendent, immaterial entity is the real productive cause, and nature – even the 'whole nature', whatever it is – is subordinate to this productive cause as an instrumental cause, is the one also entertained by Alexander. *Quaestio* II.3 does not broach this issue. All it speaks about is the divine power reaching the recesses of the sublunary domain from the celestial bodies. Where this divine power (called also a psychic power) originates from, is simply not addressed here.

The *De principiis* – and a host of other texts of Alexander – attest that Alexander followed a particular interpretation of Aristotle's account rather closely, according to which the Prime Mover causes motion by being an object of love and striving. I am quoting here in this regard what we find in the *De prinicipiis*:

> **T15** (75) The mover imparting the first motion in this way is perfect in all respects; it is, then, devoid of all motion[50] and better than all beings.
>
> (76) The divine body is moved with the natural[51] motion essentially proper to it by its desire for this mover and its longing to imitate it. By this motion it imitates this substance, which is unmoved, for the eternity of the motion inborn[52] in the divine body, its continuity and permanence in one and the same state, are similar to the life-span[53] of that [mover] and its duration.
>
> (77) For since it is not possible that a natural body should be immovable, and this is the state of the divine body,[54] the regularity and continuity of its natural motion resemble the absence of motion of that thing which imparts motion[55] to it by its [i.e. the divine body's] impulse to imitate it [i.e. the mover].[56]

Indeed, such an interpretation is only to be expected in Alexander. Genequand in a note to (77) remarks that we find the same interpretation also in *Quaest.* II.18 p. 62, 33 – 34 and p. 63, 20 – 21, and I.25 p. 40, 17 – 21.[57] What we should note, however, is that this apparently lands Alexander in a paradoxical, or even untenable position. One can sum this up in the following way. Nature, according to **T3** above is not a productive cause in the full sense of the term. This is the case also for celestial nature, which is responsible for celestial revolutions, and through this, for the incessant coming-to-be and perishing of sublunary bodies. Then, celestial nature will need a productive cause which is responsible for the natural motion of the heavens. This efficient or productive cause cannot be on a par with the cause of the natural motions of sublunary elements. In their case, as Aristotle sets out, the efficient or productive cause of these natural motions is the item that is responsible for the generation of these elemental masses in the first place.[58] The celestial body is eternal, ungenerated and incorruptible. The causal account of the natural motion of these bodies provided by Alexander interprets Aristotle in a way in which the First Mover is responsible for this motion – but its responsibility is couched in terms which put it on a par with a final cause. If there is no proper productive cause behind the operation and causal efficacy of the celestial body, its status as an instrumental productive cause will be in jeopardy.

Simplicius' further testimonies about Alexander's commentary on book II of the *Physics* provide rather meagre additional information. There are two or three mentions of the commentary on this book which might appear relevant in this regard, but on a closer look they remain inconsequential. In one (Simpl. *In Phys.* 366, 15 – 29) Simplicius reports that Alexander argues that the passage starting at *Physics* 198a31 picks up the argumentation conducted in 198a21 – 24, the intervening lines (198a24 – 31) sorting out what kind of identity relations can hold between causes of different kinds (what something is – i.e. the form – and for the sake of what it is – i.e. the final cause – is the same item, and where motion is first from – i.e. the moving cause – is the same in species as these). The other issue broached in these intervening lines by Alexander's lights is sorting out the difference of productive causes, "if indeed one is unmoved and the other is moved, and of the latter one is imperishable, the other perishable."[59] (Simpl. *In Phys.* 366, 21 – 23)

It is noteworthy that Alexander switches from Aristotle's formulations about 'the mover', 'where motion is first from' to speaking about productive causes. Aristotle introduces the three types of moving cause first with a distinction

50 The English translation has "it is, then, **a species** devoid of all motion," only to admit in a note that "this is odd, and might result from the two meanings of εἶδος in Greek (form and species), moreover it occurs only in [manuscript] Z." (Genequand 2001, p. 157). In the French translation Genequand (2017) decides on following the other manuscripts, and leaves out the word altogether.

51 The English translation has 'essential'.

52 The French translation (Genequand 2017, p. 74) has *intrinsèque* here.

53 'Life-span' (*durée de vie* in the French translation) may well go back to αἰών, cf. *De caelo* I.9 279a18 – 28.

54 "I.e. it is a natural body," (Genequand 2001., p. 157, *ad loc.*)

55 "of that thing which imparts motion" – *dans cette chose motrice* in the French translation (Genequand 2017, p.. 74).

56 Genequand (2001), p. 83.

57 Genequand (2001), p. 157, with minor changes drawn from Genequand (2017), as indicated in the preceding footnotes above.

58 Aristotle *Physics* VIII.4 255a30 – 256a2.

59 "… τῶν μεταξὺ παρεμβεβλημένων εἰς διορισμὸν τῆς ταυτότητος τῶν αἰτίων καὶ τοῦ ποιητικοῦ αἰτίου τῆς διαφορᾶς.εἴπερ τὸ μὲν ἀκίνητόν ἐστι τὸ δὲ κινούμενον, καὶ τούτου τὸ μὲν ἄφθαρτον τὸ δὲ φθαρτόν."

between those that are unmoved, and those that are in motion, and the latter is divided into the imperishable and the perishable ones among them. Aristotle closes this with listing the three different inquiries: one is about unmoved items, which fall outside the scope of physics, another one about eternal moving bodies, and yet another one about the perishable ones.

Alexander's remark then that the productive cause can be distinguished into these three types shows that he takes the investigation into the unmoved supra-physical movers to be an investigation of productive causes. Nevertheless, the worry does remain: in what sense are these movers, or causes of motion productive causes? As we shall see, Alexander can talk about a cause which need not be a productive cause in the full sense of the term as the cause productive of motion.[60] In that case, however, we cannot accept this testimony of Simplicius' at face value and claim that the Prime Mover is a fully-fledged productive cause by Alexander's lights.

The other pair of testimonies is similarly inconclusive. The context of these is a comment on Aristotle's claim in *Physics* 198a5 – 13, that chance and spontaneity are accidental causes of things that are caused by nature and intellect. But then whatever might be claimed to be caused by chance or spontaneity the corresponding non-accidental causes, nature and the intellect, should have a prior claim of being causes of such things. This holds about a lot of things, leading all the way to the universe. Here it is instructive to compare Aristotle's actual statement to Simplicius' report about Alexander.

First, Aristotle:

> Since spontaneity and chance are causes of things when – though intellect and nature might be responsible for them – something else becomes accidentally their cause, and nothing which is accidental is prior to what is *per se*, it is clear that an accidental cause cannot be prior to a *per se* one. Spontaneity and chance, therefore, are posterior both to intellect and nature. Hence, if most of all spontaneity is the cause of the heavens, it is necessary that intellect and nature are prior causes both of many other things and of this universe.[61] (*Physics* 198a5 – 13)

The final claim of the passage then is apparently transcribed by Alexander in terms of productive causation:

> **T16** the first causes are productive of the first things among existent things, and the first among existent things came to be by the first among causes, which are the intellect and nature. If intellect and nature are causes of anything at all, they will be [causes] of those things that are most according to the intellect, as the heavens and this universe are.[62] (Simpl. *In Phys.* 354, 22 – 26)

As a result, this latter formulation speaks about the heavens and this universe – the first of existing things – as generated by intellect and nature. But in the very next sentence the claim about intellect and nature is formulated much more cautiously, without stressing the productive causal efficiency of intellect and nature. That may even have been discarded. The context introduced intellect and nature as productive causes. This presupposition may still be in effect, then talk about the causal efficacy of nature and intellect in the next sentence will stay in that original frame. On the other hand, one might want to claim that the second sentence's talking only about causation, without type of causation mentioned, may have released the original presupposition.

Most importantly, however, we should keep in mind the context of Aristotle's claims – a dialectical context, in a refutation of those natural philosophers who claim that spontaneity is responsible for the generation of the cosmos. As a result, neither Aristotle, nor his commentator Alexander is under obligation to give a worked-out alternative to the proposal they reject. It is sufficient if they identify a crucial shortcoming. Aristotle and Alexander only need to provide the key instance of their proposal, that intellect and nature, much rather than spontaneity, are causally responsible for the existence of the heavens and of this world. Accordingly, Simplicius' testimony can be used only with utmost caution as evidence about Alexander's notion of nature.

3. Nature, soul and the object of desire

After this impasse in the comments on book II we need to turn to Alexander's take on book VIII and also to the final comment on book I – and as we shall see to the commentary on *De caelo*. Alexander has already remarked on in a comment on book II that Aristotle's definition of nature includes also the soul as the nature of living entities. In the

60 See **T22, T23 and T24** below.

61 ἐπεὶ δ' ἐστὶ τὸ αὐτόματον καὶ ἡ τύχη αἴτια ὧν ἂν ἢ νοῦς γένοιτο αἴτιος ἢ φύσις, ὅταν κατὰ συμβεβηκὸς αἴτιόν τι γένηται τούτων αὐτῶν, οὐδὲν δὲ κατὰ συμβεβηκός ἐστι πρότερον τῶν καθ' αὐτό, δῆλον ὅτι οὐδὲ τὸ κατὰ συμβεβηκὸς αἴτιον πρότερον τοῦ καθ' αὐτό. ὕστερον ἄρα τὸ αὐτόματον καὶ ἡ τύχη καὶ νοῦ καὶ φύσεως· ὥστ' εἰ ὅτι μάλιστα τοῦ οὐρανοῦ αἴτιον τὸ αὐτόματον, ἀνάγκη πρότερον νοῦν αἴτιον καὶ φύσιν εἶναι καὶ ἄλλων πολλῶν καὶ τοῦδε τοῦ παντός.

62 "διότι, ὥς φησιν Ἀλέξανδρος, τὰ πρῶτα αἴτια τῶν πρώτων ἐν τοῖς οὖσίν ἐστι ποιητικὰ καὶ τὰ πρῶτα τῶν ὄντων ὑπὸ τῶν πρώτων αἰτίων γέγονεν, ἅπερ ἐστὶ νοῦς καὶ φύσις. εἰ δὲ ὅλως ἐστὶν αἴτιά τινων νοῦς καὶ φύσις, τούτων ἂν εἴη οἷς μάλιστα τὸ κατὰ νοῦν ὑπάρχει, οἷος ὁ οὐρανός ἐστι καὶ τόδε τὸ πᾶν."

course of the arguments of book VIII about motion and time, that neither of them had a beginning, nor will they ever end, and about the claim that eternal motion requires an unmoved mover, Alexander contrasts the natural motion of celestial bodies to the motion of sublunary elements:

> **T17** Alexander inquires here how the circularly moved body will be still natural, if, as Aristotle says, a natural body has a principle of being affected, but the circularly moved body is impassive.[63] (Simpl. *In Phys.* 1218, 20 – 22)

After providing a first proposal Alexander formulates another one as follows:

> **T18** "Or it is better – he [Alexander] says – in the case of the divine to understand natural motion not as [it is understood] in the case of inanimate bodies, but as in the case of things that move by virtue of the soul, which are not moved by something external but have in themselves the moving principle and the cause."[64] (Simpl. *In Phys.* 1218, 27 – 30)

This, however, leads to a further difficulty:

> **T19** "But if this is [the answer] – he says -, why it does not have the principle of rest and of motion in contrary [directions]? Or – he says -, it will not move to contrary [directions] because there is no contrary motion to circular motion; and it does not rest because it does not move to such [locations] in which that which came to be must come to rest, nor does it need rest. For those things which move by themselves and are of the nature to stop, have the capacity of stopping by themselves."[65] (Simpl. *In Phys.* 1218, 30 – 37)

At this point we encounter a natural motion of an element which – unlike the natural motion of the other elements – does not rest on the capacity of being moved. Rather, it is like the motion of an entity endowed with a soul, which is actively responsible for the entity's motion. At the same time, the last lines quoted above set out a crucial difference between the motion of the celestial bodies and the motion of sublunary animals. The motion of the latter is variegated to a very large extent. These animals can move in contrary directions and can also make a stop. Not so the celestial bodies: their motion conforms fully to the simple and uniform natural tendency of the celestial body. This leads over to Simplicius' further remark, which he bolsters with a quote from Alexander's commentary on *De caelo*:

> **T20** "We endeavour to show that the nature of the divine body and its soul are not different, but [they are] as the heaviness of earth and the lightness of fire." And a little further on: "What else would be its nature besides this [i.e. besides its soul]? For the soul is more perfect nature, and it is reasonable that the nature of the more perfect body is also more perfect."[66] (Simpl. *In Phys.* 1219, 3 – 7)

Note that this signature doctrine of Alexander's resolves the problem we have faced in book II. Sublunary natures are moving causes only in a restricted sense, because their causal operation rests on the causal efficacy of some external moving cause. Causal chains in the sublunary realm invariably lead all the way up to the causal impact of the motions of the celestial bodies. These celestial bodies, on the other hand, are responsible for their own motion the way sublunary living beings are.

Nevertheless, this proposal, if formulated in these crude terms, runs into insuperable difficulties again. First of all, this will revoke Alexander's assertion about all the natures there are that they are subservient, instrumental causes. And, as the reverse side of this very problem, if the nature of celestial entities, which is identical to their soul, could bear full causal responsibility for the motion of these entities, the case for the existence of a separate unmoved mover would become moot.

Once, however, it is admitted that the celestial bodies are animate, and there is no distinction between their nature and soul, Alexander can specify a further, external mover of the motion of celestial spheres. It is the object of desire, just as for the locomotion of mortal animals:

63 Ἐπιζητεῖ δὲ ὁ Ἀλέξανδρος ἐν τούτοις, πῶς ἔτι τὸ κυκλοφορητικὸν σῶμα φυσικὸν ἔσται, εἰ τὸ μὲν φυσικόν, ὡς ὁ Ἀριστοτέλης φησίν, ἀρχὴν τοῦ πάσχειν ἔχει, τὸ δὲ κυκλοφορητικὸν ἀπαθές ἐστι.

64 "ἢ ἄμεινον, φησίν, ἐπὶ τοῦ θείου ἀκούειν μὴ ὡς ἐπὶ τῶν ἀψύχων σωμάτων τὴν κατὰ φύσιν κίνησιν, ἀλλ' ὡς ἐπὶ τῶν κατὰ ψυχὴν κινουμένων, ἃ οὐχ ὑπό τινος ἔξωθεν κινεῖται, ἀλλ' ἐν αὑτοῖς ἔχει τὴν κινητικὴν ἀρχήν τε καὶ αἰτίαν."

65 "ἀλλ' εἰ τοῦτο, φησί, πῶς οὐχὶ καὶ στάσεως ἀρχὴν ἔχει καὶ τῆς εἰς τὰ ἐναντία κινήσεως; ἢ εἰς τὰ ἐναντία μέν, φησίν, οὐ κινήσεται, ὅτι μὴ ἔστι τις ἐναντία κίνησις τῇ κυκλοφορίᾳ· οὐκ ἠρεμεῖ δέ, ὅτι μήτε ἐπὶ τοιαῦτα κινεῖται, ἐν οἷς ἀνάγκη στῆναι τὸ γενόμενον, μήτε δεῖται στάσεως· ὅσα γὰρ τῶν κινουμένων ὑφ' ἑαυτῶν καὶ ἵστασθαι πέφυκε, ταῦτα καὶ τοῦ ἵστασθαι ἐξ αὑτῶν ἔχει τὴν δύναμιν".

66 "ἡμεῖς δὲ ἐπιχειροῦμεν δεικνύναι τοῦ θείου σώματος οὐκ ἄλλην μὲν τὴν φύσιν, ἄλλην δὲ τὴν ψυχήν, ἀλλ' ὡς ἡ βαρύτης τῆς γῆς καὶ τοῦ πυρὸς ἡ κουφότης" καὶ μετ' ὀλίγα· "τίς γὰρ ἄλλη παρὰ ταύτην ἂν εἴη φύσις αὐτοῦ; τελειοτέρα γὰρ φύσις ἡ ψυχή· εὔλογον δὲ τοῦ τελειοτέρου σώματος καὶ τὴν φύσιν εἶναι τελειοτέραν."
The passage is fr. 129f in Rescigno's (2008) edition of the fragments of Alexander's commentary on the *De caelo* books II – IV. Rescigno collects in this fragment the evidence for this signature doctrine of Alexander's from the commentary. Cf. there esp. fr. 129d = Simpl. *In De caelo* 379, 18 – 381, 2.

T21 "For even if – he says –, being animate, the circularly moved body is moved by virtue of the soul in it, it still needs also something else that provides for it the principle of motion; for regarding all animate beings, there is something external to them that becomes their cause and the principle of the animate motion with respect of place, if indeed the motion of animate beings in respect of place comes to be by a desire for something.[67] (Simpl. *In Phys.* 1354, 29 – 34)

There is a crucial difference though between the two cases: the item that is the object of desire for a mortal animal, triggering its motion to some particular location can be different on different occasions. Not so for celestial entities – the object of desire for them is just as eternal as the circular motion which is triggered by it. Furthermore, this may be coordinate with an additional difference between the mode of operation of these objects of desire. At this point this is still quickly passed over. All that is said is that "there is something external to them that becomes their cause and the principle of the animate motion with respect of place." How on a particular occasion the object of desire of a mortal animal becomes the object of desire that it is, easily can have some causal history, whereas in the case of the object of desire of the celestial entity although there can be some causal connection between the desiring entity and the object of desire, grounding the desire itself, but this cannot be broached by referring to some change that the object of desire is responsible for. The desire of the celestial body is not triggered by the celestial body attaining some specific status, or position, or taking part in some change. Indeed the only change it has, its circular motion cannot possibly be responsible for the desire which causes this motion.[68]

Most importantly, much to the chagrin of Simplicius, all Alexander asserts is that this object of desire is responsible for the motion of the celestial spheres, but does not seem to allow for any further causal role in its case. In book VIII Simplicius quotes Alexander to this effect on two occasions. First as a comment on the claim "The prime mover causes eternal motion and for an infinite time" (*Physics* 267b24-26) Simplicius remarks:

T22 interpreting these words, Alexander says "Indeed the prime mover is the productive cause of the motion of the divine body, which [body] is ungenerated."[69] (Simpl. *In Phys.* 1361,31-33)

Then, a page later he returns to the issue, saying:

T23 Since Alexander as well as certain other Peripatetics seem to hold that Aristotle believes that the final cause of the heaven is a moving [cause] too, but not a productive one, as the above cited words of Alexander made clear, when he said that "the prime mover is the productive cause of the motion of the divine body, which [body] is ungenerated", ...[70] (Simpl. *In Phys.* 1362,11-16)

only to introduce his own, emphatically Neoplatonic interpretation in which the prime mover is also the productive cause of the heavens, and indeed of all there is in the natural world.

*

We can now take stock. Nature, as it is stressed by Simplicius several times, as an internal cause is an instrumental cause, always in thrall to some external cause. This is also the case for souls, which are the nature, i.e. the internal principle of motion and rest for the animals whose soul they are. But

67 "κἂν γὰρ ἔμψυχον, φησίν, ὂν τὸ κυκλοφορητικὸν σῶμα κινῆται κατὰ τὴν ἐν αὐτῷ ψυχήν, ἀλλὰ καὶ ἄλλου τινὸς δεῖται τοῦ τὴν ἀρχὴν αὐτῷ τῆς κινήσεως παρέχοντος· ἐπὶ πάντων γὰρ τῶν ἐμψύχων ἔξωθέν τι ὂν αἴτιον αὐτοῖς καὶ ἀρχὴ γίνεται τῆς κινήσεως τῆς ψυχικῆς τῆς κατὰ τόπον γινομένης, εἴ γε ἐφέσει τινὸς ἡ κατὰ τόπον γίνεται τῶν ἐμψύχων κίνησις."

68 Cf. also Alexander's comments about the accidental motion of the souls of embedded celestial spheres, communicated to them by the spheres containing them, contrasted to the accidental (self-) motion of the souls of sublunary animals, whose bodies are in different locations as a result of their motions, in which their soul also takes part, see Simpl. *In Phys.* 1260,22-35 and 1261,30-1262,4, the assertion about the additional motion of the planetary spheres further clarified at 1356,33-1357,9.

69 καὶ ὁ Ἀλέξανδρος ταῦτα τὰ ῥήματα ἐξηγούμενος "τὸ γοῦν πρῶτον κινοῦν, φησί, τῆς τοῦ θείου σώματος κινήσεως αἴτιόν ἐστι ποιητικὸν ὄντος ἀγενήτου."

70 Ἐπειδὴ δὲ καὶ ὁ Ἀλέξανδρος καὶ οἱ ἄλλοι τινὲς τῶν Περιπατητικῶν δοκοῦσι νομίζειν τὸν Ἀριστοτέλη τοῦ οὐρανοῦ τελικὸν αἴτιον καὶ κινητικόν, οὐ μέντοι ποιητικόν, ὡς καὶ ἡ πρὸ ὀλίγου παρατεθεῖσα τοῦ Ἀλεξάνδρου λέξις ἐδήλωσεν εἰπόντος ὅτι "τὸ πρώτως κινοῦν τῆς τοῦ θείου σώματος κινήσεως ποιητικόν ἐστιν ὄντος ἀγενήτου," Note that at the end of the commentary on book I Simplicius cautions those Peripatetic interpreters who deny productive efficacy to the prime mover, thinking that in this they conform to Alexander's authoritative interpretation, and quotes the following statement of Alexander: **T24** "The first form would also be cause as a productive cause. For he [Aristotle] says in the Metaphysics that this thing, namely the fifth body, moved by it [i.e. by the first form] moves the other things which are in generation and destruction. It is then productive in this way. In so far as everything attains its proper perfection by the desire for it, as he has just said [i.e. in Physics I.9], and in so far, as he also said in the Metaphysics "it moves as being loved" [Λ.7 1072b3], it would be the cause as the end and that for the sake of which; for the object of desire is such." (Simpl. *In Phys.* 268, 17 – 24: "τὸ δὲ πρῶτον εἶδος καὶ ὡς ποιητικὸν ἂν εἴη αἴτιον. λέγει γὰρ ἐν τοῖς Μετὰ τὰ φυσικά, ὅτι τοῦτο τὸ κινούμενον ὑπ' αὐτοῦ, τοῦτο δέ ἐστι τὸ πέμπτον σῶμα, τὰ ἄλλα κινεῖ τὰ ἐν γενέσει καὶ φθορᾷ. οὕτως μὲν οὖν ποιητικόν. καθόσον δὲ πάντα τῇ τούτου ἐφέσει τῆς οἰκείας τελειότητος τυγχάνει, ὡς καὶ μικρῷ πρόσθεν εἴρηται, καὶ καθόσον, ὡς αὐτὸς εἴρηκε πάλιν ἐν τοῖς Μετὰ τὰ φυσικά, 'κινεῖ δὲ ὡς ἐρώμενον', εἴη ἂν ὡς τὸ τέλος καὶ τὸ οὗ χάριν αἴτιον. τοιοῦτον γὰρ τὸ ὀρεκτόν."

then although the souls of celestial bodies too need some further external cause, this external cause nevertheless is restricted to the role of a final cause by Alexander's lights. In this capacity it is "productive" of motion, but strictly speaking is not a proper productive cause. As a consequence of this division of labor, all other natural motions of the universe can be referred back to the primordial natural motion of the heavens, and that too will have an external prop – which however is not a productive cause on a par with the productive causes of physical reality, not qualifying as a productive cause even in the way as crafts of craftsmen can serve as productive causes.

Concluding afterthought

In closing we need to consider why we should trust this account. It rests on quite a narrow evidentiary basis, crucial parts of which are provided by a source, who in this instance definitely has an axe to grind. Put crudely: we are at the mercy of Simplicius. What should be added nevertheless is that this crude assessment may be premature. Simplicius in **T23** above asserted that

> Alexander as well as certain other Peripatetics seem to hold that Aristotle believes that the final cause of the heaven is a moving [cause] too, but not a productive [one],

and he invoked Alexander's own words in **T22** to substantiate this claim. We should definitely keep in mind that we are dependent on Simplicius for this crucial bit of information. But neither should we lose sight of the fact that there is little room for maneuver for staking out a position about the causal efficacy of the Prime Mover. It has to be productive of motion, as Alexander's words quoted in **T22** assert – otherwise it could not possibly qualify as a prime mover. It has to be the cause of motion as an object of striving and thought, as *Metaphysics* Λ.7 asserts.[71] This can easily be taken as settling the causal status of this entity as that of a final cause. Both characterizations can be queried. One should indeed note, for what it's worth, that Alexander's words, quoted by Simplicius do not assert that the Prime Mover is a 'moving' (κινητικόν) cause, as Simplicius paraphrases it in **T23**, but as a 'productive cause of motion' (κινήσεως αἴτιον ... ποιητικόν).

But the only charge one can raise against Simplicius' presentation is that he did not pay attention to whatever such reservations Alexander may have had – if the words quoted in **T22** indeed could be taken as indicating any reservation at all. Moreover, it is clear what Simplicius intends to accomplish by taking Alexander's position as strictly conforming to these two available causal types. He needs Alexander – and the 'certain other Peripatetics' – as a convenient foil against which he can formulate his own position. In this he – almost like chiding the position he ascribed to Alexander – says

> one must keep in mind that what is moved by something else necessarily has its subsistence also from something else, if indeed substance is superior to motion. (Simpl. *In Phys.* 1363, 2-4)[72]

To put it otherwise: by his own lights Simplicius interpreted Alexander here in the most charitable way. We are certainly entitled to exercise caution. But this cannot go in the direction of assimilating Alexander's stance to that of Simplicius. We, on our part, should exercise that amount of interpretative charity when assessing Simplicius' presentation that he must have selected the strongest possible pieces of evidence for reporting on Alexander's position, against which he intended to situate his own exegesis of Aristotle.[73]

---

71 Cf. in this regard Alexander's assertion in **T21**, which rests on Aristotle's account of animal motion in *De anima* III.10.

72 ἐκείνῳ δὲ χρὴ προσέχειν τὸν νοῦν, ὅτι τὸ ἑτεροκίνητον καὶ τὴν ὑπόστασιν ἑτέρωθεν ἔχειν ἀνάγκη, εἴπερ κρείττων ἡ οὐσία τῆς κινήσεως.

73 This is a fundamentally revised version of the presentation I gave at the Symposium in Athens. I am grateful to the organizer and the audience for the opportunity and for feedback. I have been helped at each turn along the way of writing this paper by Orna Harari – with whom I am in continuous discussion in the context of the project of collecting, translating and interpreting the fragments of Alexander's commentary of Aristotle's *Physics*. Some of the translations of fragments from this commentary – specifically the ones from book VIII – are by her, and the others are the result of our collaboration. I am also grateful to Frans de Haas, who let me see the final version of his paper in this volume, and who raised the crucial issue that I now try to address in my Concluding afterthought.

Bibliography

Bonitz, H. (1849): *Aristotelis Metaphysica*, Part Two. Bonn: Ad. Marcus.

Caston, V. (2012): *Alexander of Aphrodisias On the Soul: Part 1: Soul as Form of the Body, Parts of the Soul, Nourishment, and Perception.* London: Bloomsbury.

Genequand, C. (2001): *Alexander of Aphrodisias on the Cosmos*. Leiden-Boston-Köln: Brill.

Genequand, C. (2017): *Alexandre d'Aphrodise: Les principes du tout selon la doctrine d'Aristote*. Paris: Vrin.

Lennox, J.G. (2001): "Teleology, Chance, and Aristotle's Theory of Spontaneous Generation". In: Lennox, J.G.: *Aristotle's Philosophy of Biology.* Cambridge: Cambridge University Press, pp. 229-249. (Originally published in the *Journal of the History of Philosophy* 20 [1982], pp. 219-238.)

Rescigno, A. (2008): *Alessandro di Afrodisia: Commentario al De Caelo di Aristotele: Frammenti del secondo, terzo e quarto libro*. Amsterdam: Hakkert.

Ross, W. D. (1953): *Aristotle's Metaphysics*, 2 vols. Oxford: Clarendon (lithographical reprint with corrections of the 1st ed. of 1924).

Sedley, D. (2000): "Metaphysics Λ 10". In: Frede, M. – Charles, D. (eds.): *Aristotle's Metaphysics Lambda: Symposium Aristotelicum*. Oxford: Clarendon Press, pp. 327-50.

Sharples, R. W. (1992): *Alexander of Aphrodisias: Quaestiones 1.1-2.15*. London: Duckworth.

Nature and Soul as Principles of Motion and Change:

Simplicius, Alexander of Aphrodisias, and Philoponus on Aristotle's *Physics* II. 1-3[1]

Melina G. Mouzala

Department of Philosophy
University of Patras

Abstract

Given that the soul too is a principle of movement and change in ensouled bodies according to Plato and Aristotle, both Simplicius and Philoponus, in their comments on Aristotle's *Physics* II. 1-3, raise the question about the distinction between nature and soul considered as principles. In their attempt to find an answer to this question they set out to explain what kind of principle or source of change nature is in Aristotle's natural philosophy, by comparing it with the soul. Endeavouring to explain from his perspective the relation of nature to soul, Simplicius is implicitly involved in dialectic with the theses of Alexander of Aphrodisias and the Stoics on certain aspects of this issue. He further uses the analogy between the ship and the helmsman to expose his theory about the soul as a separate actualization and dispute Alexander's conception of it as an inseparable actualization. When explaining nature, both Philoponus and Simplicius place special emphasis on the notion of ζωή, which they use as an intermediate between nature and soul. In his exegesis of the Aristotelian definition of nature, Philoponus uses a language that depicts nature as a dynamic and active inner source or principle of motion that orders and thoroughly directs the behaviour of each natural thing. He additionally claims that the definition of nature offered by Aristotle will also embrace the nature of the ensouled bodies which is called by him ζωή and is their soul. Simplicius, on the other hand, argues that nature differs from soul in that it is a sort of *propensity for being moved* which resides in the substrate, therefore it is not a principle in the strict sense, whereas soul is a principle because it is set apart from what is moved by it. According to Simplicius, nature represents a kind of ζωή that is associated with the Aristotelian εἶδος. It is the *lowest level of life* and the *life of the form* which is related to the form in all the ways that are determined by the frame of the Aristotelian theory of causality.

---

1 Earlier versions of this paper were presented at the 18th annual Conference of the International Society for Neoplatonic Studies, June 10-12, 2021; at the Conference "Aristotle Across Boundaries", June 8-9, 2023, Verbania, Italy; at the 20th annual Conference of the International Society for Neoplatonic Studies, June 14-17, 2023, Catania, Italy; and at the International Symposium "Nature and Human Nature in Ancient Greek Philosophy and its Reception", October 3, 2023, Netherlands Institute at Athens, Athens. I would like to express my heartfelt thanks to the participants and attendants of these conferences for their helpful comments.

in: Mouzala, M.G. (ed.) 2025: *Nature and Human Nature in Ancient Greek Philosophy and Its Reception.* Leiden: Sidestone Press, pp. 91-120.

Preliminaries

Nature is defined by Aristotle in *Physics* II. 1, 192b20-23 as a sort of source and cause of motion/change and its cessation (ἀρχῆς τινὸς καὶ αἰτίας τοῦ κινεῖσθαι καὶ ἠρεμεῖν) in that to which it belongs primarily and of itself, *per se*, and not *per accidens* (transl. Charlton, modified). According to a line of interpretation proposed by Solmsen, when Aristotle defines nature and designates natural things as having the principle of movement in themselves, nature seems to take over the function which Plato assigned to soul. He believes that the Platonic world soul is the more obvious antecedent of Aristotle's nature.[2] On the other hand, it has been claimed that Plato had replaced the Ionian notion of φύσις, especially as a principle of motion, with the notion of ψυχή as it was conceived of in the metaphysical theories of Greek philosophers who flourished in Italy (the Ἰταλικοί).[3] So, according to this viewpoint, it seems that Aristotle set out to reconstruct the thread that binds the philosophical thought of his time with the pre-Platonic philosophical doctrines within the tradition inherited from his predecessors. However, the clear-cut distinction of the functions and tasks of nature and soul in Aristotle remains an issue, since there is a major ontological field, that of the theory of principles of motion and change, in which nature and soul somewhat overlap. This obscurity led the ancient commentators on Aristotle's *Physics* to focus on the problem, positing the crucial question of how nature differs from the soul.

Given that the soul too is a principle of movement and change in ensouled bodies, according to both Plato and Aristotle himself, Simplicius raises the question as to what the distinction is between nature and soul considered as principles.[4] Simplicius poses this question twice in his comments on Aristotle's *Physics* II; the first in his comments regarding *Physics* II. 1, 192b8, and the second in those regarding *Physics* II. 2, 193b 22. Simplicius' treatment of the question is rather more noteworthy in the latter case. In his comments on *Physics* II. 2, he offers a bold reading of the theory of nature, as expressed by Aristotle in *Physics* II.1, and presents a radically new understanding of the difference between nature and soul. In his reception of Aristotle's theory, he elaborates and develops what is stated by Aristotle up to this point of his treatise, enriching his theory with highlights from the tradition.

I. Simplicius on Nature and Soul in his Commentary on *Physics* II.1: the Hierarchy of Lives

I will initially examine his first approach to this problem, as set out in his comments on *Physics* II. 1. Simplicius poses the following crucial question: "In what sense does Aristotle mean that animals and plants exist by and because of nature (φύσει καὶ διὰ φύσιν), since they are ensouled and are what they are because of soul?".[5] He implies the very first sentence of *Physics* II.1, namely 192b 8-12, where Aristotle explains that those things which exist by nature are the animals and plants and their parts, and the simple bodies, i.e. the four elements. Simplicius raises the objection that, in fact, when we define an animal, we say that it is a being with soul and sensation (οὐσίαν ἔμψυχον αἰσθητικήν), and the plant has been given its psychic character by the vegetative soul (ὑπὸ τῆς φυσικῆς ἐψύχωται ψυχῆς), which causes it to take nourishment, to grow, and reproduce its like (ὅμοια). Therefore, he stresses that it is surprising that Aristotle himself, a little further on, in his *Physics* (192b 13-15), says that things which change by increase and decay or diminution suffer this change, in so far as they are natural things, while in his *De anima* 415b 23-416a 15, he says that it is appropriate for the vegetative soul to nourish and to give increase and diminution. And even further on, in his *Physics* 193a 11-13 and 193b 9-11, Aristotle says that when pieces of wood are planted in the earth, they put forth shoots because of their own nature, although the shoots and the whole process of their production belong to them because of the soul.[6] The definition of the soul, given in the *De anima*, which calls it "the first actuality of a natural body with organs, potentially possessing life",[7]

2 Solmsen (1960), pp. 95-102.

3 Lebedev (2019), p. 666; (2022); pp. 691-692. Aristotle, *Metaphysics* 987a10; 987a29-31; 988a23-27. According to Lebedev, the Ionian *physis* is a self-moving and self-evolving substance which in Plato is replaced by the soul. Within the same line of interpretation, in the Aristotelian doxography the Aristotelian matter (*hylē*) is a misleading equivalent of the Ionian *physis*, since the latter does not need an external causa movens. The concept of passive matter allows for the introduction of the creationist notion of a *dēmiourgos*-craftsman who imposes order upon matter through his organised and purposeful creative activity. Lebedev notes that this idea was invented by the Western Greek metaphysics "as a polemical counterpart of the self-moving and self-evolving Ionian *physis*" (2022, p. 691). Aristotle's theory of nature as well as his theory of first principle must be differentiated from both Plato and the pre-Platonic *physiologoi*, for two reasons: a) in contradistinction to the Platonic theory of the *Timaeus*, the creationist approach is absent from the Aristotelian theory of first principle or first unmoved mover b) a distinctive feature of the Aristotelian *physis*, which distinguishes it from the Ionian *physis*, is its teleological character, especially when associated with form and not matter. This character in the *Timaeus* is attributed to the *dēmiourgos*' activity.

4 Simpl. *In Phys.* 286. 20-22. All references to Simplicius' Commentary on Aristotle's *Physics* II are to the page and line of the Berlin Academy Edition (*CAG* IX) and follow the translation of Fleet (1997).

5 Simpl. *In Phys.* 262. 13-14.

6 Simpl. *In Phys.* 262. 14-22.

7 Aristotle, *De anima* 412a 27-412b 1; cf. 412b4-6; 412b15-17. For the definition of soul in *De anima*, see Owens (1971); Bolton (1978); Charlton (1980); Menn (2002); Johansen (2014).

fits both plants and animals, but not the simple bodies such as earth and fire etc., since these do not have organs. So, according to Simplicius the following question arises:

> "Why, then, at this point, when he wants to discover the difference between things that do
>
> and things that do not exist by nature—since it is in the distinction that nature
>
> is to be found—does he include animals and plants, namely the very things that are
>
> characterised by soul, among things that exist by nature?".[8]

Simplicius' answer to this question entails an interpretation that combines the Aristotelian conception of nature with the Aristotelian theory of soul and is based on the notion of ζωή (*zōē*). In Simplicius' interpretation ζωή is a middle term or a transitive term between these notions, at least with regard to all natural organic bodies, with the exception of the simple bodies and their compounds, and general inanimate bodies. As we will see a few lines below, it is Aristotle who first associates ζωή (*zōē*) with both nature and soul in different contexts of his theory, specifically with nature in his *Physics* and with soul in his *De anima*. This apparently enables Simplicius to approach not only the soul but also nature and their relationship through that proper and common conceptual field, namely ζωή.

Simplicius' own conception of the essence of nature plays a vital role in his solution to the problem of the distinction between nature and soul, both considered as principles of motion. According to his theory exposed in his commentary on Aristotle's *Physics* II. 2, nature is the lowest level of life (ἐσχάτη ζωή). This kind of life, which is equal to the lowest potentiality, is the growth of the enmattered form from matter and the movement towards that form viewed according to the potentiality of the form. Both these natural processes, ἔκφυσις (growth) of the enmattered form from matter and κίνησις (movement) towards it according to its potentiality, are considered to be the lowest potentiality and the lowest life, which are tantamount to nature.[9] In contradistinction to this lowest kind or level of life, the primary potentiality and the primary life which subsists according to the first movement of Being, is the "bubbling over, as it were, from primary Being into the separating out of the Hypostasis of Form and *the movement outwards from Being to Actuality* (ἡ ἀπὸ τοῦ εἶναι εἰς τὸ ἐνεργεῖν ἔκστασις)" (Simpl. *In Phys.* 289. 26-29).

I shall analyse this theory in my treatment of Simplicius' solution to the problem of the distinction between nature and soul as it appears in his commentary on *Physics* II.2. I refer to it now only to show that ζωή is not a notion exclusively associated with the soul, but he also uses it to explain what the essence of nature is. This is not an original approach; it is based on Aristotle himself, who in *Phys.* 250b 11-15 states that motion is "like a sort of life as it were to all naturally constituted things" (transl. Chase, 2012). In his commentary on *Physics* VIII, when he explains the meaning of Aristotle's statement, Simplicius once again defines nature as the last of lives (ἐσχάτη τῶν ζωῶν ἡ φύσις). The commentator notes that when Aristotle uses the words "a sort of life as it were to all naturally constituted things", he expresses himself with exactness and in a manner consonant with Plato, who in his *Laws* 895c clarifies that ζῆν is attributed to those things that move from within and by themselves. It is thus a general assumption that when a thing moves itself, we speak of it as alive. Furthermore, Simplicius associates this assumption with all physical things; since the latter have nature as the principle of motion within them, they too could rightly be said to be alive (ζῆν), in accordance with their inner aptitude for motion.[10] We may note that in his exegesis motion appears as the middle term and a transitive notion between life (ζωή) and nature (φύσις) or life (ζωή) and natural things (φυσικά).

In the next stage of his syllogistic, Simplicius infers what kind of life nature is from the relation between nature and natural things and introduces his own conception of nature as the lowest level of life. Since nature has its being in a physical body as its substrate, it is, as it were, more 'alive' (ζῶν) than it is a 'life' (ζωή) in the proper sense of the term. In his view, nature is not a *life* in the proper sense of the term, but it is *alive* to the degree that it has its being in a physical body that is alive, with this body being its substrate. Since nature resides in a physical body as its substrate and has its being in it, the relation of nature to life depends on this physical body which is only alive and not life. Nature is more "alive" than "life", similarly to its substrate.[11] Simplicius clarifies that Plato's *Laws* 895c refers to the life that is

8 Simpl. *In Phys.* 262. 22-28.

9 Simpl. *In Phys.* 289. 29-31; cf. 287. 17-21.

10 Simpl. *In Phys.* 1119. 3-8; 11-16. I follow the translation of Chase (2012). Cf. Simpl. *In De caelo* 677.12-13.

11 Cf. Proclus, who in his *Elements of Theology*, prop. 188, recognises an ontological scale within the philosophical context of life (ζωή). The pure principle is the first und unparticipated Life (πρώτη καὶ ἀμέθεκτος ζωή), while that which is consequent upon it, is not only a principle of life but also a living thing. Soul is not the first and unparticipated Life. Therefore, soul is at once a principle of life and a living thing («ἅμα ἄρα ζωή ἐστι καὶ ζῶν ἡ ψυχή») (transl. Dodds).

self-moved in the proper sense, and the properly said self-moved life is only the psychic life. For this reason, he praises Aristotle for saying that physical motion, and consequently nature, is a sort of life (οἷον ζωήν) and not simply life (ἁπλῶς ζωήν). Simplicius draws an analogy which shows that life in the proper sense (κυρίως ζωή) differs from physical motion, which is only a sort of life (οἷον ζωήν τις), in the way that soul differs from nature. Life in the proper sense has the same ratio (λόγον) to physical motion as the soul has to nature.[12] The analogy may be illustrated as follows:

ψυχή: φύσις::κυρίως ζωή: φυσική κίνησις

or

ψυχή: φύσις::κυρίως ζωή/ἁπλῶς ζωή: οἷον ζωή

The equation "φυσική ἔνδοθεν κίνησις (internal physical motion)= οἷον ζωή τις (a sort of life, as it were)" is later implicitly transformed by Simplicius to the equation "φύσις (nature)= οἷον ζωή τις (a sort of life, as it were)". He finally specifies the sort of life nature is with the equation: φύσις (nature)=ἐσχάτη τῶν ζωῶν (the last of lives) (Simpl. *In Phys.* 1119.8). In Simplicius' view the crucial difference between nature and soul is that nature, as it is said in *Phys.* 192b 34, always resides in a substrate (ἐν ὑποκειμένῳ ἐστὶν ἡ φύσις ἀεί) as moving cause, whereas soul is set apart from what is moved because it properly has the power of moving.[13]

Life is also generally acknowledged as an essential characteristic of the soul, not only by Aristotle and his teacher Plato, but also by most of the representatives of pre-Platonic thought.[14] Simplicius in his comments on *Physics* II. 2 (*In Phys.* 285. 34-286. 6) stresses that both Aristotle himself and Plato followed the same method in their effort to find out the soul, i.e., they discovered what the soul is from the difference between what is ensouled and what is soul-less. He mentions two Platonic passages. Plato in the *Phaedrus* states: "All body which is moved from outside itself is soul-less, while what is moved from within itself is ensouled, this being the nature of soul" (245e4-6). Also, in *Laws* 895c it is said that that which is moved from within itself we say to be alive (ζῆν). Aristotle in his explanation of his own definition of soul involves the definitions of both nature and life (ζωή, ζῆν). After the definition of soul in *DA* 412a27-28, Aristotle recalls the definition of nature in his effort to explain what a natural body is and, further, he introduces the notion of life in order to explain what a natural body possessing life is.[15] Since the ensouled are distinguished from the soul-less bodies by living, the role of life in our understanding of what soul is becomes crucial and the definition of soul is bound with the explanation of what life is. Moreover, life belongs to those things that are more knowable than soul to us, because when we gaze upon nature, we see different aspects of life all around us; so, obviously, to start our investigation of soul from the notion of life means to employ the method which Aristotle proposes in *De anima* 413a 11-13. He uses the notion of life to determine what the ensouled body is and defines ζῆν (life) as that which distinguishes the animate from the inanimate: "We take, then, as our starting point for discussion that it is life which distinguishes the animate from the inanimate".[16] Furthermore, it is said there that since the term *life* is used in various senses, if it is present in but a single one of these senses, namely intellect (νοῦς), sensation (αἴσθησις), locomotion (motion from place to place) and rest (κίνησις καὶ στάσις ἡ κατὰ τόπον), the motion concerned with nutrition (κίνησις ἡ κατὰ τροφήν) and decay and growth (φθίσις τε καὶ αὔξησις), then we speak of a thing as living. Hence all plants are supposed to have life, since they have within themselves a faculty and principle, whereby they grow and decay in opposite directions.[17] And this form of life can be separated from the others, though in mortal creatures the others cannot be separated from it. This becomes evident in the case of plants, for they have no other faculty of soul at all.[18] According to Philoponus, life is likely to be characteristic of soul, and having characterised the soul by life, Aristotle divides the latter into different senses since a thing may be said to be alive

12 Simpl. *In Phys.* 1119. 8-11; 16-20.

13 Simpl. *In Phys.* 286.36-287. 4.

14 Sisko (2019), pp. 3-4; cf. McKirahan (2010), p. 30.

15 Miller (1999, p. 311) remarks that when Aristotle tries, after the definition of soul, to explain what a natural body is, in *De anima* 412b 10-17, he clearly recalls the account of nature in *Physics* II.1, which distinguishes between things that exist by nature and things that exist by other causes. He then divides natural bodies into living and non-living. Themistius (*In De anima*, 41.40-42.2) clearly explains this divisional process: "...since in the case of bodies some are natural, others not, and some natural bodies have life, while others do not, the soul is neither the entelechy of body in general, only of natural body, nor of natural body in general, only of that which is also alive" (transl. Todd, 2013). Polansky (2007, p. 173) notes that there are early stages of the definition of the soul in *De anima* 412a11-16, in which we can recognise a progression from substance to bodies to natural bodies to living natural bodies; soul enters only when the stage of natural bodies having life is reached, but further investigation of soul requires that this stage be explained in all its parameters. Owens (1971, p. 127) notes that since the distinction between two kinds of bodies, living and non-living, is central, "life" seems to be regarded as the distinguishing attribute that must be explained, and it must be explained by soul.

16 Aristotle, *De anima* 413a 20-22; I partly follow the translation of Hicks (1907) and partly that of Smith (1931).

17 Aristotle, *De anima* 413a 22-28.

18 Aristotle, *De anima* 413a 26-413b1.

in many ways. Each of the powers of soul is a life and makes things that share in it live.[19] On the other hand, it is sensation primarily which constitutes the animal; for, provided that they have sensation, even those things which are devoid of movement and do not change their place are called *animals* and are not merely said to be alive.[20]

Aristotle defines life (ζωή) in *DA* 412a14-15 as the power of self-nourishment and of independent growth and decay, and soul is the first actuality of a natural body with organs, potentially possessing life (*DA* 412a27-28). Thus, Simplicius traces an apparent inconsistency between *Physics* and *On Soul*. It is surprising, according to him, that Aristotle himself in *Phys.* 192b 13-15 says that things which change by increase and decay or diminution suffer this change, in so far as they are natural things, while in his *De anima* 415b23-416a9 he asserts that the plant has been given its psychic character by the vegetative soul (ὑπὸ τῆς φυσικῆς ἐψύχωται ψυχῆς), which causes it to take nourishment, to grow, and reproduce its like (ὅμοια). Simplicius attempts a solution to the problem of determining the principle of motion in things that are considered both natural and ensouled, by establishing a hierarchy of lives among animate or ensouled and inanimate things. Natural things are all finally reduced to a compound of form and matter and this reductionist approach indicates that all things which are ultimately analysed in a compound of matter and form, are by nature (φύσει) and have a nature (φύσιν).

Fleet translates as if the term *life* (ζωή) in Simplicius 262.31-263.4 equates with soul.[21] This is probable if we take into account the definition of soul in the *De anima*, which Simplicius refers to a few lines earlier in his comments.[22] However, in my view, it is equally likely that the term *life* (ζωή) Simplicius uses in this passage of his comments on *Physics* II.1 means the complex which consists of nature and the specific faculties or parts of soul by which each ensouled body is endowed according to its kind. In other words, *life* (ζωή), concerning all the kinds of animate things referred to here, equates with soul plus nature (life=soul+nature). According to a line of interpretation, the idea that soul (*psychē*) is the equation "*physis* + f", in the sense that soul performs the same functions as nature, such as nutrition, growth, as well as some additional, such as impulse, perception, etc., can be traced back to the Stoic Hierocles.[23] However, in my reading, Simplicius here seems to conceive of a new complex, *life* (ζωή), which is constituted by those kinds of soul that each animate body possesses, plus nature. He first forms the hypothesis that only the simple bodies are natural, then he assumes that even if animals and plants have soul as well-the former a desiderative one (ὀρεκτικήν), the latter a vegetative one (φυτικήν)-they also have the nature that was the subject of the enquiry, the nature which also the simple bodies have.[24] He sets out to explain this situation by recognising a climax or a scale of lives among the bodies or natural things that are ensouled. According to his interpretation, the more perfect bodies, which have more perfect life, have as well the less perfect life. For example, man has a rational, a desiderative and a vegetative soul and the nature which is the object of enquiry. The irrational animal has all the other parts or faculties of soul except the rational; the plant has the vegetative soul and nature; and the simple bodies and their compounds, in so far as they are just compound bodies such as stones, wood, bones and in general inanimate bodies, have only nature, whatever that nature is. This last conclusion is necessary, according to Simplicius' exegesis, since the soul supervenes

19 Philoponus, *In De anima*, 233. 26-234.2; 234.22-26 (transl. Charlton, 2005). Thus, the soul is determined by the capacities of nutrition (θρεπτικῷ), sensation (αἰσθητικῷ), thought (διανοητικῷ), and motion (κινήσει), according to what is stated in *DA* 413b12-13. In *DA* 414a 31-32, Aristotle enriches this schema since this time he mentions five faculties or powers (δυνάμεις) of the soul instead of four, the nutritive (θρεπτικόν), the sensitive (αἰσθητικόν), the appetitive (ὀρεκτικόν), the locomotive (κινητικὸν κατὰ τόπον) and the intellective (διανοητικόν). In *DA* 416a19 Aristotle adds one more faculty, which he calls 'generative' (γεννητική). However, he identifies the nutritive with the generative faculty of the soul because he says that nutrition and generation (or reproduction) are due to one and the same psychic power (cf. *DA* 432b10-11). Furthermore, in 432a 15-17 he states that the soul in animals is defined by virtue of two faculties, that of discrimination (τῷ κριτικῷ), which is the task of thought and perception, and the faculty of originating local movement (τῷ κινεῖν τὴν κατὰ τόπον κίνησιν). Some lines further, in 432a 22-b7, Aristotle begs the question, in what sense we are to speak of parts of the soul and how many we should distinguish, because in a sense there is an infinity of parts. In this passage, he says that some thinkers distinguish three parts of the soul, the reasoning (λογιστικόν), the passionate (θυμικόν) and the desiderative (ἐπιθυμητικόν), while others distinguish only two, the rational (λόγον ἔχον) and the irrational (ἄλογον). In the same passage he points out that if we follow the divisions put forward by these thinkers, we shall find parts far more distinctly separated from one another than these, namely those previously mentioned; the nutritive (θρεπτικόν), the sensitive (αἰσθητικόν), the imaginative (φανταστικόν), and the appetitive (ὀρεκτικόν). Within this enumeration of parts or faculties of soul we can see that Aristotle has added the imaginative part. For the kind of soul which is representative of humans, animals and plants and for the hierarchy among the parts or faculties of the soul, see Fleet 1997: 165, n. 29. Fleet also refers to *EN* 1102b28, where we can find the vegetative and impulsive faculties.

20 Aristotle, *De anima* 413b2-4.

21 See esp. Fleet's translation of Simpl *In Phys.* 262.33-263.2.

22 See again Simpl. *In Phys.* 262. 22-24.

23 Nawar (2020), pp. 149-150, commenting on Hierocles 1. 5-28 (LS 53B).

24 Simpl. *In Phys.* 262. 28-31.

(ἐπιγίνεται)[25] on a natural body as "the first actuality of a natural body with organs, potentially possessing life", as Aristotle himself defined it in *De anima*.[26]

Simplicius gives his final answer to why Aristotle includes animals and plants, namely the very things that are characterised by soul, among things that exist by nature, after investigating the criterion for calling a thing 'natural'. According to his explanation, if nature belongs to the simple bodies, not in so far as they have organs but because they are compounds of form and matter, and if these bodies are inherent in plants and animals-for they too are made up of the four elements-it is clear that the bodies of animals and plants are in all respects natural prior to their being those of animals and plants. So, the criterion for characterising a body as natural is that when it is analysed in its ultimate constituents, it is found to be a compound of form and matter. The bodies of animals and plants are primordially natural bodies and Simplicius believes that this may be the reason why Aristotle added the phrase "and their parts" in *Physics* 192b9. For instance, bone and wood, which can be considered as parts of animals and plants respectively, can no longer be said to have desire or a vegetative soul, but they do have a nature.[27] From what Simplicius also says, we can infer that Aristotle's main aim in *Physics* II. 1, was to point out the difference between natural things and the things produced by art, so he included in his theory animals and plants in that they are natural. Regarding the reason Aristotle says here that things which change by increase and decay or diminution, suffer this change in so far as they are natural things, although they are also subjected to increase and decay as ensouled things, Simplicius' answer is as follows. Aristotle stated that increase belongs to natural bodies, either because he had not yet determined to what things increase is proper, or because it was agreed by some to belong to certain things which are strictly speaking natural, such as fire. The wavering between two answers regarding the question whether increase is proper to natural or to ensouled things may originate from pre-Platonic thought, especially Heraclitus. Based on DK 115, Kahn speaks of a self-augmenting power of the *psychē*, associated with *logos* in Heraclitus; while based on DK 31A, 31 B, and 36 he believes that for Heraclitus everything is a form of life, and there can be no fundamental discontinuity between the realm of *psychē* and the realm of elemental transformation, all the more since in the last fragment *psychē* is integrated within a series of physical transformations.[28]

Simplicius also adds a testimony about Eudemus' exegesis of the question as to why Aristotle included animals and plants among natural things.[29] The latter states that Aristotle did so, not in so much as they are animals and plants, but because they are natural in themselves. In an extended passage of Eudemus quoted by Simplicius, we can see that Eudemus seeks to show, following Aristotle, what is common to all things considered as natural. Since we say that many things exist by nature (for instance, a horse, a man and every animal and their parts, olive and every form of plant life and their parts, grass and in general all things that grow, earth and fire and many lifeless things), the crucial question is what is it that belongs to all of them? It cannot be sensation (αἴσθησις), because this and various other features are particular to animals. It also cannot be increase (αὔξησις), because this is particular to living things (τῶν ζωτικῶν). What actually is common to all these things is that they can move (wood, bronze, fire and in general all bodies), although they do not move in the same way in all their movements. So, the common characteristic in all these things that exist according to nature is an inherent source of movement; thus, nature becomes the internal source of self-imparted movement.

II. Simplicius on Nature and Soul in his Commentary on *Physics* II.2

II.1. Simplicius in dialectic with the Stoics and Alexander of Aphrodisias

In his comments on Aristotle's *Physics* II. 2, and more specifically on the very first passage of this chapter (193b 22), Simplicius stresses that "even the lowest part of the soul, called the vegetative (φυτική), is something other than nature even according to Aristotle-even if they often call the vegetative part of the soul nature on the grounds that it is close to nature".[30] Furthermore, he states that for Aristotle all soul, even the lowest kind, is said to be "actuality of the natural body possessing organs". Therefore, the vegetative part of the soul belongs to the body which has a nature and it is something that clearly differs from its nature.[31] In my view, based on relevant research on the relationship or distinction between soul and nature as illustrated in the context of the philosophical

25 Fleet (1997: 165, n. 31) points out that the verb *epigignesthai* indicates "the distinction between Aristotle, for whom soul is an immanent entity, and Plato, for whom it is transcendent". Pseudo-Alexander uses the same verb in his commentary on Aristotle's *Metaphysics* 1033a24, to denote that *eidos* comes into existence without being generated; it supervenes (ἐπιγίγνεται) timelessly on matter, which is subjected to alteration and generation by its own nature; see Pseudo-Alexander in *Metaphysics* 495. 20-23. According to *De anima* 412b 10-17, it seems that there is an analogy between matter and body, eidos and soul, so we may infer that *epigignesthai* is also here opposed to *gignesthai*, namely it makes *gignesthai* of soul impossible.

26 Aristotle, *DA* 412 a 27 and 412b5-6. See Simpl. *In Phys.* 262. 31-263. 6.

27 Simpl. *In Phys.* 263.6-13.

28 Simpl. 263. 13-17. See Kahn (1979), pp. 237-238.

29 Simpl. *In Phys.* 263. 18-264. 3.

30 Simpl. *In Phys.* 286. 22-25.

31 Simpl. *In Phys.* 286. 25-27.

tradition that precedes Simplicius' commentaries on Aristotle, with this remark the commentator begins an implicit debate, on the one hand with the Stoics, and on the other with Alexander of Aphrodisias. The Stoics considered that plants do not have a soul but only nature, while Alexander of Aphrodisias maintained that nature and soul identify in the celestial bodies. In following I will demonstrate the main points of Simplicius' polemic against their theses and the innovation in his own approach to the distinction between soul and nature in Aristotle's philosophy of nature.

Sorabji notes that Aristotle's thesis is that animals have an inner nature, but when he talks of the inner nature of a living thing, he often means its soul.[32] This is what we can infer from the fact that when the question 'by what an animal is moved' arises, Aristotle's answer in his *Physics* is that evidently it is moved by its soul.[33] For Aristotle the rational soul distinguishes man, the locomotive and the sensitive (the latter is also desiderative) the animals and the vegetative the plants.[34] When Simplicius states "even if they often call the vegetative part of the soul nature on the grounds that it is close to nature", he is alluding to the Stoics, who distinguished between "nature" and "soul" and rejected the Aristotelian view that even plants have a soul.[35] Before Aristotle, certain pre-Platonic philosophers and Plato had attributed a soul to plants.[36] As Sorabji notes, Aristotle retains the idea that plants have souls, by extending the concept of soul and including in its activities the non-conscious processes of nutrition and growth; however, he rejects the Platonic idea that they have sensations and desires and presents sensation as the distinctive characteristic of animals.[37] On the other hand, the Stoics considered that plants have only *physis* and not *psychē*, therefore they did not recognise that all living things possess a soul, nor did they associate the soul with all vital functions.[38] According to some Stoic sources, "*pneuma* allegedly manifests itself as 'cohesion' in lifeless things, as 'nature' in plants, as 'soul' in animals and as 'rational soul' in human beings" (Reydams-Schils and Ferrari, 2014, p. 46). As Reydams-Schils and Ferrari note, from one perspective, cohesion, nature, soul and rational soul are all manifestations of *nature* in its most general Stoic sense. But from another, *nature* is a specific Stoic usage for plants.[39] Regarding the difference between nature and soul, in the Stoics we can distinguish between a physical *pneuma*, which is present in plants and embryos and is responsible for nutrition and growth, and a psychic *pneuma*, which is present in animals and men, namely generally in living beings, and is responsible for sensation and movement.[40] Nawar notes that "the difference between the *pneuma* responsible for endowing a plant with its functions (i.e. *phusis*) and the *pneuma* responsible for endowing an animal with its functions (i.e. *psuchē*) seems to be one of degree (of complexity of motion and of tension of the relevant *pneuma*)..." (2020, p. 149).[41]

Sorabji emphasises that the Stoics disagreed with the thesis that there is one kind or part of soul which can be described and conceived of as nature or equated with nature, focusing on the case of plants. He notes that long before Descartes, the Stoics rejected Aristotle's theory about the existence of a non-conscious soul in plants with merely nutritive functions.[42] From two fragments, of Galen and of Clement, we learn that the Stoics did not call the dominant principle within plants "soul" but "nature", and they considered plants to be soulless (ἄψυχα), but participants of nature.[43] Thus, they substituted nature for soul as the property of plants and contrasted soul to nature.

32 Aristotle, *PA* 1.1, 641a28; b9-10; *GA* 2.4, 740b29-741a2. Cf. Sorabji (1988), p. 222 and n. 17.

33 Aristotle, *Phys.* 254b27-33; 258a1-b9; 265b 32-266a 1. Cf. Sorabji (1988), p. 222 and n. 18.

34 Aristotle, *DA* 414a32-b5; 414b32-415a12. Fleet (1997), p. 165, n. 29.

35 Fleet (1997), p. 170, n. 111; cf. Reydams-Schils, G. and Ferrari, F. (2014), p. 46. See also Eunyoung Ju (2007), pp. 97ff.

36 Many early thinkers before Aristotle assumed that not only humans and animals but even plants have soul; for example, Empedocles (DK31B117) and Pythagoras (DK44B89). Iamblichus *VP* 99; Porphyrius *VP* 39; Diogenes Laertius, *Vitae Philosophorum* 8.23. See Huffman (2019), pp. 38-39, n. 50; Sisko (2019), p. 4. Some of the Pre-Socratics recognised that the plants possess powers one would expect to be attributed only to humans and animals. The author of *On Plants* (Pseudo-Aristotle; DK59A117) reports that some early thinkers, like Anaxagoras, Empedocles and Democritus, acknowledged that plants are moved by desire, they perceive, and feel pain and pleasure; in addition, they considered that plants also possess mind and knowledge; see DK59A117; Sisko (2019), p. 4; cf. Sorabji (1974, p. 66, n. 11). See also Plato, *Timaeus* 77A-B.

37 Sorabji (1974), pp. 65-66. Aristotle, *DA* 411b 27-30.

38 Nawar (2020, p. 149) notes that *psychē* was required for some higher functions, such as impulse, sensation and others, which we would more naturally nowadays characterise as standard psychic functions.

39 Reydams-Schils and Ferrari (2014), p. 46. So, we must consider that the Stoic usage of the term or the label "nature" may be either general or too specific.

40 Veillard (2020), pp. 147-148, and n. 7, 8. See Hierocles 1.5-33; 4.38-53 (=LS 53B). See also Galen, *Adversus ea quae a Juliano in Hippocratis aphorismos enuntiata sunt*, vol. 18A, p. 266. 9-13 (Kühn); in the latter passage Galen states that every plant is ruled by nature, whereas every animal is ruled by both nature and soul. Veillard (2020. P. 147) notes: "The Stoic conception of soul draws from their cosmology. A soul is a hot breath (*pneuma enthermon*) by which we become animate and able to move. This special kind of breath called soul is produced by the sudden cooling (*psuxis*) of a dense kind of pneuma called nature (*phusis*)".

41 According to his analysis of Hierocles 1.5-28 (= LS 53B), it seems that *psychē* performs the same functions as *physis* (e.g. nutrition, growth) as well as some additional ones (e.g. impulse, perception); see Nawar (2020), p. 150. See also *SVF* 2. 715; 716.

42 Descartes, 'Reply to objections brought against the *Second Meditation*', §4, in the fifth objection, translated by Haldane and Ross, vol. 2, p. 210. Cf. Sorabji (1997), p. 2.

43 Galen, *PHP* 6.3.7 (*SVF* 2.710); Clement, *Stromateis* 2.20 (*SVF* 2.714).

Sorabji claims that this Stoic elimination and replacement of the term *soul* from the plants may help to explain why Simplicius and Philoponus can take nature and soul to be distinct agencies in living things. He adds that despite this distinction, the two commentators believe that living things can be acted on by both soul and nature, but they also believe that this calls for an explanation[44]. Fleet also points out that Aristotle might have been prepared to say that souls were one kind of nature, but after him the Stoics contrasted nature with soul and ascribed to plants a *nature* which they did not identify with soul, thus rejecting Aristotle's ascription of soul to plants and substituting nature as something different. Fleet also believes that this is somehow associated with Simplicius and Philoponus' treatment of soul and nature, as if they must be considered as distinct causes, albeit both working towards the same end in living things.[45]

Sorabji, in his Introduction to Fleet's translation of Simplicius, states that "Aristotle might arguably have been willing to treat the souls of living things as one kind of nature", adding that Alexander, as we can infer from what Simplicius testifies about his view in his Commentary on Aristotle's *De caelo,* "takes this to have been Aristotle's view, at least for the case of the supposedly living heavens" (Sorabji 1997, p. 2). In fact, in the fragment from his lost Commentary quoted by Simplicius, Alexander appears to equate the nature and power (δύναμιν) of the divine celestial body with its soul. Simplicius exposes Alexander's exegesis as follows:

> "We are trying to prove that the nature of the divine body is not different from its soul, but it is like the heaviness of earth and the lightness of fire. For, just as when we say that these things are moved by nature, we are saying that they are moved in accordance with these powers, and their motion in accordance with their own powers is not something different from motion in accordance with nature, so too the nature of the divine body would reasonably appear also to be the power of its soul. For what else besides this could its nature be? For soul is more complete than nature, and it is reasonable that the nature of the more complete body, in accordance with which nature and soul the body moves in a circle, also be more complete".[46]

According to the quotation of Alexander by Simplicius in his *De caelo*, the former proceeds to a comparison between nature and soul, adding that soul is more complete than nature and that it is reasonable that the more complete body (meaning the celestial body) is endowed with the more complete nature. In the parallel passage within Simplicius' commentary on Aristotle's *Physics* (1218. 36-1219.11, Diels), in which Simplicius quotes the same passage from Alexander of Aphrodisias, and especially in 1219. 6, one can read "soul is a more complete nature" instead of "soul is more complete than nature" which one reads in Simplicius' commentary *In De caelo* (380. 36, Heiberg). I agree with Mueller, the translator of part of the latter commentary (Simpl. *On the Heavens* 2. 1-9), that Diels' text offers a more reasonable reading of what Alexander appears to say in Simplicius' commentary *In De caelo*, in Heiberg's text.[47] If we combine the two texts, then Alexander's argument in Simplicius' *In De caelo* should also be read as follows: "soul is a more complete nature and it is reasonable that the nature of the more complete body will be more complete; therefore, the nature of the divine body is reasonable to be its soul". In any event, for Alexander in the case of the celestial body, the body's nature is both the nature and soul in accordance with which the body moves in a circle (cf. Simpl. *In Phys*. 1218. 36-1219.7). Simplicius addresses his criticism at two points in Alexander's theory regarding the relationship between soul and body on the one hand, and soul and nature on the other. Firstly, Simplicius criticises Alexander's view that souls in mortal bodies are actualizations inseparable from bodies. Simplicius testifies in both his commentaries, on the *Heavens* and the *Physics*, that when Alexander states that the natural motion of the heavens is like the motion of entities moved according to soul, he says this in accordance with his doctrine about the soul, as he thinks that the soul is an inseparable actuality of bodies, just as nature is also such an inseparable actuality of bodies.[48] Alexander, in his *De anima*, declares in all ways that soul is a form of the body and not a substance "itself just on its own" (*autē kath' autēn*) and that this becomes evident to us from the soul's activities. He stresses that no soul activity can occur apart from a bodily change and if it is not possible to conceive of any activity of the soul apart from its bodily change, then clearly the soul is something that belongs to the body and is inseparable from it. For if it were separate, it would be superfluous, since it would not be able to engage in any of its own activities on its

44 Sorabji (1997), p. 2.
45 Fleet (1997), pp. 164-165, n. 27; cf. p. 170, n. 111 and n. 112.
46 Alexander apud Simplicius, *In Aristotelis De caelo commentaria*, 380. 29-381.2 (Heiberg). In general outlines, with some deviations, I follow the translation by Ian Mueller (2004). Cf. Simpl. *In Aristotelis Phys.* 1218.36-1219.11 (Diels); Philoponus, *In De anima* 101.37-102.4 (Hayduck).
47 Mueller (2004), p. 133, n. 79.
48 Simpl. *In De caelo*, 378. 27-29; 380. 13-15. Cf. Simpl. *In Phys.* 1219. 9-11. In all my references to Simplicius on *Physics* 8.4, I follow the translation by Bodnár (2012).

own.[49] Simplicius declares with all certainty that exactly the opposite view has been demonstrated by many well-known men. According to his criticism, although Aristotle says that the soul is an actualization, he recognises two kinds of actualization, one inseparable and one separable, and in the *De anima* he definitely speaks of the rational soul as a separable actualization.[50] Secondly, Simplicius disputes Alexander's position that in celestial and divine bodies nature and soul do not differ. In the context of this objection, he emphatically expresses his opinion on the clear-cut distinction between soul and nature, regarding all natural things.

After quoting Alexander, Simplicius in *In De caelo* criticises his interpretation and asks how it may be harmonised with Aristotle's views, given that the latter clearly thinks that nature differs from soul (nature is one thing and soul another).[51] This is proven by the different definition of nature in the second book of his *Physics* compared to the definition of soul in the second book of his *De anima*. In the former,[52] Aristotle defines nature as a starting point of motion and rest for that in which it exists (ἐν ᾧ ἔστι), whereas in the latter, he defines soul as the actualization of a natural organic body, potentially having life.[53] Simplicius poses the following question: "So if all soul is the actualization of a natural body, and a natural body is one thing, the actualization– and most of all the separable actualization– is another, how could nature and soul be the same?".[54] According to his testimony, Alexander considers the soul to be an inseparable actualization, and since nature is inseparable from a natural body and in a way comes to be the same thing as form, he jumbles nature and soul together, thinking that the name of actualization suits both, so that he also thinks that power (δύναμιν) and soul (ψυχήν) and nature (φύσιν) are the same.[55]

I believe that Simplicius' explanation of Alexander's thesis, which he takes to be a misinterpretation of Aristotle, does not properly consider the starting point of this thesis, which provides an interesting justification for it. Alexander does not arbitrarily conflate nature and soul, thinking that the name of actualization suits both, but he starts his reasoning from his thesis, reported by Simplicius, that, "the οἰκεία ψυχή (its own soul), *if it is an actualization*, is rather associated with form and power" (Simpl. *In De caelo*, 380, 13-15; my italics). Therefore, as we can also infer from Simpl. *In De caelo* 380. 29- 381. 2, which I quoted above, Alexander intrinsically associates in the same relationship the οἰκεία ψυχή, the form and the natural power or powers (δύναμις, δυνάμεις) or the οἰκείας δυνάμεις (their own powers) of the things that are naturally moved in accordance with these powers. Alexander, as we can understand especially from Simpl. *In De caelo* 380. 34-35, does not seem to distinguish regarding the motion of the divine celestial body the power of the soul from those powers that we conceive in a completely natural way, like the heaviness of earth and the lightness of fire. In addition, Alexander in his *De anima* exposes his theory about the inseparability of the soul considered as form. He has devoted the arguments of section 11.14-17.8 of his *DA* to demonstrate that the soul is a form. According to his further argumentation, if the soul is a form, it is inseparable from the body whose soul it is, it is non-bodily, and it is incapable of undergoing change on its own, since every form is of this sort (*DA*, 17. 9-11). Whereas a body is a composite that exists on its own, a form is a form of something else, since this is the sort of thing a completion and a culmination are (τοιοῦτον γὰρ ἡ ἐντελέχειά τε καὶ τελειότης). A form cannot be without that of which it is the form, just as a limit cannot be apart from that of which it is the limit; therefore, the soul cannot be separated and exist on its own (*DA*, 17. 11-15).[56] This thesis, which represents a Peripatetic interpretation, is disputed by the central claim of the Neoplatonist commentators that the rational soul is separable from the body, although as soul it must

49 Alexander of Aphrodisias, *De anima*, 12.8-10; 12. 21-24. I follow the translation of Caston (2012). On other translations and commentaries of Alexander's *De anima*, see de Haas (2015), p. 242. On the distinction between Alexander's *De anima* and his lost commentary on Aristotle's *De anima*, see Caston (2012), pp. 1-2; Kupreeva (2012), pp. 112-113; de Haas (2015), p. 242, n. 2. On Alexander of Aphrodisias' doctrine of soul and its reception, see Kessler (2011), pp. 1-93. Caston (2012, p. 91, n. 107) notes that by using the phrase "itself just on its own" (*autē kath' autēn*), Alexander stresses that soul is not an independent substance that can exist itself just on its own but only the kind of *ousia* that the form is (see Alexander, *DA* 11.14-12.7). According to Caston, Alexander's use of this Platonic terminology here shows an added emphasis to his rejection of substance dualism, namely of the distinction between the Form of *F* and the many things which are *F*. I believe that in this way Alexander rather exhibits his rejection of a radical body-soul dualism, such as the Platonic.

50 Simpl. *In De caelo*, 380.16-19. See Aristotle, *De anima* 3. 4-5.

51 Simpl. *In De caelo*, 381. 2-6.

52 Aristotle, *Physics* 192b 20-23.

53 Aristotle, *De anima* 412b 5-6.

54 Simpl. *In De caelo*, 381.6-9.

55 Simpl. *In De caelo*, 381. 9-13.

56 I believe that the thesis that the limit cannot be apart from that of which it is the limit alludes to the thesis testified by Aristotle in *Metaphysics* 1028b 17-18; 1090 b5-11: there are some who think that since the point is the limit and the extremity of the line, as the line is of the surface, and as the surface is of the solid, there must exist such natures and these are *ousiai*. Aristotle criticises this thesis, claiming that the limits cannot be separate substances. Asclepius (*In Metaph.* 379. 2-4) ascribes this thesis to the Pythagoreans; according to Pseudo-Alexander (*In Metaph.* 462. 23- 25) when Aristotle refers to the proponents of this thesis, he means Plato and his environment; Syrianus (*In Metaph.*179. 5-10) in his comment speaks of those who consider the limits as Forms and substances, which in my reading means that he includes Plato and his followers among them.

be considered as an actualization of the body.[57] Simplicius' argument about the distinction between nature and soul against Alexander, in his Commentary on Aristotle's *De caelo* is based on the distinction between a natural thing/a natural body and its separable actualization, since he takes the existence of a separable actualization as granted; by contrast, in his Commentary on Aristotle's *Physics* he develops an argumentation that focuses on the differences between ensouled and natural things.

II.2. Simplicius' Arguments about the Difference between Nature and Soul in his Commentary on *Physics* II.2

Simplicius believes that since all soul, even the lowest kind, is said by Aristotle to be "the actuality of the natural body possessing organs",[58] we can infer that the vegetative part of the soul belongs to the body which has a nature, being something clearly different from its nature.[59] Simplicius puts forward three arguments which demonstrate that soul does not identify with nature, along with two arguments which show that even if both soul and nature are principles of motion of the bodies in which they are inherent and co-exist, soul is something different from nature because it operates in a totally different way. He then sets out to show what kind of principle nature is for each natural thing. All three arguments the commentator uses to demonstrate that nature is not identified with soul, share as a common basis the idea that the range of natural things is not coextensive with the range of ensouled things. Firstly, while soul is the ultimate actuality of the natural body possessing organs, it is not only bodies with organs that have a nature, but also homoeomerous substances and the four elements. Secondly, we give the name "ensouled" (ἔμψυχα) to things that have within themselves the cause of growth, increase and the propagation of their kind, while we designate as "natural" (φυσικά) also things which are not like this, such as rocks, other minerals, lifeless bodies and simple bodies. Thirdly, all body has a nature (including the materials of artefacts like the material of the statue) and is natural just like the wood of the bed; but not all body is ensouled. For these reasons, nature could not be soul.[60] Simplicius then proceeds to a comparative evaluation of nature and soul, emphasising that nature is inferior even to the lowest part of the soul, the vegetative soul, since such soul supervenes on the natural body as form on matter.[61]

Thus far Simplicius has formulated the arguments which soundly allow the inference that nature cannot be identified with soul. Immediately thereafter, to increase the expectation for the answer he will provide according to his own understanding, he repeats the question "how then did Aristotle present the difference between nature and soul?" (Simpl. *In Phys.* 286.36-287.1). Simplicius presents two reasons and correspondingly two arguments which precisely demonstrate the difference between nature and soul, strictly considered as principles of motion. The first argument explains that the relationship between soul, as a cause and principle of motion, and what it moves, is completely different to that between nature and what is moved by nature, whereas the second shows that nature as a principle is completely different from soul because it is a source of passive movement.

II.2.1. Simplicius' First Argument about the Difference between Nature and Soul

The first argument refers to *Physics* 192b 22, where Aristotle used the phrase "in which it resides" (ἐν ᾧ ἔστιν) with regard to nature, which Simplicius characterises as sufficient for what he aims to demonstrate. The same argument also refers to *Physics* 192b34, which according to Simplicius, contains a clearer phrase than the latter with regard to nature: "in a substrate" (ἐν ὑποκειμένῳ). Whereas nature is a principle or cause of change in those things in which it resides *per se* and not *per accidens*[62] and it resides in each of the natural things as in a substrate, all soul is set apart from what is moved by it, because it properly has the power of moving («ψυχὴ γὰρ πᾶσα κινητικὴν ἔχουσα κυρίως δύναμιν ἐξῄρηται τοῦ κινουμένου»).[63] We can find a relevant explanation of the way in which soul moves in Simplicius' comment on Aristotle's *Physics* 192b15-31. In this context, Simplicius is attempting to clarify the meaning of the phrase "*per se* and not *per accidens*", which is used in the definition of nature in *Phys.* 192b 22-23. Within this reasoning framework Simplicius draws an analogy between the helmsman who moves the ship and the soul which moves the body, or in other words, an analogy between on the one hand the helmsman and the soul and

57 Cf. Tiuryn (2016), p. 32. Within the frame of the biological conception of the soul in Aristotle, which Sorabji emphasises, one may consider the following suggestion by the latter: if the most appropriate account of the soul is the one which picks out the various capacities by which living things differ from each other (see *DA* 415a 12-13), which are also called "parts of the soul" (*DA* 413 b7; b27-32; 429a10-13; 432 a19), then a reasonable thought would be that soul *is* these capacities (Sorabji, 1974, pp. 64-65; *his* italics). From this perspective, soul as first actuality is a capacity which must be inseparable from this thing of which it is an actuality. Johansen (2014, pp. 41-42) also stresses that by "parts of the soul" Aristotle clearly has in mind capacities and that the capacities which make up the various souls are also the capacities by which the different souls differ from each other. On the relation between these capacities or parts of the soul and a unified account of the soul as a whole, see Johansen (2014), pp. 45ff.

58 See again Aristotle, *De anima* 412b 4-6.

59 Simpl. *In Phys.* 286. 25-27.

60 Simpl. *In Phys.* 286. 27-34.

61 Simpl. *In Phys.* 286. 34-36.

62 Simpl. *In Phys.* 266. 27-31.

63 Simpl. *In Phys.* 287. 1-4.

on the other the ship and the ensouled body. According to his explanation, we must first understand that what belongs to anything *per se* (καθ'αὑτό) is inseparable from it, while what is separable does not belong to it *per se*, but *per accidens*. Something belongs *per se* to another thing when it forms an essential part of the being of its subject or is included in the definition of its subject.[64] For instance, if the ship has the helmsman within itself moving it, it does not have him *per se*. This is because the helmsman does not complete the ship's nature, since any ship, just to be a ship, would have no need of someone outside to move it. Otherwise, its helmsman could not be separated from it and removed. As mentioned above, none of the things that belong to anything *per se* can be separated from it, if the thing itself is to remain what it is.[65] Simplicius concludes that even if the helmsman, in moving the ship, moves himself, he does not do so either *per se* or primarily.[66]

The Neoplatonists frequently use the analogy between the relationships *helmsman* (or *steersman* or *sailor*): *ship* on the one hand, and *soul*: *body* on the other, usually with relation to the major issue of the separability of the soul from the body.[67] The use of this analogy by the Peripatetic and Neoplatonic commentators probably alludes to Aristotle's enigmatic and controversial remark at the end of the first chapter of the second book of his *De anima*, that "it is not clear whether the soul may not be the actuality of the body as the sailor is of the ship" (413a3-10, esp. 8-9; transl. Hicks 1907). Tracy (1982, p. 97) notes that this enigmatic sentence has posed a notorious problem for commentators from Alexander to W.D. Ross. Ross, who emended the text by inserting ἤ before the phrase ὥσπερ πλωτὴρ πλοίου, commented on his emendation that it is surprising to find this suggestion made here, since it flatly contradicts the thesis Aristotle has been maintaining some lines above; namely that soul is clearly inseparable from its proper body as axeness is from the axe or sight from the living eye (*DA* 412b27-413a4).[68] Tracy notes that Aristotle's words in *DA* 413a 8-9 suggest that he may be referring to a simile which someone had actually put forward before him. However, he declares that he found no trace in the Pre-Socratics or in Plato of the use of this simile as it is referred to in Aristotle. Nonetheless, he thoroughly investigates the use of the verb "to steer" (κυβερνᾶν) and the noun "steersman" (κυβερνήτης) in the Pre-Socratics, Plato and the contemporary to Aristotle Attic comedy (Menander).[69] The evidence from these pre-Aristotelian sources shows that the soul-steersman metaphor had already been established as a *locus communis* before Aristotle.

Turning back now to Simplicius' approach to the soul-helmsman analogy in his comment on Aristotle's *Physics* 192b15-31, the latter raises an objection against Alexander of Aphrodisias' opinion, who supports that the soul moves itself like a helmsman by moving the body in which it resides, as the helmsman moves the ship. Simplicius makes a distinction between the local movement of the soul on the one hand, and the desires (βουλήσεις), processes of thought (διανοήσεις), processes of opinion (δοξάσεις) and impulses (ὁρμαὶ πᾶσαι) on the other. He then states that although one might perhaps agree that the local movement of the soul takes place in this way, i.e. neither *per se* nor primarily, nevertheless its desires, its processes of thought and opinion and its impulses all occur when it moves itself primarily and *per se* and not through an intermediate, for its very essence is self-motion.[70]

Fleet maintains that when Simplicius introduces the idea of motion in the explanation of the phrase "in which it is present in a primary manner, *per se* and not *per accidens*", in *Physics* 192b 22-23, he uses the distinction between a natural entity, the man, and the artefact, the ship, to show that whereas the former has its source of motion within itself *per se* and primarily, the latter does not.[71] I believe the point is not the distinction between a natural entity and an artefact, but between something which moves *per se* and primarily and something which does not, because here he introduces an analogy between an artefact, i.e. the ship, and the body, which is a natural entity. So, if the ship has the helmsman within itself moving it, but it does not have him *per se*, because the helmsman is separated from it and can be removed and because any ship, *qua* ship, would have no need of someone from without to move it, we can infer that this has serious consequences for the status of the helmsman's own movement while he is within the ship and moves

64 Simpl. *In Phys.* 267. 20-22; 267.33-268. 1-2.

65 Cf. Simpl. *In Phys.* 267. 20-22: "For what belongs to anything *per se* is inseparable from it, while what is separable does not belong to it *per se*, but *per accidens*".

66 Simpl. *In Phys.* 268. 7-12.

67 See Plotinus, *Enn.* 4.3.21.3-21; Porphyry, *Ad Gaurum* 47.5-48.8 (Kalbfleisch 1895); Themistius, *In De anima* 43. 21-34; Simplicius, *In De anima* 96. 1-15; Philoponus, *In De anima* 224.21-225.31.

68 See Tracy (1982), p. 97. See also Easterling (1966); Hardie (1968), pp. 81-83; Lefèvre (1972), pp. 137-140; (1978), pp. 23-25; Bos (2003), p. 304.

69 Tracy (1982), pp. 99-102.

70 Simpl. *In Phys.* 268. 12-18. Johansen (2007, pp. 284-285) notes that in *De anima* 415b 21-27 Aristotle suggests the reason why he does not just want to say that the soul is the efficient cause of locomotion; it is only certain animals which have locomotion, so if the soul were the efficient cause of locomotion only, then the assertion that the soul is the efficient cause of the living body would be true only for some kinds of living being. But he himself seeks a general account of the causal role of soul that applies to all living beings. Johansen points out that the best way of presenting as general the thesis that the soul is a cause in all three senses, formal, final and efficient, is to apply it to the kind of soul that all living beings have, namely the nutritive soul. See also Johansen (2012). For the nutritive faculty of soul as the most natural, see J.G. Lennox (2021).

71 Fleet (1997), p. 167, n.52.

it. As Fleet correctly notes, although the helmsman is in the ship, he is in fact an external mover.[72] Given that the helmsman is an external mover of the ship, which means that he does not move it *per se* and primarily (or he is not a source of motion *per se* and primarily, since he moves the ship by using the ship's equipment), when he moves the ship, he does not move himself either *per se* or primarily. If we apply this inference to the analogy between the helmsman and the soul, what would be the line of reasoning?

When the soul moves the body, it does not move it *per se* and primarily because it is an external mover, since the body as a natural entity already has the source of its motion within it. Being an external mover, the soul does not belong *per se* to the body, i.e., it is separated from it. Furthermore, this means that when the soul moves the body, it also moves itself but neither *per se* nor primarily. This would be the conclusion according to Simplicius, if one accepts the analogy drawn by Alexander between the soul which moves itself in moving the body, and the helmsman who moves himself in moving the ship. This conclusion would imply that it is disputed if the soul's very essence is self-motion. Furthermore, if on the grounds of this conclusion it is disputed that the soul's very essence is self-motion, the analogy drawn by Alexander between the soul and the helmsman would also imply the rejection of the Platonic theory that the soul is the source of all motions[73]. However, Simplicius shall discuss the conclusion that the soul moves itself neither *per se* nor primarily, only if it is strictly confined within the bounds of local movement. But even this does not mean that the soul's essence is not self-motion, because the rest of the psychic motions, such as desires, processes of thought and opinion, and impulses, all occur when it moves itself primarily and *per se* and not through an intermediate.[74] Frede notes that both Aristotle and the scholastic Aristotelians believe that the soul is that in virtue of which a living body is alive, but Aristotle rejects the Platonists' conception of soul, according to which the soul not only is that in virtue of which a body is alive, but is also the proper subject of what we might call the mental functions, activities like believing or desiring. According to the Platonist conception it is the soul which is thinking or feeling, for instance anger, and the living organism can be said to do these things only in so far as its soul is doing them.[75] On the contrary, Aristotle's approach to the soul is clearly different when he states: "it would appear that in most cases soul neither acts nor is acted upon apart from the body: as, e.g., in anger, confidence, desire and sensation in general" (*DA* 403a5-7; transl. Hicks). The attributes of the soul (τὰ τῆς ψυχῆς πάθη) appear to be all conjoined with the body. Thought, if anything, would seem to be peculiar to the soul. Still, if thought is a sort of imagination or not independent of imagination, then even thought cannot be independent of the body.[76] It would be better not to say that the soul pities or learns or thinks, but that the man does so with the soul.[77]

According to Alexander's thesis as exposed in his *De anima*, one might learn that the soul is a form of the body and not a substance itself just on its own from its activities, which cannot occur apart from the bodily changes. He stresses that no soul activity can occur apart from a bodily change, just as there could not be motion from natural tendencies either, since the body engages in these activities in virtue of the power within it (Alex. *DA*, 12. 7-11). Alexander draws a distinction between the powers of the soul and the changes of the body; but he then shows that these necessarily interweave. Being nourished, growing, and generating another like oneself occur in virtue of a soul power, but the changes belong to the body. An animal perceives through the perceptual organs, which are bodies, and desires themselves plainly occur when a certain body undergoes change. Appetites (ἐπιθυμίαι), passions (θυμοί), and rage (ὀργαί) occur in animals in the same way; in fear as well, there is an alteration and contraction of a body. Representation also occurs through the body, if at any rate it depends on perception in activity; also, in striving (ὁρμαί) what undergoes change is a body. Even thinking (φρονεῖν) would itself be something that occurs through a body too, since it does not occur without representation. Alexander's conclusion is that if it is not possible to conceive of any activity of soul apart from a bodily change, then clearly the soul is something that belongs to the body and is inseparable from it (Alex. *DA*, 12. 12-22). Caston aptly remarks that Alexander insists on *both* an activity in the soul *and* a corresponding change in the body (his emphasis) and he applies this necessary combination to all modifications (πάθη) of the soul, aiming at a twofold target; he wants to sustain Aristotle's view that the soul does not itself undergo change and in parallel

72 Fleet 1997: *ibid.*

73 Plato, *Phaedrus* 245c-246a.

74 S. Menn (2002, 91ff.), commenting on Aristotle's definition of soul, remarks that the Aristotle of the *De anima* still thinks, like all other Greek philosophers, that the soul moves the body, but he denies that the body moves or acts upon the soul. Menn points out that Aristotle is already denying the Platonic self-motion of soul and the description of νόησις as the soul's undisturbed self-motion, while accepting that the soul is moved via the body; still, in the *De anima* 406 b 10-11 he says that one would rather say that the soul is moved by the sensibles [sc. than by itself], if it is moved at all.

75 Frede (1995), pp. 96-97.

76 Aristotle, *De anima* 403a 8-10.

77 Aristotle, *De anima* 408b13-15.

maintain that all psychological activity involves change in the body.[78]

When Simplicius uses the analogy between the soul and the helmsman in his comment on Aristotle's *Physics* 192b15-31, he relies on the similar analogy between the soul and the sailor which Aristotle uses in *DA* 406a4-6, but as a Neoplatonist he reaches a different conclusion. Aristotle uses this analogy within the frame of his programmatic aim to show that it is quite impossible for soul to have the attribute of motion at all. In *DA* 406a3-8 Aristotle shows that even if we think of the soul as one of the things that are not moved directly, namely through themselves, but indirectly, through something else, in the sense that they are in something else which is moved, like the sailor who is in the ship, again we would necessarily acknowledge that the soul does not move as something which moves *per se*. The ship moves of itself, whereas the sailor moves only because he is in something else which is moved. Simplicius blames Alexander (and implicitly Aristotle himself) for claiming that the soul moves itself like a helmsman by moving the body in which it resides, as the helmsman moves the ship (*In Phys.* 268. 12-14); because even if the helmsman, in moving the ship, moves himself, he does not do it either *per se* or primarily. According to Simplicius, the soul moves itself neither *per se* nor primarily, only if it is strictly confined within the bounds of local movement; therefore, the analogy cannot apply to the soul. In his comment on *Phys.* 195 a3, Simplicius offers his own explanation for Aristotle's thesis that soul does not move and is unchanged.[79] Soul, even if it is changed, has the agent of change within itself. Simplicius believes that this is the reason why Aristotle prefers to call the soul unchanged. An additional reason for Simplicius, would be that Aristotle thinks that only those things that are altered in body are changed.

On the other hand, Alexander in his *De anima* uses the analogy between the soul and the helmsman (or the pilot) with another aim. He mainly tries to show that those who say that the animal's soul is a form, but a form in the way a substance is, which is separable by itself just on its own as the pilot of the ship is, on the grounds that the pilot is also a form and culmination of the ship (εἶδος τῆς νεὼς καὶ τελειότητα), do not speak correctly.[80] Both Alexander and Simplicius agree that the helmsman/pilot is separable from the ship, but they utilise the analogy between the *helmsman: ship* and *soul: body* relationships differently. Alexander uses a series of arguments to dispute not only that the soul is the form of an animal in the way that the pilot is a form of a ship, but also that the pilot is the form and culmination (εἶδος καὶ τελειότης) of the ship.[81] He puts forward the thesis that the soul bears more of an analogy to the shape of the ship instead.[82]

Another objection Simplicius raises against Alexander's conception of the relationship between nature and soul is associated with Alexander's thesis that Aristotle included the soul in his description or definition of nature. He quotes the following words by Alexander: "We should note that he included the soul in his description of nature, since according to him the soul is the actuality of the natural body with organs, while nature strictly and primarily resides in simple, not organic, bodies".[83] Simplicius responds to this statement by raising the objection that soul is the actuality (*entelekheia*) of the natural organic body, but nature would not be the actuality of the natural body; the former would be a source of some changes, and the latter of others. One of the main differences between nature and soul according to Simplicius is that nature resides in the substrate body, since that in which it resides primarily is called the substrate, as Aristotle clarifies in *Phys.* 192b34, whereas not all soul resides in a substrate; for intellect is separable, as Aristotle himself proclaims in *De anima*.[84] Simplicius then testifies regarding the relevant Aristotelian theory of *nous* in *De anima*,[85] that according to Alexander's interpretation, the intellect Aristotle refers to there is not the logical faculty of the human

78 Caston (2012), p. 92, n. 108. See also Aristotle, *DA* 405b31ff.

79 Simpl. *In Phys.* 317. 14-20.

80 Alexander, *DA* 20.26-29.

81 Alexander, *DA* 15. 9-26; 20. 26-21. 21.

82 Alexander, *DA* 21.8-9.

83 Alexander apud Simplicius, *in Phys.* 268.18-21. Alexander may mean that since soul is the actuality of the natural organic body, if we need to define what a natural body with organs is and what its actuality involves, we must necessarily include the soul in that definition. Also, if we need to define simple, not organic, bodies, we must say that they are soulless, namely we must again refer to the soul.

84 Aristotle, *De anima* 429b5; 430a 17ff. See also Simpl. *In Phys.* 268. 22- 26.

85 Regarding the theory that intellect can exist outside the body, Polansky (2007, p. 363) notes that in *De anima* 430a 15, as commentators observe, Aristotle borrows the comparison to light from the Sun-Good analogy in Plato's *Republic* 506dff. Since the Good is considered to be the ultimate cause of all other things and of all understanding and it is outside us, he assumes that the Platonic background may tempt some interpreters to put intellect outside humans.

soul but the divine *nous*.[86] Nonetheless, he formulates his acute criticism of Alexander's position about the relation between nature and soul, by emphasising that even if Alexander wants to understand it not as the psychic but as the divine intellect, he matches that argument with his own opinion of the soul in a most unconvincing and polemical manner. Finally, he presents his own position, saying that he too agrees that the soul is a source of change, and a more powerful source (ἀρχή) than nature, and not only a source but a fountainhead (πηγή),[87] but not present in what is moved as in a substrate. To the contrary, according to Simplicius, Aristotle wants the term "in a substrate" to be added to nature when he says "each thing is a substrate and nature is in a substrate".[88] For Simplicius, the assumption that the soul does not reside in what is moved by it as in a substrate indicates that the soul has activities separable from the body, as Aristotle states in *De anima*,[89] demonstrating that it also has its essence separable from the body.[90]

We have already seen that Simplicius, in his comments on *De caelo* 284a14-b6, also raises an objection against the two relevant theses on soul of Alexander of Aphrodisias. There, Simplicius disputes Alexander's belief that the soul is an inseparable actualization. Furthermore, he disputes Alexander's suggestion that since nature is inseparable from a natural body and in a way comes to be the same thing as form, the name of (inseparable) actualization suits both, and consequently nature and soul must be considered the same.[91] In the same comment on *De caelo* Simplicius also claims, as here in his comment on *Physics* 192b 15, that nature by itself is not sufficient to cause a complete and natural local motion,[92] since not even the motion of the four elements which is produced by their inclination in relation to the entirety (of the universe) is a complete and natural motion in the sense that the cause of their motion is inherent in them; their motion resembles falling rather than a kind of pulling, since it is brought to fulfillment by a power produced in the particular by the universe.[93] Simplicius maintains that these elements, since they are only natural things, do not contain in themselves the cause of motion in the strict sense, since nature is not self-moving, but causes motion by being moved by something else. Consequently, according to Simplicius, nature cannot be said to be more a mover than a thing moved. He describes the way in which we must understand the nature and soul of parts in relation to their wholes;[94] the universe which is natural and has soul is moved in the strict sense by soul and through the intermediary of nature.[95] At this point we must remember that Simplicius, in his comment on Aristotle's *Physics* 195a3, denies that nature is an efficient cause in the strict sense, since this kind of cause must be separate and distinct, and implies twice that nature must be considered as an instrumental cause, also noting that this is a thesis of Alexander. He clarifies that an instrumental cause is that which is both changed by something else and itself changes another thing and characterises this kind of cause as a contributory cause in that it both undergoes and produces change.[96]

II.2.2. Simplicius' Second Argument about the Difference between Nature and Soul

Simplicius' second and more crucial argument regarding the difference between nature and soul is presented in passage 287. 9-17 of his Commentary on Aristotle's *Physics* II. 2. Simplicius' argumentation in support of the radical difference between nature and soul culminates in this final and most compelling argument, which is aimed

86 Philoponus (*In De anima*, 539. 27-39) assumes that Aristotle is not speaking here of the divine intellect. Moreover, he believes that Alexander misunderstood because Aristotle draws an analogy between intellect and light as a disposition (*hexis*), by saying that there is a kind of intellect that makes all things as light does. According to Philoponus, Alexander did not pay close enough attention to Aristotle's statement. Aristotle adds the words "for in some way also light makes potential colors actual colors" (*De anima* 430a 16-17). However, God does not make all things *in some way*, but he makes all things in every way.

87 We can take an idea for the distinction between soul as ἀρχή and its conception as πηγή in Hermias Alexandrinus, *In Platonis Phaedrum Scholia*, 116. 7-12 (Couvreur); Hermias, commenting on *Phdr*. 245c9, states: "He has done well to call [the soul] *source* and *principle* for it is characteristic of a source to as it were share what is its own spontaneously with things that are other than itself and of a principle to be as it were set over and the master of the things under it" (transl. Baltzly and Share 2018).

88 See again Aristotle, *Physics* 192b 34.

89 Aristotle, *De anima* 415b8ff.

90 Simpl. *In Phys.* 268. 26-269.4. Fleet (1997, p. 167, n. 56) notes that this is the account of the soul that a Platonist would support. According to him, Simplicius is stressing that there is a clear distinction to be made between soul and nature; one must understand that nature resides in the substrate body as an immanent principle, whereas soul is separable and transcendent. Fleet claims that "Simplicius is calling in Aristotle in support of his Platonist position, exploiting Aristotle's view that at least some intellectual activity is separable from the body".

91 See again Simpl. *In De caelo*, 381. 6-13.

92 Cf. Simpl. *In Phys.* 268. 14-15.

93 Simpl. *In De caelo*, 381. 21-28.

94 Simplicius (*In De caelo*, 381. 28-31) notes that parts which are torn asunder from their wholes are deprived of their source of life in the universe and their complete nature, but they are said to have a nature insofar as when they move, they are such as to be again in contact with the universe. Mueller (2004: 133, n. 85) suggests that Simplicius takes issue here with the doctrine that elements have their nature only when they are in their natural place. Cf. Philoponus, *In Phys.* 195. 30-32; 198. 12-13; 199. 16-19.

95 Simpl. *In De caelo*, 381. 31-32. For Proclus' conception of nature as instrumental cause, from a different perspective, see Marinescu (2023).

96 Simpl. *In Phys.* 317. 23-28; 318. 16-20.

towards persuading those who remained unconvinced by his first. Their counterargument is that the vegetative and irrational parts of the soul also reside in bodies as substrates.[97] As stressed by Simplicius in response, Aristotle does not say that nature is a source of change for bodies in the same sense that both he and Plato say that the soul is. For according to both, the soul is what moves bodies, but nature is not a source of movement in respect of moving but of being moved, and of cessation of movement not in respect of stopping but being stopped. That is why natural things are not said to be moved by themselves; for if they could move themselves, then they could also stop themselves. He adds that, if nature were a principle of movement in the sense of causing movement, it would not in this respect differ from the soul and the primary moving cause.[98]

Still, Simplicius' argument here makes a firm distinction between the soul and the primary moving cause. Furthermore, if we compare it with what he elsewhere attributes to Aristotle about his conception of the soul as a moving cause, we can reach the conclusion that the commentator sketches a *scala* of moving causes, which illustrates their hierarchy, based on the criterium of unchangeability. In his comment on passage 195a 3 of *Physics* II. 3, Simplicius draws a distinction, saying that the principle of change is twofold, the self-changing (*autokinētos*) and the unchanged (*akinētos*). That which is changed by something else could clearly not be a principle of change. The self-changed could be a principle of change in that it has the agent of change within itself. However, it is not a principle of change in the strict sense, because it remains the same and yet is changed. At this point by using the verb βούλεται (*In Phys.* 317.15), Simplicius stresses that for Aristotle being the principle of change in the strict sense (*kyriōs*) means being an unchanged changer, so that the efficient cause in the strictest sense (*kyriōtaton*) of things that come-to-be would be that which is unchanged, eternal and always remaining enduringly the same, namely the august Intellect.[99] Soul comes below Intellect, explains Simplicius; for even if soul is changed, it has the agent of change within itself. As I already noted, according to his view, this is the reason why Aristotle prefers to call it unchanged, since he also thinks that only those things that are altered in body are changed. So, the soul as self-changed could be a principle of change in that it has the agent of change within itself, but even according to Simplicius' aforementioned analysis, it is not a principle in the strict sense, because it remains the same and yet is changed.[100]

From the above analyses one may infer two distinct criteria to determine the place of a moving cause in the hierarchy of moving causes. The first is the separability of the moving cause from the things it moves. The second is the changeability of the moving cause. According to the first criterium, being a moving cause in the strict sense means being separate and distinct from the things that are moved by it. Simplicius maintains that soul is set apart from what is moved by it because it properly has the power of moving it and must be considered as a separable actualization of the natural body possessing organs. In this sense, soul is more of a moving cause than nature because the latter resides *per se* and not *per accidens* in each of the natural things as in a substrate. Nature is an internal principle of change, inseparable from the natural things, and that makes it a moving cause subordinated to soul. On the other hand, the issue becomes rather more complex if the criterium of changeability is taken into account. Soul with relation to nature is a principle and separate source of active movement whereas nature is the internal principle of passive movement; and furthermore, nature, according to Simplicius, would properly be characterised as the instrumental cause and not an efficient cause in the strict sense because it is both changed by something else and itself changes another thing. But from the Neoplatonic perspective, which is the basis of Simplicius' argumentation, soul as self-moved is also both a changer and something changed, although it has the agent of change within itself. Therefore, soul is not an efficient cause in the strict sense either, since it is not an unchanged changer or an unmoved mover, and is placed below the primary moving cause, the "august Intellect", which in Aristotelian terms is the "prime unmoved mover".

III. Simplicius' Conception of Nature as a Sort of Propensity for being moved[101]

One of the most characteristic aspects of Simplicius' explanation of the Aristotelian nature is his view that nature seems to be a sort of propensity, ἐπιτηδειότης καὶ εὐφυΐα (*epitēdeiotēs kai euphyia*), for being moved and regulated. According to this view, the propensity seems to be, as it were growing upwards from below and inviting the regulative causes because of its own fitness.[102] The commentator points out that it is clear what Aristotle

97 Simpl. *In Phys.* 287. 4-7. Cf. *De anima* 412a 17-21.

98 Simpl. *In Phys.* 287.7-13; 16-17.

99 Simpl. *In Phys.* 317. 9-10; 14-17. Simplicius stresses that therefore that which is unchanged and subsisting eternally, being productive and a cause of change in the strict sense, is primary; Simpl. *In Phys.* 318. 15-16. Alexander also stresses that the efficient cause in the strict sense must be separate and distinct; Alexander apud Simplicius, *In Phys.* 317. 27-28.

100 Simpl. 317. 17-20; 12-14.

101 This section, with slight modifications, derives from section V.2 of Mouzala (2019).

102 Simpl. *In Phys.* 287. 13-15.

primarily means by the word *nature* when he defines it as the principle of change in the sense of being changed, not causing change, and when he says that the nature resides in the substrate.[103] According to the definition given in passage 192b 20-23, 'nature is a principle and cause of being changed and its cessation'. But, according to what was previously stated, that which resides in the substrate would not in the proper sense be a principle that moves the substrate, because the moving or the efficient cause in the strict sense must be separate and distinct from what is to be moved.[104]

Simplicius' first and main argument that nature is a sort of propensity for being moved is the Aristotelian reference to the principle of change in the sense of being changed and not causing change, within the definition of nature offered in *Physics* II.1. His second argument is based on what is referred to in passage 255b 29-31 of book VIII of the same treatise. In the latter passage, when discussing the four elements, Aristotle states: 'It is clear that none of these things moves itself. But they do have a principle of movement, not in the sense of acting or causing movement, but of being moved'.[105] Simplicius notes that since it is acknowledged that the elements are not moved by themselves, Aristotle asks what it is that moves the elements; for he wants moving by themselves to be particular to animals that have a soul, which he defines as a source of movement (*archēn kinētikēn*).[106] The commentator also makes reference to two other Aristotelian passages in order to articulate his argument. Firstly, he alludes to passage 255a 24-26 in book VIII of the *Physics*, where Aristotle states: "Similarly that which can by nature be changed is that which is potentially of a certain quality, quantity or position when it has within itself such a source". According to Simplicius,

103 Simpl. *In Phys.* 287. 26-29; Arist. *Phys.* 192b 21-22; b34. Sorabji (1988, p. 220) correctly points out that the word *kineisthai* stands indifferently for the intransitive *being in motion* and for the passive *being moved.* Lang (1998, pp. 40-41) notes that since the forms are homographic, the verb *kineisthai* may be either middle or passive, and that the choice between them is crucial because the middle voice implies that nature is a self-mover, whereas the passive voice clearly indicates being moved (i.e., moved by something). She argues that the verb here must be passive: what is by nature must be moved by something. Her main argument is that *kineisthai* is always passive, not middle (or reflexive), in both Plato and Aristotle and, furthermore, is never used to express self-motion (Lang, 1998, pp. 42-43). Furley (1994, pp. 3-14) notes that to anyone who reads the *Physics* incautiously it might appear that since nature is declared to be an internal source of change and rest, all the things specified at the beginning of *Phys.* II.1 should be self-movers: living things and their parts, plants, and simple bodies, earth, water, air, and fire. Furley stresses that, of course, this turns out to be too generous, since we are told explicitly in *Phys.* 255a 5-10 that the bodies that move by nature up or down cannot be said to move themselves. Fritsche (2010, pp. 7-31) maintains that in the entire corpus of Aristotle's writings the expression 'principle of motion' most probably never means a passive principle. By examining several relevant Aristotelian passages, he sets out to prove that this expression in *Physics* 192b 14 and 20-23 is used in the sense of a mover. Furthermore, with regard to Simplicius' interpretation of nature as passive principle, it is worth remembering that in *De Generatione et Corruptione* 323a 15-20, there is the statement that the mover is said to act (*poiein*) and the acting thing to impart motion (*kinein*). Nevertheless, Aristotle invites us to draw a distinction, for not every mover can act, if the term 'agent' (*poioun*) is to be used in contrast to 'patient' (*paskhon*) and 'patient' is to be applied only to those things whose motion is a qualitative affection...in the sense that they are altered (trans. H.H. Joachim, 1922). Joachim (*Aristotle, On Coming-to-be*, p. 147) notes that the term *poioun in the strict sense* applies only to a body which causes a change of *pathos* (affection) in another body. So, we can infer that *kinein* is a wider term than *poiein*; and based on this reasoning we can also infer that *kineisthai* is not identified with *paskhein* but is a wider term than the latter.

104 Simpl. *In Phys.* 287. 29-30.

105 Simpl. *In Phys.* 287. 30-33. Sorabji (1988, p. 220), when referring to the passage *Phys.* 255b 30-31, notes that this idea of passivity illustrated in it, to wit, the idea that nature is an internal source of change, a source not of causing motion, but of passively undergoing it (*paskhein*), had been prepared for in the earlier account of nature in *Physics* II.1, when Aristotle had described it as a source of *kineisthai*; see *Phys.* 192b 21. Simplicius, in his comments on *Physics* VIII.4, repeatedly stresses that being moved is a kind of being affected; see Simpl. *In Phys.* 1210. 21; 1220. 22. In his comment on *Phys.* 255 b 24, he further notes that since none of these [sc. the elements] are moved by themselves, but by something else, an objection presents itself, asking how these physical [bodies] are said to have in themselves their nature as the principle of motion, if they are not moved by themselves, from within, but by something else, from outside. Simplicius argues that Aristotle resolves this objection precisely by saying that these are said to have 'the principle of motion' not as [the principle] of 'causing motion, nor of producing [motion]', but of 'being moved' and 'being affected'. He explains that not only that which moves from itself is said to possess a principle of motion, but also that which is of a nature to be moved. For the term 'motion' is common both to the mover and to that which is moved; but if motion is in that which is moved, as it has been proved in *Physics* III.3, motion is more proper to that which is moved; see Simpl. *In Phys.* 1217. 34-1218. 7.

106 Simpl. *In Phys.* 287. 33-288. 1. See *Phys.* 254b 33-255a 20, especially 255a 4-10; see also Simpl. *In Phys.* 1207. 26-30; 1208. 8-10; 1208. 28-31; 1209. 5-6; 1209. 20-24. Simplicius notes that Aristotle proves by several arguments that it is impossible that the elements are moved by themselves. The first argument is the one that it is the sign of life (*zōtikon*) that something moves itself. The commentator proves that this is a common assumption, by adding a reference to Plato's *Laws* and *Phaedrus*: "For we all say that for something to move itself is the same as to live, as Plato says in the tenth book of the *Laws*, '-Are you asking me whether we say that something lives when it moves itself. -Indeed' (see *Laws*, 895c). And, Aristotle says, it is the property of ensouled beings that they are moved from themselves. This is also said by Plato in the *Phaedrus*: 'That for which motion is from outside-he says- is without soul, that for which it is from within, is ensouled' (see *Phaedrus*, 245e). If, then, these bodies (i.e., the elements) are without a soul, and the ones which move themselves are ensouled, these would not be moved from themselves"; see Simpl. *In Phys.* 1209. 26-35.

Aristotle is clearly referring here to the nature of the thing which can be changed (*kinēton*), meaning that it is an inherent principle of being changed.[107] Secondly, he alludes to passage 284b 30-34 in Book II of the *De caelo*, where Aristotle states the following: "In none of the soul-less entities can we see the origin of the source of movement".[108] Simplicius refers to the same passage in his comment on *De caelo* 284b 6-285a27, where he reminds us that in 284b 32-34 Aristotle clearly says that "we do not see in anything without soul that from where their motion starts". He also invokes the way in which Alexander interprets Aristotle on this issue. Simplicius presents a quotation from Alexander, where the latter makes a distinction between the starting point of motion (ἀρχὴ κινήσεως) and the principle which causes motion (κινοῦσαν ἀρχήν) or the kinetic power (κινητικὴν δύναμιν) that exists within the moving thing. According to this quotation, Alexander believes that by "archēn kinēseōs" Aristotle might mean the kinetic power, since things without soul also have a certain starting point of motion, at least if they are natural bodies, but they do not have a principle which causes motion nor a kinetic power (*dynamis*) in themselves, since what moves them is external; however, they do have a certain passive principle and power of being moved.[109] Simplicius clarifies that things without soul have a nature to move, not on their own, but by one thing being moved by another, as is demonstrated in the *Physics*.[110] Finally, he formulates the reasoning of his second argument that nature is a sort of propensity for being moved as follows: "If, then, the four elements are natural entities and do not have within themselves the origin of the source of movement, i.e., the moving cause, it is clear that it is not in this sense that nature as a cause of movement is said to be a source of movement, but as a source of being moved".[111] The thesis that physical bodies are said to possess the principle of being moved because they possess the capacity and the propensity or the aptitude for being changed into something, is also expressed in Simplicius' Commentary on *Physics* VIII.4.[112]

Simplicius expresses a similar thesis, which places the emphasis on nature interpreted as a kind of propensity (*epitēdeiotēs*), in his Commentary on *De caelo*. There he states that nature is a kind of life (*zōē tis*) which is in a bodily substratum and is suitable and naturally conducive (*epitēdeiotēs kai euphyia*) to a body's being moved by soul through the intermediary of nature when nature transmits the kinetic power of the soul into a body.[113] In a previous work I supported the view that the key-word in Simplicius' explanation of *epitēdeiotēs* is *euphyia*, a word which in its etymological structure contains as a constituent, apart from the 'nature', the 'eu' (*εὖ*), which means the good nature or the good disposition for something. Given that *epitēdeiotēs* is *euphyia* for being moved, in my interpretation, nature as *epitēdeiotēs tis* is neither the material nor the formal cause; in other words, it cannot be identified with either

107 Simpl. *In Phys.* 288. 1-3; cf. Simpl. *In Phys.* 1211. 31-37.

108 Simpl. *In Phys.* 288. 3-6. Irwin (1988, p. 94) claims that Aristotle explains the 'origin of change' only in *Physics* II. 3, when he introduces the doctrine of the four causes, and specifically in passage 194b 29-30 (cf. 195a 22-23), where in his view, the 'efficient cause' is described in terms very similar to those applied to nature in *Physics* II.1. In my view this is not true, because the definition of nature in *Physics* II.1 obviously emphasises the idea that this principle, which can be considered either passive or active —that depends on the interpretation—, is inner or inherent, whereas in the *Physics* II. 3, we see that Aristotle describes only the relation between the agent and its effect, or between the producer and its product, and determines what is primarily called "efficient cause".

109 See Alexander apud Simplicius *In De caelo*, 387. 5-11. Cf. Simpl. *In Phys.* 1209. 23-27; 1211. 15-16.

110 Simpl. *In De caelo*, 387. 11-12. Aristotle, *Physics* VIII.4.

111 Simpl. *In Phys.* 288. 6-9. In his Commentary on *Physics* VIII. 4, Simplicius remarks that the case of the elements is problematic, because it seems absurd that they should be moved by something else when they perform their natural motion (*kata physin kinēsin*), since they are said to possess the principle of their motion in themselves (for animals were said to be moved by themselves on this very same account), while to assert that they (heavy and light bodies) are moved by themselves is to say something impossible; see Simpl. *In Phys.* 1209. 20-24. Cohen (1994, p. 153) notes that if the natural motions of the elements are caused by another, rather than having an internal source in their natures, it might seem that they do not proceed from an internal principle, and so ought not to be counted as *natural* motions in the first place. He points out that Aristotle's main task is to explain how elemental motions can be natural, granted that they have an external cause. But the difficulty, according to Cohen, is that he has to come up with an answer to this question that is compatible with the account of nature in *Physics* II.1, which seems to require an internal principle for natural motions. McGuire (1985, pp. 244-245) stresses that in fact the solution offered by Aristotle is that since a simple body can only begin to move relative to the removal of the last hindrance, the removal of the hindrance is the true initiator of its motion. Only living things can be self-movers; the change that a simple body exhibits, is one of undergoing motion. McGuire notes that the simple bodies, even though they undergo motion according to their nature and manifest activity, are not self-initiators of their own natural impulses.

112 Especially in passage 1218. 7-10 of Simplicius' Commentary on the *Physics*, we can find the most detailed explanation of the real meaning behind the statement that nature is the *principle of being moved*.

113 Simpl. *In De caelo*, 381. 32-35: "ἡ γὰρ φύσις ζωή τίς ἐστιν ἐν ὑποκειμένῳ τῷ σώματι ἐπιτηδειότης οὖσα καὶ εὐφυΐα πρὸς τὸ κινεῖσθαι τὰ σώματα ὑπὸ ψυχῆς καὶ διὰ μέσης ἑαυτῆς τὴν τῆς ψυχῆς δύναμιν τὴν κινητικὴν εἰς τὸ σῶμα διαπορθμεύουσα". For an examination of the meaning of *epitēdeiotēs* see Mouzala (2019), pp. 77-80.

matter or form.[114] But it could be successfully described as something that prepares the linkage between matter and form, as a *sine qua non* presupposition of their joining.[115] Simplicius believes that his exegesis in *In De caelo* 381. 32-35, about soul as the principle of motion which moves a body through the intermediary of nature when nature transmits the kinetic power of the soul into this body, is compatible with the Aristotelian thesis that soul is the actualization of a natural body, and that which Aristotle himself propounds in *De caelo* 284b 32-34 and 285a 28-29. According to Simplicius, what Aristotle clearly says in the above passages is that things which have soul, and not natural things, have a starting point of motion. Moreover, he testifies that Alexander also interprets Aristotle in this way.[116] To reinforce his argument, Simplicius also invokes Plato, who considered these things even before Aristotle, since in the tenth book of the *Laws* he says that the ninth motion, which, being moved by something else, moves other things, is nature, and it has its existence in being naturally conducive to being moved, not in causing motion.[117] Simplicius' answer to the question of what local motions nature and soul cause the heaven to have, is that the soul through the intermediary of nature makes the heaven move in a circle.[118]

IV. Philoponus on Nature and Soul in his Commentary on Aristotle's *Physics* II.1

In his explanation of Aristotle's definition of nature in *Physics* 192b20-23,[119] where one reads that natural things clearly have in themselves the source of their own movement and rest, Philoponus stresses that both animals and inanimate things when they move are not moved by something outside but have the mover in themselves.[120] Aristotle, in *Physics* 192b 18-19, speaks of an innate or natural impulse (ὁρμὴν μεταβολῆς ἔμφυτον) which both sorts of natural things, animate and inanimate, or living and non-living, have.[121] In the case of the inanimate things, Philoponus identifies nature with the natural inclination (φυσικὴ ῥοπή)[122] within them; e.g. stones on being released

114 Mouzala (2019), pp. 79-80.

115 On the other hand, in passage 1045a 30-33 of his *Metaphysics*, Aristotle mentions as the cause of this union of what is potentially with what is actually in the case of things which are generated, apart from the agent, the essence of matter and form: 'For there is no other cause of the potential sphere's becoming actually a sphere, but this was the essence of either' (trans. W.D. Ross, The Internet Classics Archive). But here it is easy to assume that the *essence* of matter and form is the *nature* of matter and form; see also Mouzala (2008), pp. 86-95; Mouzala (2016), p. 127, n. 15.

116 Simpl. *In De caelo*, 381. 35- 382. 5.

117 Plato, *Laws* 894c 2-8; Simpl. *In De caelo*, 382. 5-8.

118 Simpl. *In De caelo*, 382. 8-11.

119 Aristotle, *Physics* 192b 20-23: "For nature is the principle and cause of motion and rest to those things, and those things only, in which she inheres primarily, as distinct from incidentally" (transl. Wicksteed and Cornford 1957).

120 Philop. *In Phys.* 195. 24-27. All references to Philoponus' Commentary on Aristotle's *Physics* are to the page and line of the Berlin Academy Edition (*CAG* XVI) and follow the translation of Lacey (1993).

121 McGuire (1985, p. 242) notes with regard to ὁρμὴν ἔμφυτον that every natural individual, living or non-living, is 'accordingly natured' with its own innate or natural impulse for change and this impulse is present in all natural things from their inception and is thus an intrinsic part of what they are and "a source of their characteristic behaviors".

122 Lacey (1993, p. 147, n. 23) notes that the word *rhopē* is a key-term in Philoponus which partly anticipates his notion of *impetus*, developed in his later works as an internal force bestowed upon agents by an outside agent, God. However, according to Lacey, *rhopē* is limited to the upward or downward, quasi-levitational or-gravitational, tendencies of the four elements, fire, air, earth and water, and does not apply to the *impetus* when this is connected with projectiles or the celestial bodies. Sorabji (1988, p. 233, and n. 19) also notes two things about the term *rhopē* used by Philoponus in 195. 24-32 of his Commentary on Aristotle's *Physics*: 1) he explained the fall of rocks and rising of flames by reference to their inner nature, without any suggestion that that nature was *impressed*. Sorabji makes this inference from the fact that Philoponus calls this inner nature an "innate inclination" (*physikē rhopē*); the word *physikē* which determines *rhopē* means "innate" and is connected etymologically with *physis*. The inner nature that causes the fall of rocks and rising of flames is not yet described in this passage as being impressed by God 2) the word *rhopē* is standardly confined to an *upwards* or *downwards* inclination. Zimmermann (2010, pp. 161-162) points out that *rhopē* is often used by Philoponus for *impetus* and adds that he dismissed Aristotle's misgivings about admitting internal movers in inanimate bodies. He stresses that while Aristotle had balked at the idea of making weight a 'mover', i.e. a cause or source of motion, for Philoponus it is the natural inclination (*physikē rhopē*) of the four elements that causes fire to rise and stones to fall. Krafft (1982, p. 60; 1988, pp. 69-71) believes that it was the Christian belief in the creation of the universe by God which prompted Philoponus to interpret all moving forces —including the natural tendencies of heavy, light and celestial bodies to move in a certain natural way— as forces imparted to these bodies by the creator of the universe; cf. Wolff (2010), p. 147. Sorabji also notes that Philoponus in his *De opificio mundi*, which has been dated some thirty or forty years later than the first edition of the *Physics* Commentary, exposes his *impetus* theory grounded on the belief that God created the universe: "It is God who implants a motive force in the sun, moon and other heavenly bodies at the time of creation. It is God who then implants the downward inclination (*rhopē*) in earth and the upward inclination in fire. It is God who implants in animals the movements which come from the soul within them" (Sorabji, 1988, p. 232). For a discussion of the theories of dynamics before Philoponus and the possible origins of Philoponus' *impetus* theory see Wolff (2010), pp. 140ff. Sorabji (1988, pp. 234-235) mentions another passage from Philoponus' Commentary on Aristotle's *Physics* (690. 20-27) where he treats the rotation of the heavens as due to an innate power, just like the innate inclination which causes the fall of the rocks and the rising of the flames, without mention of this power being impressed. Sorabji suggests that in order to understand how the earlier treatment of celestial motion and of the fall of rocks differs from *impetus* theory, it is important to distinguish between two senses of *impetus*. *Impetus* in the strict sense is identified with an internal force impressed from without, while in a looser sense *impetus* means a force internal to the moving body, whether impressed from without or not. If we ignore the requirement of impression, we will find many examples of *impetus* already in the *Physics* Commentary, having the sense of 'internal forces'.

are not moved downwards by the releaser (for he has merely released them) but it is the natural inclination in them which brings them down. In the same way, fire when released from [being] below is borne upward by the nature in it; and then all these inanimate things rest after being borne to their own masses (οἰκείας ὁλότητας) and their own places (οἰκείους τόπους) by the nature in them.[123] Aristotle, in *Physics* 255b 24-28, recognises that the releaser does have a causal role in giving rise to the stone's movement downwards, operating as a *per accidens* cause. So, the external cause acts as an accidental cause of motion.[124]

McGuire notes that Aristotle defines nature as both a 'source' and a 'cause' (*Phys.* 192b 21) of what an individual is and does, and his use of ἀρχή in the sense of 'source' combines well with his use of ὁρμή, but the relation between these notions is also relevant to his account of different sorts of δύναμις in his *Metaphysics*. According to him, the relation to this ontological context raises the question whether the Aristotelian 'impulse' is itself a completely developed ability for change. The answer to this question is crucial in guiding our decision whether Philoponus' thesis that "inanimate things naturally possess a δύναμις–a power or ability for change" deviates from the Aristotelian conception of the issue.[125] At *De caelo* 268b14-16 we are told that all the natural bodies are capable of moving of themselves with respect to place, which means that all the natural bodies, including the simple bodies, have an inherent capacity which is the inner source of their natural motions. However, McGuire stresses that the simple bodies can by their nature move in one determinate direction alone, i.e. to proceed to and reach their respective places, only if they are not impeded, so they possess only a 'one-way ability'. He argues that what a simple body does not possess by nature is an inner source for initiating its coming to rest prior to its arriving at its natural place.[126] This means that we have to make a distinction between animate and inanimate things and to consider that, strictly speaking, only animate things can be self-movers.[127] According to *Physics* 255b 29-31, the change of a simple body is one of undergoing motion (πάσχειν).[128]

123 Philop. *In Phys.* 195. 24-32.

124 Cf. Lacey (1993), p. 147, n. 22; see especially the connection between the necessity of the role assigned by Aristotle to the external cause and the role of the prime mover in moving the celestial bodies.

125 McGuire (1985), p. 242.

126 McGuire (1985), pp. 242-243.

127 A simple body or an inanimate thing cannot initiate its own motion but, as McGuire (1985, p. 244) puts it, it can only begin to move relative to the removal of the last hindrance, so the true initiator of its motion is the cause of the removal of the hindrance.

128 McGuire (1985, p. 245) concludes that the simple bodies, even though they manifest activity, are not self-initiators of their own natural impulses, and for Aristotle this means, "that they possess a non-active source of change by virtue of which they undergo motion according to their natures, i.e., 'reduce to act' their innate impulse to move in a determinate direction".

Sorabji examines the suggestion that Philoponus dispenses with Aristotle's auxiliary causes of natural motion. More specifically, he discusses the interpretation according to which Philoponus sought to eliminate Aristotle's generator as well as his obstacle-remover from among the efficient causes of natural motion. Then, by referring to Philoponus' comment in 195. 27-29 which we have previously referred to, he notes that "this rejection of the obstacle-remover as a cause is, admittedly, an important difference from Aristotle. For... if the fall of rocks calls for no such causes, this will affect the strategy for arguing that celestial motion requires God as an external final cause".[129] It has been claimed that Philoponus wishes to attribute to nature an enhanced self-sufficiency.[130] Sorabji points out that whereas Aristotle viewed a rock's inner nature as a cause of its being *passively* moved (*paskhein*)[131] by auxiliary agencies, Philoponus insists that its inner nature has an activity (*energeia*) and acts (*poiei*).[132] McGuire stresses that Philoponus' language in his approach to the Aristotelian definition of nature in *Physics* II. 1 depicts nature "as a dynamic inner source, shaping, ordering, and thoroughly directing the determination of a thing's behavior".[133] It is worth mentioning that Philoponus replaces the infinitive *kineisthai* of the definition with the phrase *archē kinēseōs* in his commentary and he generally interprets nature as an active principle of motion.[134] Lammer, commenting on Philoponus' *In Phys.* 195. 24-29, emphasises that "here, the account of nature as a principle of suffering motion by two external causes is dismissed straight away and replaced by an active understanding of nature as a natural inclination (φυσικὴ ῥοπή)".[135] In his comments on *De Generatione et Corruptione* 336a 6-12, Philoponus also stresses that the efficient cause in a strict sense is not acted upon. He then clarifies his thesis about nature as efficient cause: "And indeed we would not say that nature is acted upon, insofar as it is efficient cause, but if at all, [that] its underlying substrate [is acted upon], while [nature] itself always imparts motion" (Philop. *In De Gen. et Cor.* 287. 29-288.1; trans. Kupreeva, 2005). From Philoponus' words we can infer that he recognises that nature is an efficient cause in the strict sense, namely, in the sense that it is always active and it always imparts motion, hence is never acted upon.

Philoponus interprets the Aristotelian definition of nature in *Physics* 192b 13-14 and 20-23 with reference to the teleological perspective of the Aristotelian notion of

129 Sorabji (1988), pp. 241-242.

130 Cf. Lacey (1993), p. 147, n. 22.

131 Aristotle, *Physics* 255b 29-31.

132 Sorabji (1988), p. 242.

133 McGuire (1985), p. 250.

134 See Philop. *In Phys.* 195.24-26; 196.6-8; 196. 13-16;196. 21-26;197. 9-10; 197. 30-33; 198. 9-10; 198. 22-23; 198. 30-32; 199. 12-16; the most indicative passage amongst these is 196. 13-16.

135 Lammer (2015), pp. 122-123.

eidos and its relation to nature. This perspective which places the emphasis on the idea that nature always aims towards an end (*telos*), endows nature with a specifically active causal role. In the former passage where Aristotle uses the term στάσις, nature is presented as a source not only of change but also of stability (στάσεως). Philoponus justifies this definition by saying that nature moves things in order to bring them into the state of possessing the form and halts them in order to preserve them in the state of possessing the form.[136] Thus, nature has a twofold activity corresponding to a twofold aim. On the one hand, it moves things with the objective of having them acquire form, and on the other, it halts things aiming at the preservation of the form they have assumed. In the latter passage, according to Philoponus, when Aristotle uses the word ἠρεμία, one must understand it as meaning not only the rest which is contrasted with change,[137] but stability as well, for nature is a cause not only of rest after change but also of things which are in any way at all without moving always stationary (e.g., the centres of the heavenly spheres and the standing still of their poles). Philoponus interprets Aristotle's statement that nature is a source not only of change but also of rest by emphasising that nature always pursues some end. This means that it does not move things that are moved simply on this very account, in order that they should move, but in order that they should reach some end and form. So, since nature pursues some end, when it brings the moved to this it naturally halts it, having attained the end, in order to preserve it in the state, on account of which it originally moved it.[138]

Philoponus states in his comments that nature is not only a formal cause but also an efficient and a final one and invokes Aristotle's thesis, presented later in his *Physics*,[139] that the three causes often come together.[140] McGuire notes that these relationships are important for Philoponus since he wishes to preserve and reinforce Aristotle's claim that nature is an inner source of change and staying unchanged. He also notes that if nature is conceived as embodying the formal, productive, and final aspects of change, a relationship between change and rest can be made out. According to his view, Philoponus puts the relationship succinctly, since his approach implies that nature causes motion of the natural thing aiming at the realization of the form and causes the thing to stand still so as to remain in that form.[141] In my view, Philoponus' approach of nature as cause of motion and standing still of natural things combines the three causal roles, but places the emphasis on the final causality and the teleological aspect of nature's activity. With his analysis, Philoponus contributes to our understanding of Aristotle's teleological causal perspective. Nature not only causes and allows change in order that the end, i.e., the form or the "completion of the formal characteristics of the nature itself", may be realized, but also seems to have a kind of providence or protective care, and "causes the thing to stand still in order that it may remain in that form".[142] There are at least two important issues on which Philoponus diverges from Aristotle and develops his own conception of nature, attempting either to criticise and improve the latter's theory or simply to modify and supplement it. The first issue is the Aristotelian definition of nature. Philoponus believes that this definition does not signify the essence of nature, namely what nature is, but merely its activity (*In. Phys.* 197. 30-33). We will see later how he proposes to remedy this deficiency. The second issue concerns the natural inclination (φυσικὴ ῥοπή) of inanimate natural things and its importance for the explanation of their inherent and natural capacity to move. Although Philoponus understands the Aristotelian subdivision of natural things into those that are self-movers or self-changers and those that are not, and is aware of the fact that Aristotle conceives of the simple bodies as being passively moved, he highlights his own different approach to the natural inanimate things, within the frame of his own dynamic conception of nature as a source of change. He interprets the natural inclination within them as a natural power which makes the inanimate things to be, like all the natural things, both the dynamic source and subject of their own change.[143]

Philoponus uses the verb στοχάζεται to describe the relation between nature and the end which it pursues. This verb means to aim at something and entails a purposeful and rational activity. From the use of this verb, we could infer that Philoponus construes nature as a rational power or at least a power, the behaviour of which is aimed towards rationally selected goals, with chosen concrete plans to implement. This would mean that Philoponus construes nature as an efficient cause in the sense of an agent that aims

136 Philop. *In Phys.* 196.13-15.

137 According to Simplicius, not all cessation (στάσις) is rest (ἠρεμία); only that which comes after movement is. See Simpl. *In Phys.* 264. 26.

138 Philop. *In Phys.* 196. 17-26. Simplicius also focuses on the teleological aspect of the Aristotelian *eidos* when it is considered as an end at which nature always aims, saying that the change of each natural thing and its cessation do not originate from outside, nor are they without limit, but rather the change proceeds as far as the limit of the appropriate form and then ceases. He thus relates the limit of each change to the limit of the appropriate form, which means that not only the result of change but also change itself is determined by the appropriate form. See Simpl. *In Phys.* 264. 16-18.

139 Aristotle, *Physics* 198a 24-27.

140 Philop. *In Phys.* 195. 2-5.

141 McGuire (1985), p. 246. We can assume that nature causes both change and rest of natural things within the frame of its objective to make the things attain the form and preserve it; in this way, it acts as a productive and efficient cause and also embodies in its causal activity both the formal and final aspects of change.

142 Cf. McGuire (1985), *ibid.*

143 Cf. McGuire (1985), pp. 246-247.

to achieve certain goals and makes goal-directed choices. However, in his Commentary on Aristotle's *De anima*, Philoponus clarifies that nature does not act purposefully but its activity has always *by nature* (φυσικῶς) the character of aiming towards some τέλος: "...nature does everything for the sake of something. For even if it does not know the things it does and does not propose concerning them, still by nature its activity has an eye to some end" (Philop. *In De anima*, 264. 20-22; transl. Charlton 2005). Simplicius testifies that Alexander of Aphrodisias, in his lost commentary on Aristotle's *Physics*, supported the view that nature does not work by choice or by any reason within it because it is an irrational power. But this, according to Alexander, does not mean that nature produces at random and not for the sake of something, because *for the sake of something* is not the term applied only to coming-to-be based on reason and choice. This term is applied also to everything that comes-to-be according to some regularity (κατὰ τάξιν) and because of something else (ἄλλου χάριν).[144] Philoponus' view seems to be similar to that of Alexander.

We can also find Philoponus' understanding of both the distinction and the relationship between nature and soul in his exegesis of the Aristotelian definition of nature. Philoponus believes that Aristotle added the word 'primarily' to the definition of nature in *Physics* 192b 20-23, to distinguish between soul and nature as principles of motion. According to his view, the rational soul too moves the animal and such a source of motion is not outside but in the moved itself. But the rational soul does not move primarily but through the irrational soul, and neither does the irrational soul move the animal primarily, but rather by moving its nature. So, this is what primarily causes motion, the nature of the moving thing.[145] Philoponus clarifies that by 'primarily' he means 'proximately'. In case of perception, sight moves desire and this moves the natural capacities and these move the animal.[146] The rationale which leads to the distinction between soul and nature encompasses both the rational and irrational soul:[147] "if then not even the irrational soul moves the animal primarily, still less does the rational, so that even if the soul, both the rational and the irrational, moves the animal, and this moving cause is in the moved, yet since it does not move it primarily, that is proximately, for this reason soul is not nature".[148] Thus, he identifies the cause which moves primarily with nature and, conversely, the main characteristic of nature is that it moves primarily, i.e., proximately, what it moves.[149] Furthermore, if according to his view the rational soul does not move primarily but through the irrational, and neither does this move the animal primarily but by moving its nature, then we can assume that for Philoponus too, nature is an intermediary and instrumental cause, as it is for Simplicius, because it moves by being moved.[150] Macierowski and Hassing remark that if primarily (πρώτως) means immediately (προσεχῶς) for Philoponus, then it follows that at least at this stage of his exposition, nature must move without the mediation of instruments.[151]

Philoponus also refers to the example of the ship and the helmsman who moves it, to show the difference between soul and nature as movers. We noted that Alexander of Aphrodisias and Simplicius also use the same example.[152] Similarly, Philoponus also draws an analogy between the soul and the helmsman. A ship too has the mover in itself, the helmsman who moves it, but the helmsman is not nature, because he does not move it primarily but through the rudder, and the rudder moves the ship from outside. The source and the cause of movement is not in the rudder, but in the helmsman, because he is the one who moves the ship through the rudder as an instrument. Nature too moves things through instruments, nevertheless it belongs in those things which it also primarily moves. But the helmsman is not in the rudders but moves them from outside, and moves the ship too from outside, if it

144 Simpl. *In Phys.* 310.36-311.1 and 311. 20-25.

145 Philoponus (*In Phys.* 196. 30-32) describes the way in which perception moves to show that nature is the ultimate mover in the chain of moving causes, i.e. that which moves primarily. Perception moves the animal towards something, either sight or hearing or one of the others (for it is having seen something that we are moved towards it), but sight does not move the animal primarily.

146 Philop. *In Phys.* 196. 32-197. 1.

147 Philoponus, in his comment on *De anima* 430a 23, points out that only the intellect is both immortal and eternal. The irrational and vegetative soul is only immortal, but not eternal; this kind of soul is called immortal although it is destructible, because it is not destructed *qua* soul, but in so far as it inheres in a body. According to Philoponus, this is the reason why Plato states that every soul is immortal, and that this also applies to the irrational and vegetative soul. See Philop. *In De anima* 541. 6-12.

148 Philop. *In Phys.* 197.1-5.

149 Macierowski and Hassing (1988, p. 97, n. 56 and 57) note that Philoponus, unlike Aristotle, takes the term πρώτως (primarily) and προσεχῶς (immediately) as identical in meaning, so that it is nature and not soul that moves primarily. They think that the best examples of nature within the comments of Philoponus on *Physics* are the natural inclinations which move the elements in their natural motions (195. 29-31), the grower in plants and animals (195.33-196.1), the changer of quality (196. 1-3), and the natural powers which Philoponus mentions in 196. 33- 197.1. Simplicius (*In Phys.* 267. 22) understands πρώτως in the definition of nature differently from Philoponus. In his thorough exegesis of this term, he shows that it means that nature belongs to or exists in the natural things without any intermediate.

150 See again Simpl. *In. Phys.* 317.23-28; 318. 16-20; *In De caelo*, 381. 31-32; 382.10.

151 Macierowski and Hassing (1988, p. 97, n. 57) note that it is not entirely clear whether the term 'instruments' includes only the powers or faculties of the soul, such as sensation and appetite, or whether bodily parts are also included, as suggest the examples of the pilot and rudder that Philoponus uses in the following comment; 197.5 ff.

152 See again Simpl. *In Phys.* 268. 7-14.

moves it through the rudder and this is outside.[153] We can assume that for Philoponus, both soul and nature move through instruments, but while nature belongs in those things which it also primarily moves, soul moves from outside both the organs through which it moves and the things which are moved by it. Macierowski and Hassing maintain that this exposition seems to be a revision of what Philoponus has stated previously, that nature moves primarily. Here we can identify the thesis that nature may move through instruments, provided it is present primarily in the instruments through which it moves. The question is whether by 'instruments' here we must understand the natural powers and inclinations. In any case, according to their interpretation, this prepares the admission of irrational soul to the rank of natural principle.[154]

Philoponus proceeds almost immediately to revise his thesis that soul is not nature, claiming that perhaps it is possible to say that soul too is nature in the case of animals so far as they are animals. He justifies this deviation from his previous thesis by saying that if soul is the cause of the movement of animals *qua* animals primarily and not *per accidens*, and is in them, and not only inanimate things are natural but also animals and animate things *tout court*, then this too seems to be nature, unless we are to say that animate things *qua* animate are not natural. Philoponus clarifies that when he says that "perhaps soul too is nature", he does not mean the rational soul but all the rest of the soul, because it is this which proximately moves natural things. Furthermore, he maintains that perhaps it was also because of the rest of the soul that Aristotle used the term πρώτως (primarily); otherwise, thought (διάνοια) too moves by being in the moved, but not primarily, since it is within the rational soul.[155] Lacey argues that Philoponus' claim explains why thought does not move things primarily, but would surely leave it unexplained why the rational soul should not do so. He assumes that we seem to need some further premise, such as that the rational soul only moves things by stimulating desire, which belongs to the rest of the soul.[156] I believe we can find this missing premise if we go back to Philoponus' exposition in 196. 26-30, where he explains that the rational soul does not move primarily but through the irrational, and neither does this move the animal primarily but by moving its nature. As I noted before, in the same comment (196. 30ff.) he explains that perception moves desire and this moves the natural capacities and these move the animal. Therefore, Philoponus' view that soul too is nature is restricted only to the case of animals *qua* animals and is based on two criteria: a) it is justified by the fact that soul is the cause of the movement of animals *qua* animals primarily and not *per accidens*; namely it fulfills the same causal presuppositions with nature, as these are determined in the Aristotelian definition of the latter; b) it concerns not the rational soul but all the rest of the soul, namely the irrational soul, because it is this which *proximately* moves the animate natural things. Philoponus uses (*In Phys.* 197.19) here the term *proximately* with regard to the irrational soul only in comparison with the rational soul, and not with nature. What proximately moves all natural things *qua* natural is nature, but what proximately moves animals *qua* animals is their irrational soul. However, it seems that the irrational soul in the case of animals *qua* animals operates as their nature, as far as it is this which primarily (in the sense of προσεχῶς) moves their natural capacities. As such, without contradicting his main thesis that nature (or the inherent natural powers) is what proximately moves all natural things, Philoponus puts forward the complementary thesis that the irrational soul is for the animate natural things *qua* animate a kind of nature, since it is within them and operates as the cause that moves them primarily and not *per accidens*. From this perspective, indeed, the definition of nature should also apply to soul.

V. Philoponus and Simplicius on nature as *zōē* in Aristotle's *Physics* II. 1-2

It is important that both Philoponus and Simplicius use the notion of *zōē* (life) to describe and explain what nature is.[157] I shall attempt to analyse and compare their approaches to nature through the notion of life. Philoponus stresses that the definition of nature in *Physics* 192b 21-23 does not signify what nature is but the activity of nature; when we learn that nature is the source of movement and rest, we do not learn what it is but what it does. He argues that if we aim to also give the definition of nature's essence itself, we must say that nature is a life or a power which has descended into bodies (δύναμις καταδεδυκυῖα διὰ τῶν σωμάτων), and which moulds (διαπλαστική) and manages (δοικητική) them, being a source of change and rest for that "in which it belongs primarily, *per se* and not *per accidens*".[158] For Philoponus it is clear that nature manages both animate and inanimate things, for each thing has a natural power holding together its being, as it would have perished and gone over into not being if there were nothing holding it together.[159] Thus, according to him, nature is a power which has descended into bodies, both animate

153 Philop. *In Phys.* 197. 5-12.

154 Macierowski and Hassing (1988, p. 97, n. 58).

155 Philop. *In Phys.* 197.13-21.

156 Lacey (1993), p. 148, n. 36.

157 Frede (1995, p. 97) attributes to later Platonists the following theses regarding the soul, the body and their relation to nature : a) under the influence of Stoicism, they give up the assumption that our soul makes us alive b) they come to think, as Aristotle does, that bodies, whether alive or not, are part of nature, so they can be explained in terms of it c) they retain the notion of the soul as the thinking self and the proper subject of the mental functions which is distinct from the body.

158 Philop. *In Phys.* 197. 30-198. 1.

159 Philop. *In Phys.* 198. 2-4.

and inanimate, and has a triple effect on them. It moulds them, manages them and holds together their being. The difference between animate and inanimate things with regard to nature, is that the providence of nature is more manifest in the animate, exactly as the form is. Philoponus also states that, in accordance with the above theses, the definition of nature offered by Aristotle clearly will also embrace the nature of the animate, which is its soul, given that the life of animate things is nothing other than soul.[160]

The propositions of Philoponus allow us to produce the following reasoning. The nature of the animate things is their soul; the life of animate things is nothing other than soul; therefore, the nature of the animate things is their life, which is their soul. Regarding the animate things, all three principles, nature, soul and life, are equated; but nature is life too in relation to the inanimate things. Nature as life is that which moulds and manages the natural bodies, and its presence in them becomes manifest as a natural power which holds together their being. If there were nothing like it to hold them together, they would have perished. In my view, there are two issues in Philoponus' exegesis which seem to have a special significance for the character and innovation of his interpretation. The first is the expression δύναμις καταδεδυκυῖα διὰ τῶν σωμάτων (a power which has descended into bodies) and the second his reference to the providence of nature. Lacey[161] notes that if we understand the word καταδεδυκυῖα as "diffused",[162] this suggests the Stoic notion of diffusion, whereas if we understand it as "descending", it suggests Philoponus' later idea of power as coming down from the Christian God. My main reservation with the second interpretation is that in 198. 3, Philoponus speaks of a "natural power" that holds together the being of each natural thing. In my view, this remark by Philoponus applies to all natural bodies and implies an inherent power and not something that is given from without. Macierowski and Hassing believe that Philoponus' formulation is consonant with a general philosophical context, which we may infer from the examination of the notion of nature and life in the Stoics, Plotinus, Proclus, and in *De Mundo*.[163] They note that the verb is used often in its literal meaning, 'to sink', and claim that a search for forms of the verb καταδύ(ν)ειν in Plato, the Stoics, Plotinus and Proclus found no instances "in a theological or natural philosophical context". Furthermore, Macierowski and Hassing believe that in all probability Philoponus used the term deliberately, given that he was a Monophysite Christian who was concerned with reconciling Aristotelian with biblical teaching. Finally, they adopt the thesis that although he employed a formulation which reflects the impact of Stoic and Neoplatonic sources, his intention was to bring Aristotle's theory into agreement with the biblical doctrine of creation.[164] McGuire, on the other hand, stresses that Philoponus' definition of nature, at least in Renaissance commentaries on Aristotle, is considered to be Platonic, either wholly or partially, but he believes that this evaluation somehow ignores the subtle nuances in Philoponus' explanation.[165] Lacey refers to a statement by L. Siorvanes during a private conversation, that δύναμις καταδεδυκυῖα is perfectly acceptable as a Neoplatonic phrase, with the specific participle (καταδεδυκυῖα) being used to refer to the descent of souls into bodies.[166] According to a certain line of interpretation, his terminology as well as his tendency, when analysing the definition of nature, to explain soul as a kind of nature, show that the roots of his inspiration are on the one hand Platonic and on the other Neoplatonic.[167] Based on the similarity of nature to soul recognised and put forward by Philoponus, Lammer claims that his notion of nature (φύσις) as life (ζωή) correlates with the conception of soul as life and as self-moved in Plato's *Laws*. He also associates Philoponus' conception of nature as δύναμις with the conception of soul as immortal and self-moving principle and as δύναμις in Plato's *Phaedrus*. He believes that the participle καταδεδυκυῖα in Philoponus' language may recall aspects of the fall of the soul in the *Phaedrus* as well as some similar contexts in Plotinus' *Enneads*.[168]

To the best of my knowledge, we can find a use of a form similar to the participle καταδεδυκυῖα with regard to nature

160 Philop. *In Phys.* 198. 4-8.

161 Lacey (1993), p. 148, n. 43.

162 See McGuire (1985), p. 247; 264, n. 11. He notes that he found the 16th Century latin translation of Joannes Baptista Rasarius suggestive for this rendering of καταδύω.

163 Macierowski and Hassing (1988, p. 85) summarise as follows the resume of their research: "In Plotinus and in the commentary of Proclus on Plato's *Timaeus*, we find an account of cosmic soul or life, pervading all things, and understood as a product of demiurgic activity. In the Stoic passages, we find a notion of nature as a power pervading matter or all things. This power shapes or forms that in which it works: it is characterised as *diaplastic, eidopoetic, cosmopoetic*. It is self-subsistent and is called spirit or god. In *De mundo*, this power is not self-subsistent but is the instrument of a divine being".

164 Macierowski and Hassing (1988), p. 85.

165 McGuire (1985, pp. 264-265, n.11) argues that Philoponus does not juxtapose a Platonic conception of nature to Aristotle's. He is rather adapting the Platonic notion of "directed self-activity" to Aristotle's view that all individual natural things, animate and inanimate, have a natural impulse.

166 Lacey (1993), p. 149, n. 43.

167 Cf. Lammer (2015), p. 124. Conversely, nature in Plotinus is a reflection or an offspring of a parent principle, which is the (higher) Soul; see Gerson (2012), pp. 17, 29 and n. 1, 2; Wilberding (2022), pp. 321- 322, 331.What we call "nature" is a soul, offspring of a prior soul having a more powerful life; see Plotinus. *Enn.* 3.8.4.15-22. For the Plotinian conception of nature as a life-like power that appears last among the creative causes of the world, see Golitsis (2019), p. 242.

168 Lammer (2015), p. 124. Plato, *Laws* 894a8-896a5; *Phaedrus* 246a-248e. Plotinus, *Enn.* 1.6.8. 14; 1.8.13.23.

in Proclus' commentaries on Plato's *Timaeus* and on Plato's *Parmenides*. In *In Timaeum* I, 10. 5-11.20 Proclus presents the various ways in which the ancient philosophers used the term φύσις, *nature*, and the meanings they attributed to it. Within this framework, he sets out to explain Plato's use of the term *nature* and the meanings he attributed to it; he further remarks that Plato "stopped short of identifying nature outright with soul" (*In Timaeum* I, 10. 15-16).[169] During this exposition, he takes the opportunity to put forward the distinction between nature and soul as he conceives it: "intelligible soul and nature are two different things, for nature is what belongs to bodies, deeply embedded in them and existing as something inseparable from them, whereas soul is separable and is rooted within itself..." (*In Timaeum* I, 10. 24-27; transl. Tarrant 2006). Proclus uses the participle δύνουσα (κατ'αὐτῶν) which is relative to Philoponus' καταδεδυκυῖα. He also presents in this passage a hierarchy of causes, the gradations of which are described through the following five determinations: τὸ αὐτό, τὸ αὐτοῦ, τὸ αὐτοῦ καὶ ἄλλου, τὸ ἄλλου, τὸ ἄλλο (*In Timaeum* I, 11. 1-2).[170] According to Proclus, nature which is differentiated from soul is the last one of the causes that construct the sensible bodily world, so it is placed beneath the soul; but it is full of formal principles and properties through which it directs immanent things and it gives the lead to the whole cosmos through its own powers, preserving the heaven at its own highest point, governing generation through the heaven, and everywhere securing links between particulars and universals; it pervades all things unhindered and breathes life into them.[171] Martijn stresses that according to this passage the main difference between soul and nature lies in their different relations to body: "Nature is not only intrinsically and essentially related to bodies (τῶν σωμάτων, ἀχώριστος ἀπ'αὐτῶν) but is also physically immersed in them (δύνουσα κατ'αὐτῶν)" (2010, p. 29). We can recognise that Philoponus attributes to nature similar characteristics as Proclus, with emphasis on government or administration, the preservation of cohesion, and providential care. Also, in *In Parmenidem* III. 794. 3-11, Proclus uses the participle δύνασα (κατὰ τῶν σωμάτων) and describes how nature acts, as follows: "Nature, when it descends into bodies, acts as you might imagine a carpenter descending into his pieces of wood, hollowing them out from inside, straightening, drilling, and shaping them. Such is the way of Nature, infusing itself into bodies, dwelling in their solid masses, and breathing its movement and its reason-principles into them from inside" (transl. Morrow-Dillon, slightly modified). This image, as Martijn notes, "is clearly concerned primarily with portraying the immanence of Nature" (2010, p. 49). According to an important line of interpretation, Proclus' analysis in *In Timaeum* I, 10. 4-11.20 determined the framework for all subsequent approaches to nature in Neoplatonism henceforth.[172] This will be verified also from my analysis of Simplicius' conception of nature as *zōē* later in this chapter. Indeed, the origin of Philoponus' use of καταδεδυκυῖα can be traced to Proclus' terminology, all the more because Proclus also describes the relationship between nature and the bodies in a similar way.

Macierowski and Hassing declare that their concern is not with the details of Philoponus' theology, meaning obviously the question of how far he is influenced by his Christian beliefs, but with a major philosophical issue; the relation between his understanding of the definition of nature and Aristotelian formal causality. They argue that Philoponus' formulation implies a notion of nature incompatible with Aristotle's understanding of nature as formal cause; according to their remark, for Aristotle form is a principle and cause, whereas for Philoponus, form is a product and effect of something prior to form.[173] I believe that Philoponus' approach to *nature* (meaning also *zōē*) as the principle and cause of the bodies and of the form is perfectly compatible with its Neoplatonic background, since the Neoplatonists considered the productive principle and cause prior and superior to its effect.[174] In my view, Philoponus' words δύναμις καταδεδυκυῖα διὰ τῶν σωμάτων explain the word *zōē*, which determines the essence itself of nature. Philoponus himself states in *In Phys.* 197. 33-34 that he will formulate the definition of the essence of nature itself. It is obvious that *zōē* is a power prior to anything that a body can have, because it is a power which moulds and manages the bodies; it is also a natural power which holds each thing's being together. As such, I agree with Macierowski and Hassing that for Philoponus, nature as *zōē* is prior to form, and that form seems to be a product and effect of it, like anything else which, when considered with regard to its principle (*archē*), appears to depend on it. In my reading, *zōē*, being the essence of nature, is a principle (*archē*) on which the natural body and its form depend, but nature as *zōē* appears to be and behave like a natural power (*In Phys.* 198. 3). I do not recognise

169 I follow the translation of Tarrant (2006). On Proclus' exposition of the theories of ancient philosophers on nature in his commentary on the *Timaeus* and on his own conception of the relation between nature and soul, see Martijn (2010), chapter 2, pp. 24 ff.

170 Tarrant believes that it is tempting to find a correspondence between this fivefold metaphysic and the Platonic and Neoplatonic system of five causes. In two cases one can find an equation and in three cases a possible relevance: "In two cases they can be equated: paradigmatic cause = paradigm (itself/same), creative cause = demiurge (its own); a looser connection may perhaps be postulated between final, formal and material causes and (respectively): soul (its own and another's), physical nature (another's), the sensible world (other)" (2006, p. 105, n. 62).

171 Proclus, *In Timaeum* 1.11. 9-27. See also Golitsis (2019), pp. 244-245.

172 Golitsis (2019), p. 247.

173 Macierowski and Hassing (1988), p. 85.

174 Cf. Lernould (2012), pp. 68-69.

anything which manifests a specific influence of Christian beliefs, whereas I believe that this phrase, as Siorvanes noted, can be acceptable as one which bears a Neoplatonic philosophical background (including the influence of the Stoics). Philoponus' language here represents a significant conceptual layer derived from the combination of the preceding Neoplatonic tradition and his own inspiration, which reflects a philosophical metaphor with reference to the notion of descending. The words καταδεδυκυῖα διὰ τῶν σωμάτων may have two alternative meanings; either that nature as *zōē* is a broader power in the upper place of the ontological climax, which uses the inferior level of the bodies as instruments or mediums[175] to manifest; or that this power which Philoponus names *zōē* penetrates each body until its ultimate constituents. In any case, Philoponus' reference to the "providence of nature" (*In Phys.* 198. 6) shows that his approach to nature significantly differs from the Peripatetic thesis of Alexander of Aphrodisias, testified by Simplicius, that nature is an irrational power which does not work by choice or by any reason within it, although it always produces for the sake of something (ἕνεκά του).[176]

It is crucial moving on to investigate Simplicius' conception of nature as *zōē*, to see that he also understands it as something prior to form, but from the perspective of his own interpretation of nature, as a propensity for being moved. Simplicius notes that earlier thinkers clearly also had some similar conception of nature, viewed in terms of the propensity of each thing for change, according to which natural entities are characterised. Since all the natural entities have matter and form, some of these thinkers ascribed such a potentiality to the matter, claiming that this was a nature by which natural entities are constituted to be changed, since they were seeing that natural things were most changed in their matter (as for example a bed is changed in terms of the wood). Others were claiming that *nature* is that in terms of which natural entities have their being, meaning the form in this case, since the form is the mark of each thing by which each thing subsists and is said to be just what it is, and for this reason assumed that the form was the nature.[177] However, Simplicius emphasises that Aristotle did not think it right either to call *matter per se* "nature", for *matter per se* is an impotent substrate, or to call the form "nature", for this is natural but not nature. Rather, he designated as nature the propensity of matter for appropriate movement and change, when it changes from one form to another; for the loss and reception of the form happens to matter according to its natural propensity.[178] Simplicius' explanation of Aristotle's conception of nature highlights that matter and form are both natural, but neither is nature and in the same way, nor is the compound. But still there is a scale and a climax regarding the relation of matter, form, and the compound to nature. Form rather than matter would be nature because of its character and power. And the compound rather than matter would be nature because of the form, since it becomes an entirely natural individual thing when it receives the form; for matter *per se* is indeterminate and lacking in definition.[179]

Simplicius attempts to explain and further specify the designation of nature as the cause and inner principle of change in all natural bodies. Nature, being a propensity (*epitēdeiotēs*) for the existence of the form, in a way pre-exists the form by being present in the matter in potentiality, as one would expect; and it gives within itself a prior indication of the form, being its nature and its growth, as it were, and its sprouting from the matter.[180] This thesis is further explained through the exegesis of the relationship between nature, life and form, and more specifically of the way in which nature is conceived of as the life of the form. What does it mean for nature to be the life of the form? Nature, being the life of the form, is not only its growth, but also its cohesion and continuation once it has come-to-be, and its rising up to act and be acted upon, according to its natural constitution.[181] Simplicius' analysis in *In Phys.* 289. 21-35 is crucial for our understanding of nature as a *propensity for the existence of the form* (ἐπιτηδειότης πρὸς τὴν τοῦ εἴδους ὑπόστασιν), as the *lowest level of life* (ζωὴ ἐσχάτη) and finally as the *life of the form* (ζωὴ τοῦ εἴδους). Nature as a *propensity for the existence of the form* (289. 22-24) acts like a productive cause of the form since in a way (πως) it pre-exists the form, but it is present in the matter only in potentiality (δυνάμει),[182] and that makes it an idiosyncratic productive cause, since the Aristotelian productive cause is always in actuality. In addition to this causal role, nature also possesses the character of the production itself of the form, since it is φύσις αὐτοῦ, namely the *nature* (φύσις) of the form in the sense of its *genesis*,[183] and further its ἔκφυσις (growth) and ἀναβλάστησις (sprouting) from the matter (*In Phys.* 289. 24-25; 34). Furthermore, nature as the *life of the form* (ζωὴ τοῦ εἴδους) is charged with additional roles or tasks with regard

175 Cf. Aristotle, *De anima* 415b 18-20, where it is said that all the natural bodies are instruments of soul. This reference is important to my reading given that according to Philoponus (*In Phys.* 198. 6-8), the Aristotelian definition of nature also embraces the nature of the animate, which is their soul, equated with their life.

176 Alexander of Aphrodisias apud Simpl. *In Phys.* 310.31-311. 1; 311.21-25.

177 Simpl. *In Phys.* 288. 33-289.7.

178 Simpl. *In Phys.* 289. 9-15.

179 Simpl. *In Phys.* 289. 17-22.

180 Simpl. *In Phys.* 289. 22-25: "ἡ γὰρ ὕλη…προϋπάρχει μέν πως τοῦ εἴδους εἰκότως δυνάμει οὖσα ἐν τῇ ὕλῃ, προϋποφαίνει δὲ ἐν ἑαυτῇ τὸ εἶδος φύσις οὖσα αὐτοῦ καὶ οἷον ἔκφυσις καὶ ἀναβλάστησις ἀπὸ τῆς ὕλης".

181 Simpl. *In Phys.* 289. 25-26; 33-35: "διὸ καὶ οἱ ζωὴν ἐσχάτην λέγοντες τὴν φύσιν καλῶς λέγουσιν…ζωὴ δὲ οὖσα τοῦ εἴδους ἡ φύσις οὐ μόνον ἔκφυσίς ἐστιν αὐτοῦ, ἀλλὰ καὶ γενομένου ἤδη συνοχὴ καὶ διανάστασις πρὸς τὸ ποιεῖν καὶ τὸ πάσχειν ἃ πέφυκε".

182 Aristotle, in his *Metaphysics* 1049b 5-10, notes that φύσις belongs to the same genus as δύναμις. For nature as a sense of *dunamis* in Aristotle's *Metaphysics* Theta, see Gonzalez (2023).

183 For this meaning of nature, see Aristotle, *Physics* 193b 12-13.

to the form: it is not only ἔκφυσις αὐτοῦ, but once it has come-to-be, nature takes care for its cohesion and continuation and gives the form a boost to act and be acted upon according to its natural constitution (*In Phys.* 289. 33-35). This character of nature as the life of the form in Simplicius reminds us of the providential care of nature that Philoponus illustrates in his conception of nature as life. Within Simplicius' interpretive context, nature as the life of the form seems to play the role of the Aristotelian formal cause with regard to the form, since it is the formal cause which provides the bodies with cohesion and continuation. In addition, nature as the cause of the cohesion and continuation of the form ensures its preservation and appears to aim towards the development and actualization of all its active and passive capacities according to its natural constitution; from this perspective nature proves to be also the final cause of the form.

According to Simplicius' assessment, the above reasons show that those who say that nature is the lowest level of life are quite right. We can understand the meaning of nature as ἐσχάτη ζωή in Simplicius, if we base it off his description of the relationship between nature and the bodies, which is imbued with his Neoplatonic perspective and terminology. Since bodies are far removed from the indivisible and unextended essence and given that life subsists (only) in the real (or absolute) being,[184] they are lifeless and spiritless in themselves and too chilled for any kind of life. But they have within themselves the lowest (*ἔσχατον*) sort or form of life which relates to potentiality and propensity, i.e., that which we call "nature".[185] It is because of this sort of life that even lifeless bodies can be moved and changed, and what is more, grow and act upon each other, being passive.[186] Simplicius explains the phrase "καὶ εἰς ἄλληλα παθητικὰ ἐνεργεῖν" (287. 22-23) by clarifying that their activities are not pure, but involve being acted on. He stresses that this is the reason why all natural bodies can only move other things if they themselves are moved.[187] Yet what is strictly unmoved itself moves (αὐτὸ κινεῖ), as Aristotle states in *Physics* 260a1-5.[188] In Simplicius' reference to the life that subsists in the real or absolute being, it is implied that there is a contradistinction between this life and the lowest sort or form of life, which is what we call "nature". The relationship between the primary and the lowest life becomes clear in passage 289. 26-33 of his Commentary on *Physics* II. 2. Using his Neoplatonic perspective as the axis of his interpretation, in *In Phys.* 289. 26-35 Simplicius draws an analogy between the primary life and potentiality, and the lowest life and potentiality. The primary potentiality and primary life, which subsists according to the first movement of being, is the bubbling over, as it were, from primary being into the separating out of the *hypostasis* of form and the movement outwards (*ἔκστασις*) from being (*εἶναι*) to actuality (*ἐνεργεῖν*). Analogous to the movement outwards from *εἶναι* to *ἐνεργεῖν*, which is characterised as the first movement of being, is the growth of the enmattered form from matter and the movement towards that form, viewed according to the potentiality of the form; this movement is the lowest potentiality and the lowest life.[189]

We have seen that according to Proclus (*In Timaeum* I, 11. 9-12) nature is the last of the demiurgic causes that create the sensible bodily world, but even more important for its relevance to Simplicius' conception of nature as the lowest level of life (ἐσχάτη ζωή) is Proclus' statement, in *In Rem publicam* II. 311. 10-11, that nature is the last life (ἐσχάτη ζωή) of the body, a thesis also shared by Damascius.[190] Lernould, in his commentary on *Simplicius, On Aristotle's Physics* II. 1-3, interprets the commentator's theory about nature as the lowest life within the context of its Neoplatonic origin and claims that it reflects an implicit inverted correspondence between two triads, the intelligible and the natural, as follows:

Intelligible triad:

a. πρῶτον ὄν/νοητή οὐσία/εἶναι (primary being, intelligible being, being)
b. πρώτη ζωή/νοητή ζωή/πρώτη δύναμις (primary life, intelligible life, primary potentiality)
c. εἰδητικὴ ὑπόστασις/νοητός νοῦς/ἐνέργεια (hypostasis of Form, intelligible intellect, actuality)

Natural triad:

a. εἶδος/ ἐνέργεια (form, actuality)
b. φύσις/ἐσχάτη ζωή/ ἐσχάτη δύναμις (nature, lowest life, lowest potentiality)
c. τὸ ἔνυλον εἶδος κατὰ τὸ δυνάμει τοῦ εἴδους, τὸ ὄν (the enmattered form according to its potentiality, being)

---

184 I deviate somewhat from the translation of B. Fleet, because my syntax is different with regard to Simpl. 287. 17-19.

185 Simpl. *In Phys.* 287. 17-21.

186 Simpl. *In Phys.* 287. 21-23.

187 Simpl. *In Phys.* 287. 23-24; cf. Simpl. *In Phys.* 289. 15-17, where he states that the form comes-to-be according to its own nature from its opposite, and once it has come-to-be it is preserved and changed by both acting and being acted on, or rather by having a passive activity (παθητικῶς ἐνεργοῦν).

188 Simpl. *In Phys.* 287. 24-25; Diels refers to *Physics* 260a3. Fleet (1997, p. 170, n. 114) believes that the statement attributed here to Aristotle does not quite match that passage, claiming that rather it applies more generally to his doctrine of the Unmoved Mover. I believe Diels has chosen a passage indicative of this thesis.

189 In *Metaph.* 1072b 26-28, Aristotle determines life as the actuality of Intellect ("ἡ γὰρ νοῦ ἐνέργεια ζωή"), and finally identifies the first Intellect, i.e. God, with that actuality. But while Aristotle identifies life with *energeia*, considered as the *energeia* of the first Intellect or the first principle, according to the Neoplatonic approach of Simplicius, the primary life is the first movement of the primary being from *εἶναι* to *ἐνεργεῖν*.

190 Cf. Proclus, *In Parmenidem* 961.31-32 (Cousin). Cf. also Damascius, *In Parmenidem* I, 19. 7-8; III, 159. 16-17.

The intelligible triad corresponds to the triad οὐσία, δύναμις, ἐνέργεια (*ousia*, potentiality, actuality) and finally to the triad εἶναι, ζωή, νοῦς (being, life, intellect).[191]

Some characteristics of nature in Proclus that are put forward by Opsomer can also be found in Philoponus and, in a way, somewhat modified in Simplicius. "Nature is inseparable from bodies and physically immersed in them", "it precedes bodies" since it is their principle, "it serves as the proximate cause of bodies", "it is lower than soul properly speaking", "it is intermediate between soul and body", "it spreads itself out through them", "it sustains bodies by imparting structure and unity onto them and causing their movement", "it produces, conserves, and regenerates bodies and fills them with life", "it is the last of the demiurgic causes" (Opsomer, 2017, p. 152). Nature is *life* (ζωή) and a kind of δύναμις for both Philoponus and Simplicius; and, as in Proclus, for Simplicius nature is the lowest potentiality (ἐσχάτη δύναμις) and the lowest life (ἐσχάτη ζωή). Lernould also connects Proclus with Simplicius regarding the conception of the status of nature as an intermediate between soul and the corporeal. According to his interpretation, Proclus introduces nature as an intermediate *hypostasis* between the Soul and the corporeal with the same rationale that Simplicius presents in his exegesis with regard to what one should call a "principle", namely an efficient cause, in the strict sense (κυρίως): "that which is in a substrate would not in a strict sense be a principle that moves the substrate" (*In Phys.* 287. 29-30). This implies that if nature resides in a substrate, it cannot be a principle of this substrate in the strict sense (κυρίως).[192]

Philoponus and Simplicius place special emphasis on the notion of ζωή, when explaining nature. They both use the notion of *zōē* (life) as an intermediate between nature and soul, to demonstrate the bonds that conjugate the two principles. Furthermore, they both attempt to demonstrate that their explanations are in harmony with the Aristotelian definition of nature, simply bringing to the fore what in their opinion Aristotle tacitly implied as the real meaning of nature and the true relation between these two principles of change and motion, i.e., nature and soul. Especially stimulating and innovative is Simplicius' theory about nature as a *propensity for the existence of the form* (ἐπιτηδειότης πρὸς τὴν τοῦ εἴδους ὑπόστασιν), as the *lowest level of life* (ζωὴ ἐσχάτη) and finally as the *life of the form* (ζωὴ τοῦ εἴδους). Nature as ἐσχάτη ζωή in Simplicius is connected specifically with the form and not generally with the bodies. The commentator commingles the Aristotelian theory of nature and terminology with the Neoplatonic perspective and constructs a fourfold hierarchy and schema of causes. In *In Phys.* 289. 31-33 he places these causes in the following order: Being, life, nature, matter (ὄν, ζωή, φύσις, ὕλη). In my reading of this passage, nature as a sort of life and indeed the lowest level of life must be placed below life in this scale of causes. What is noteworthy is that ζωή is now made an intermediate between ὄν and φύσις and furthermore, φύσις becomes an intermediate between ζωή and ὕλη. But finally, ζωή as ἐσχάτη ζωή is commingled with nature and nature is interpreted as the *life of the form* in two senses: a) in the sense of *genesis*, sprouting from the matter, motion and growth of the form; b) in the sense of a factor which operates as formal and final cause of the form since it preserves its cohesion and continuation and simultaneously stimulates it to act and be acted upon "according to its natural constitution". Furthermore, nature as a propensity for the existence of the form (ἐπιτηδειότης πρὸς τὴν τοῦ εἴδους ὑπόστασιν [*In Phys.* 289.22-23]), can be conceived of as an efficient and productive cause of the form that pre-exists the form and is present in the matter in potentiality (δυνάμει). If we attempt to evaluate this interpretation, we would readily say that he presents an inspired renovation of the Aristotelian theory of causation with regard to nature and form. Therefore, it would not be unreasonable to say that whereas in his approach to the soul Simplicius remains faithful to his Neoplatonic background, claiming that the soul is a separate actuality with regard to the body, since both the essence and the activities of it are separable from the body, in his approach to nature he appears to be not only a Neoplatonist, but also an enthusiastic follower of Aristotle who develops his teacher's theory and surpasses his ideas.

In Aristotle's theory both soul and nature are identified with the form (εἶδος).[193] Also, both soul and nature are firmly connected with life (ζωή), the latter through motion, which is "like a sort of life as it were to all naturally constituted things".[194] Simplicius attempts to utilise and combine all these Aristotelian approaches and display the difference between soul and nature as principles of motion and change in an innovative way, albeit deeply imbued with the spirit of his inherited philosophical tradition. He effectively differentiates nature from soul by establishing and recognising a hierarchy of lives and determining nature as the *lowest level of life* or the *last life* (ἐσχάτη ζωή). His achievement is complete when he finally defines nature as *a propensity for the existence of the form* and the *life of the form*. Through these definitions he introduces a multifaceted causal relation between nature as *propensity* and *life* on the one hand, and form on the other, which brings to the fore the originality of his own approach to nature. In this way he not only

191 See Lernould (2019), pp. 128-129, n. 290. Lernould traces a similar inversion between nature and the intelligible world in Proclus, *In Timaeum* II, 139.14-140.10, regarding the *Timaeus* 35a1-4.

192 Lernould (2012), pp. 68-69.

193 Aristotle, *Physics* 193a30-b18; *De anima* 412a 19-23. See also Themistius, *In De anima*, 39. 31-40.3.

194 Aristotle, *Physics* 250b11-15; *De anima* 413a20 ff.

differentiates nature from soul, but also nature from form. But finally, at the conclusion of his philosophical survey, he somehow aligns with the Aristotelian theory of nature as a principle and cause of all natural things. While he argues that nature, contrary to the soul, cannot be a principle in the strict sense, since it resides in the substrate which is moved by it, at the same time he solemnly affirms that nature *is a principle* and *cause* with regard to the form, since he attributes to it all the necessary causal roles for the *hypostasis* of the form and the actualization of its capacities, according to its natural constitution. Consequently, nature may be regarded as a principle and cause also of the composite, of the whole natural body.

Bibliography

Standard Editions of the Greek texts

Alexandri Aphrodisiensis, *De anima Liber cum Mantissa,* Supplementum Aristotelicum, Vol. II, Pars I, I. Bruns (ed.), Berlin: Reimer, 1887.

Ioannis Philoponi, *In Aristotelis Physicorum libros tres priores commentaria*, H. Vitelli (ed.), *CAG* XVI, Berlin: Reimer, 1887.

Ioannis Philoponi, *In Aristotelis De anima libros commentaria*, M. Hayduck (ed.), *CAG* XV, Berlin: Reimer, 1897.

Simplicii, *In Aristotelis Physicorum libros quattor priores commentaria*, H. Diels (ed.), *CAG* IX, Berlin: Reimer, 1882.

Simplicii, *In Aristotelis De caelo commentaria,* J.L. Heiberg (ed.), *CAG* VII, Berlin: Reimer, 1894.

Simplicii, *In Aristotelis Physicorum libros quattor posteriores commentaria*, H. Diels (ed.), *CAG* X, Berlin: Reimer, 1895.

Themistii, *In libros Aristotelis De anima paraphrasis,* R. Heinze (ed.), *CAG* V, 3, Berlin: Reimer, 1899.

Translations, Commentaries and Secondary Literature

Bodnár, I., Chase, M. and Share, M., (2012): Simplicius, *On Aristotle's Physics 8. 1-5.* London: Bloomsbury Academic.

Bolton, R. (1978): "Aristotle's Definitions of the Soul: "De anima" ii, 1-3". *Phronesis* 23, No 3: pp. 258-278.

Bos, A.P. (2003): *The Soul and its Instrumental Body: A Reinterpretation of Aristotle's Philosophy of Living Nature. Brill's Studies in Intellectual History*, Vol. 112. Leiden-Boston: Brill.

Caston, V. (2012): *Alexander of Aphrodisias: On the Soul: Part 1: Soul as Form of the Body, Parts of the Soul, Nourishment, and Perception. Translated with an Introduction and Commentary.* London, New York: Bloomsbury.

Charlton, W. (1970): *Aristotle's Physics. Translated with Introduction and Notes.* Oxford: At the Clarendon Press.

Charlton, W. (1980): "Aristotle's Definition of Soul". *Phronesis* 25, No 2: pp. 170-186.

Charlton, W. (2005): *Philoponus: On Aristotle, On the Soul 2.1-6.* London-New York: Bloomsbury.

Cohen, S.M. (1994): "Aristotle on Elemental Motion". *Phronesis* 39, No 2: pp. 150-159.

de Haas, F. (2015): "*On the Soul,* written by Alexander of Aphrodisias". *The International Journal of the Platonic Tradition* 9, No 2: pp. 242-245.

Dodds, E.R. (1963[2]): *Proclus. The Elements of Theology. A Revised Text with Translation, Introduction and Commentary.* Oxford: Clarendon Press.

Easterling, H.J. (1966): "A Note on "De anima" 413a 8-9". *Phronesis* 11, No 2: pp. 159-162.

Eunyoung Ju, A. (2007): "Chrysippus on Nature and Soul in Animals". *The Classical Quarterly* 57, No. 1: pp. 97-108.

Fleet, B. (1997): *Simplicius: On Aristotle Physics 2.* London: Duckworth.

Frede, M. (1995): "On Aristotle's Conception of the Soul". In: Nussbaum, M.C. and Rorty, A.O. (eds): *Essays on Aristotle's De anima.* Oxford: Oxford University Press, pp. 93-108.

Fritsche, J. (2010): "Aristotele's Usage of Ἀρχὴ κινήσεως (›Principle of Motion‹) and the two Definitions of Nature in *Physics* II 1". *Archiv* für *Begriffsgeschichte,* Band 52: pp. 7-31.

Furley, D. (1994): "Self-Movers". In: Gill, M.L. and Lennox, J.G. (eds): *Self-Motion, From Aristotle to Newton.* Princeton: Princeton University Press, pp. 3-14.

Gerson, L.P. (2012): "Plotinus on Logos". In: Wilberding, J. and Horn, C. (eds): *Neoplatonism and the Philosophy of Nature.* Oxford: Oxford University Press, pp. 17-29.

Golitsis, P. (2019): "Der Begriff der *Physis* im späten Neuplatonismus". In: Koch, D., Männlein-Robert, I., Weidtmann, N. (hrsg.): *Platon und die Physis.* Tübingen: Mohr Siebeck, pp. 241-253.

Gonzalez, F.J. (2023): "From *Dunamis* as Active/Passive Capacity to *Dunamis* as Nature in Aristotle's *Metaphysics* Theta". *Apeiron* 56, No 4: pp. 785-825.

Hardie, W.F.R. (1968): *Aristotle's Ethical Theory.* Oxford: Clarendon Press.

Hicks, R.D. (1907), *Aristotle: De anima, With Translation, Introduction and Notes,* Cambridge University Press.

Huffman, C. (2009): "The Pythagorean Conception of the Soul from Pythagoras to Philolaus". In: Frede, D. and Reis, B. (eds): *Body and Soul in Ancient Philosophy.* Berlin-NewYork: Walter de Gruyter, pp. 21-44.

Irwin, T. (1988), *Aristotle's First Principles,* Oxford University Press.

Joachim, H.H. (1922, transl.), *Aristotle, On Coming-to-be and Passing-away (De Generatione et Corruptione), A Revised Text with Introduction and Commentary*. Oxford: At the Clarendon Press.

Johansen, T. (2007): "The Soul as an Inner Principle of Change: The Basis of Aristotle's Psychological Naturalism". In: Scott, D. (ed.): *Maieusis: Essays on Ancient Philosophy in Honour of Myles Burnyeat*. Oxford University Press, pp. 276-300.

Johansen, T. (2012): "The Soul as an Efficient Cause". In: Johansen, T.: *The Powers of Aristotle's Soul*. Oxford University Press, pp. 128-145.

Johansen, T.K. (2014): "Parts in Aristotle's Definition of Soul: *De anima* Books I and II". In: Corcilius, K. and Perler, D. (eds): *Partitioning the Soul: Debates from Plato to Leibniz*. Topoi-Berlin Studies of the Ancient World, 22. Berlin-Boston: De Gruyter, pp. 39-62.

Kahn, C. (1979): *The Art and Thought of Heraclitus, An edition of the fragments with translation and commentary*. Cambridge: Cambridge University Press.

Kessler, E. (2011): *Alexander of Aphrodisias and his Doctrine of the Soul: 1400 Years of Lasting Significance*. Boston: Brill.

Krafft, F. (1982): "Zielgerichtetheit und Zielsetzung in Wissenschaft und Natur". *Berichte zur Wissenschaftsgeschichte* 5: pp. 53-74.

Krafft, F. (1988): "Aristoteles aus christliche Sicht. Umformungen aristotelischer Bewegungslehren durch Johannes Philoponos". In: Bergier, J.F. (ed.): *Zwischen Wann, Glaube und Wissenschaft*. Zurich, pp. 51-85.

Kupreeva, I. (2005): *Philoponus: On Aristotle, On coming-to-Be and Perishing 2.5-11*. London: Duckworth.

Kupreeva, I. (2012): "Alexander of Aphrodisias and Aristotle's "De anima": What's in a Commentary?". *Bulletin of the Institute of Classical Studies* 55, No 1, *Ancient Philosophy in Memory of R.W. Sharples*: pp. 109-129.

Lacey, A.R. (1993): *Philoponus: On Aristotle Physics 2*. London: Bloomsbury.

Laks, A. (2000): "Metaphysics Λ 7". In: Frede, M. and Charles, D. (eds.): *Aristotle's Metaphysics Lambda, Symposium Aristotelicum*. Oxford: Clarendon Press, pp. 207-243.

Lammer, A. (2015): "Defining Nature: from Aristotle to Philoponus to Avicenna". In: Alwishah, A. and Hayes, J. (eds): *Aristotle and the Arabic Tradition*. Cambridge: Cambridge University Press, pp. 121-142.

Lang, H. (1998): *The Order of Nature in Aristotle's Physics: Place and the Elements*. Cambridge: Cambridge University Press.

Lebedev, A. (2019): "Idealism (mentalism) in Early Greek metaphysics and philosophical theology: Pythagoras, Parmenides, Heraclitus, Xenophanes and others (with some remarks on the "Gigantomachia about being" in Plato's *Sophist*)". *Indo-European Linguistics and Classical Philology* XXIII: pp. 651-704. 10.30842/ielcp230690152352.

Lebedev, A. (2022): "Anaximander and the Scientific Revolution in Miletus in the Sixth Century B.C.". *Indo-European Linguistics and Classical Philology*: pp. 688-769. 10.30842/ielcp230690152647.

Lefèvre, C. (1972): *Sur l' évolution d' Aristote en psychologie*. Louvain: Éditions de l'Institut supérieur de Philosophie.

Lefèvre, C. (1978): "Sur le statut de l' âme dans le *De anima* et les *Parva Naturalia*". In: Lloyd, G.E.R. and Owen, G.E.L. (eds): *Aristotle on Mind and the Senses. Proceedings of the Seventh Symposium Aristotelicum*. New York: Cambridge University Press, pp. 21-67.

Lennox, J.G. (2021): "Most Natural Among the Functions of Living Things". In: Korobili, G. and Lo Presti, R. (eds): *Nutrition and Nutritive Soul in Aristotle and Aristotelianism*. Berlin-Boston: De Gruyter, pp. 3-19.

Lernould, A. (2012): "Nature in Proclus: From Irrational Immanent Principle to Goddess". In: Wilberding, J. and Horn, C. (eds): *Neoplatonism and the Philosophy of Nature*. Oxford: Oxford University Press, pp. 68-102.

Lernould, A. (2019): *Simplicius: Commentaire sur la Physique d' Aristote, Livre II, ch. 1-3. Introduction, traduction, notes et bibliographie*. Presses universitaires du Septentrion.

Marinescu, R.I. (2023): "Nature as an Instrumental Cause in Proclus". *Apeiron* 56, No 4: pp. 673-692.

Macierowski, E.M. and Hassing, R.F. (1988): "John Philoponus on Aristotle's Definition of Nature". *Ancient Philosophy* 8, No 1: pp. 73-100.

Manuwald, B. (1989): *Studien zum Unbewegten Beweger in der Naturphilosophie des Aristoteles*. Stuttgart: Franz Steiner.

Martijn, M. (2010): *Proclus on Nature: Philosophy of Nature and Its Methods in Proclus' Commentary on Plato's Timaeus*. Philosophia Antiqua, Vol. 121. Leiden/Boston: Brill.

McGuire, J.E. (1985): "Philoponus on *Physics* ii 1: Φύσις, Δύναμις, and the Motion of the Simple Bodies". *Ancient Philosophy* 5: pp. 241-267.

McKirahan, R.D. (2010[2]): *Philosophy Before Socrates: An Introduction with Texts and Commentary*. Indianapolis/Cambridge: Hackett Publishing Company, Inc.

Menn, S. (2002): "Aristotle's Definition of Soul". *Oxford Studies in Ancient Philosophy*, 22: pp. 83-139.

Miller, F.D. Jr. (1999): "Aristotle's Philosophy of Soul". *The Review of Metaphysics* 53, No 2: pp. 309-337.

Morrow, G. and Dillon, J.M. (1987): *Proclus' Commentary on Plato's Parmenides*. Princeton: Princeton University Press.

Mouzala, M.G. (2008): *Ουσία και Ορισμός, Η Προβληματική της Ενότητος εις τα οικεία κεφάλαια των Μετά τα φυσικά του Αριστοτέλους* [Substance and Definition: The Problematics of Unity in the

relevant chapters of Aristotle's Metaphysics]. Athens: Harmos Editions.
Mouzala, M.G. (2015): «Κίνησις, Νους και Ζωή στην αριστοτελική οντολογική Θεολογία του Λ΄ Βιβλίου των Μετά τα φυσικά» ("Motion, Intellect and Life in the Aristotelian Ontological Theology of Book Lambda of the Metaphysics"). *Philosophein* 11: pp. 195-219.
Mouzala, M.G. (2016): "Aristotle's Criticism of the Platonic Forms as Causes in *De Generatione et Corruptione* II. 9. A Reading based on Philoponus". *Peitho-Examina Antiqua* 1 (7): pp. 123-147.
Mouzala, M.G. (2019): "Simplicius on the principal meaning of *physis* in Aristotle's *Physics* II. 1-3". *Analogia* 7: pp. 43-82.
Mueller, I. (2004): *On Aristotle: On the Heavens 2. 1-9*. London: Duckworth.
Nawar, T. (2020): "The Stoic Theory of the Soul". In: Arenson, K. (ed.): *The Routledge Handbook of Hellenistic Philosophy. Routledge Handbooks in Philosophy.* London and New York: Routledge, pp. 148-159.
Opsomer, J. (2017): "The Natural World". In: d' Hoine, P. and Martijn, M. (eds): *All from One: A Guide to Proclus.* Oxford: Oxford University Press, pp. 139-166.
Owens, J. (1971): "Aristotle's Definition of Soul". In: Plamer, R.B., Hamerton-Kelly, R. (eds.): *Philomathes.* Dordrecht: Springer, pp. 125-145.
Polansky, R. (2007): *Aristotle's De anima: A Critical Commentary*. Cambridge: Cambridge University Press.
Reydams-Schils, G. and Ferrari, F. (2014): "Middle Platonism and its Relation to Stoicism and the Peripatetic Tradition". In: Remes, P. and Slaveva-Griffin, S. (eds): *The Routledge Handbook of Neoplatonism.* London and New York: Routledge, pp. 40-51.
Sisko, J.E. (2019): "Introduction to the Volume 1". In: Sisko, J.E. (ed.): *Philosophy of Mind in Antiquity: The History of the Philosophy of Mind, Volume 1*, ed. Copenhaver, R. and Shields, Ch. London and New York: Routledge, pp. 1-22.
Smith, M.A (1931, transl.), *The Works of Aristotle: De anima*. Oxford: Clarendon Press.
Solmsen, F. (1960): *Aristotle's System of the Physical World: A Comparison with His Predecessors*. Ithaca, New York.
Sorabji, R. (1974): "Body and Soul in Aristotle". *Philosophy* 49, No 187: pp. 63-89.
Sorabji, R. (1988): *Matter, Space and Motion: Theories in Antiquity and Their Sequel.* London: Duckworth.
Sorabji, R. (1997): "Introduction to B. Fleet, *Simplicius: On Aristotle Physics 2*". London: Duckworth, pp. 1-5.
Tarrant, H. (2006): *Proclus: Commentary on Plato's Timaeus. Volume I. Book I: Proclus on the Socratic State and Atlantis. Translated with an Introduction and Notes. With a General Introduction by Dirk Baltzly and Harold Tarrant.* Cambridge: Cambridge University Press.
Tiuryn, T. (2016): "The Soul and the Steersman. Separability of the Soul from the Body in Ancient Commentators on Aristotle's *De anima*". *Studia Antyczne i Mediewistyczne* 14, No 49: pp. 31-46. PL ISSN 0039-3231
Todd, R.B. (2013): *Themistius: On Aristotle, On the Soul.* London-New York: Bloomsbury.
Tracy, T. (1982): "The Soul/Boatman Analogy in Aristotle's *De anima*". *Classical Philology* 77, No 2: pp. 97-112.
Veillard, C. (2020): "Soul, *Pneuma*, and Blood: The Stoic Conception of the Soul". In: Inwood, B. and Warren, J. (eds): *Body and Soul in Hellenistic Philosophy.* Cambridge: Cambridge University Press, pp. 145-170.
Wicksteed, P.H. and Cornford, F.M. (1957): Aristotle, *Physics, Volume I: Books 1-4*, Loeb Classical Library 228, Cambridge MA: Harvard University Press.
Wilberding, J. (2022): "Nature: Plotinus' Fourth Hypostasis?". In: Gerson, L.P. and Wilberding, J. (eds): *The New Cambridge Companion to Plotinus.* Cambridge: Cambridge University Press, pp. 312-338.
Williams, C.J.F. (1982): *Aristotle's De Generatione et Corruptione*, translated with notes, Oxford.
Wolff, M. (2010): "Philoponus and the Rise of the Preclassical Dynamics". In: Sorabji, R. (ed.): *Philoponus and the Rejection of the Aristotelian Science.* Oxford University Press, pp. 125-160.
Zimmermann, F. (2010): "Philoponus' Impetus Theory in the Arabic Tradition". In: Sorabji, R. (ed.): *Philoponus and the Rejection of the Aristotelian Science.* Oxford University Press, pp. 163-169.

Notes on the Contributors

István Bodnár is Professor of Philosophy at Eötvös University, Budapest, teaching also at the Central European University, Vienna. Apart from his numerous studies, especially in Aristotle and the commentators, he is editor of *Eudemus of Rhodes* (with W. W. Fortenbaugh, 2002) and translator of *Simplicius On Aristotle Physics 8.1-5* (with M. Chase and M. Share, 2014).

Prof. dr. Frans A.J. de Haas studied Classics, and received his PhD in ancient philosophy from Leiden University (1995). He was a visiting research fellow at the Institute of Classical Studies (London) and Research Fellow of the Dutch Royal Academy of Arts and Sciences at Utrecht University (1997-2000). Since 2003 he is Full Professor of Ancient and Medieval Philosophy at Leiden University. He has served as Dean and Academic Director of the Leiden Institute for Philosophy, and as Director of the Dutch Research School of Philosophy OZSW (2019-2023). Since 2019 he has been editor-in-chief of *Philosophia Antiqua* (Brill). He has held visiting professorships in Beijing Normal University and the Topoi project in Berlin. He has published widely on Aristotle and the late ancient commentary tradition on Aristotle. His current research project is devoted to Alexander's new design of Aristotelian philosophy.

Key publications include *John Philoponus' New Definition of Prime Matter. Aspects of its Background in Neoplatonism and the Ancient Commentary Tradition* (1997); "Aristotle and Alexander of Aphrodisias on active intellectual cognition" (2020); "Alexander of Aphrodisias on the Ancient Debate on Hylomorphism and the Development of Intellect" (2023), and *Studies on Alexander of Aphrodisias' on Mixture and Growth* (2023, edited with G. Guyomarc'h).

Fr. Nikolaos Loudovikos studied Psychology, Pedagogy, Philosophy, Theology and History of Religions at the Universities of Athens, Thessaloniki, Paris (Sorbonne 4, Institut Catholique de Paris) and Cambridge. He was a former Professor of Dogmatics and Philosophy at the University Ecclesiastical Academy of Thessaloniki, and a Professor of Dogmatics at the University Ecclesiastical Academy of Athens. He is now Professor of Religious Studies and Hermeneutics of Religion at the University of Ioannina. He is also a Visiting Professor at the Institute for Orthodox Christian Studies in Cambridge and at the Univ. of Balamand. He taught or gave lectures at more than 25 Universities around the world. He is the author of twenty-one books and numerous articles translated in ten languages. He is the Senior Editor of the international Journal *Analogia: The Pemptousia Journal for Theological Studies.* His last books in English: *Analogical Identities: The Creation of the Christian Self.* Volume I: *Beyond Spirituality and Mysticism in the Patristic Era* (Brepols 2019); Volume II: *Intermeaningfulness: Self-catholicization, Meta-narcissism and Christian Theology* (Brepols, 2024). His last book in Greek: *Techno-pithecus and Truth: Hermeneutics of Religion in the Age of Artificial Intelligence* (Athens: Armos 2024).

Claudia Marsico is a Full Professor at the University of Buenos Aires and Head of a research unit at the National Academy of Sciences in Buenos Aires. She has been a visiting professor at many universities in Belgium, Germany, Italy, and the USA, as well as Founding President of the International Society for Socratic Studies (ISSS) and current Vice President of the International Plato Society (IPS). She is author of more than twenty-five books in the field of Ancient Philosophy, including the first full translation of the extant texts on Socratic philosophies (Filósofos socráticos, Testimonios y fragmentos. I/Megáricos y Cirenaicos, Buenos Aires, 2013, and Filósofos socráticos, Testimonios y fragmentos II/Antístenes, Fedón, Esquines y Simón, Buenos Aires, 2014). She has also published many articles and chapters in national and international journals as well as books in the fields of ancient philosophy and philosophy of history, especially about Plato and the Socratic Philosophies, and its reception.

Alexandra Michalewski is Senior Research Fellow at the CNRS (Centre Léon Robin, Paris-Sorbonne). She was Co-Director with Pieter d'Hoine of a funded research project (2018-2020) on Asclepius' *Commentary on Aristotle's Metaphysics* (*Le commentaire d'Asclépius aux livres A-Γ* de la *Métaphysique d'Aristote. Textes choisis et commentaires*, Bruxelles-Paris, OUSIA, Cahiers de philosophie ancienne, 2023). As a specialist of Plotinus and the ancient Platonist tradition (*La puissance de l'intelligible. La théorie plotinienne des Formes au miroir de l'héritage médioplatonicien*, Leuven, University Press, 2014), she focuses on the question of the nature and causality of intelligible Forms and on the reception of Aristotelian metaphysics in the Middle Platonist cosmologies (*Dieu, le mouvement, la matière: Atticus et ses critiques dans l'Antiquité tardive*, Paris, Les Belles Lettres, 2024).

Melina G. Mouzala is an Associate Professor at the Department of Philosophy of the University of Patras (Ancient Philosophy; her research interests include the Platonic and Aristotelian traditions as well as Ancient and Byzantine commentaries on Aristotle). She has authored three books in Greek: *Ουσία και Ορισμός. Η Προβληματική της ενότητος εις τα οικεία κεφάλαια των Μετά τα φυσικά του Αριστοτέλους*, Athens 2007: Harmos; *Περί του καθ'ετερότητα μη όντος στον Σοφιστή του Πλάτωνος*, Athens 2007: Harmos; *Ζητήματα Γνωσιολογίας, Οντολογίας και Μεταφυσικής στην φιλοσοφία του Αριστοτέλους, Υπό το φως αρχαίων και βυζαντινών υπομνημάτων* (Athens 2013: Gutenberg). She is also the editor of six collective works, three in Greek and three in English: *Θέματα Οντολογίας-Μεταφυσικής, Φιλοσοφίας των Μαθηματικών και Λογικής, in memoriam Δημ. Μούκανου*, Athens 2018: Gutenberg; *Αυτογνωσία και Επιμέλεια Ψυχής/Εαυτού: Αρχαία·Ελληνιστική· Νεοπλατωνική· Βυζαντινή· Νεοελληνική Φιλοσοφία* (Athens 2020: Papazisis); *Αρχαία Φιλοσοφικά Θέματα στην Πατερική και Βυζαντινή Φιλοσοφία* (Athens 2023: Papazisis); *Ancient Greek Dialectic and its Reception, Topics in Ancient Philosophy*, Vol. 10 (Berlin 2023: De Gruyter); *Cognition in Ancient Greek Philosophy and its Reception: Interdisciplinary Approaches, Academia Philosophical Studies* 86 (Baden-Baden 2024: Academia Verlag/Nomos); *Nature and Human Nature in Ancient Greek Philosophy and its Reception* (in the Series *Netherlands Institute at Athens Publications*; Sidestone Press 2025).

Teun Tieleman (PhD, with highest distinction, Utrecht 1992) is Professor of Ancient Philosophy and Medicine at Utrecht University, Department of Philosophy and Religious Studies; visiting positions at Cambridge University (1993), Novosibirsk State University, Siberia (2008, 2011, 2012, 2013), UCLA (2009), the Institute for Religion and Critical Inquiry, ACU, Melbourne (2018) and Humboldt-Universität zu Berlin (2023). His research focuses on Galen of Pergamum, Stoicism (Early Stoa, Posidonius, Seneca), theories of emotion, the relation between ancient medicine and religion as well as ancient philosophy and early Christianity. He is co-director of the Gravitation-programme 'Anchoring Innovation' (2017-2027) and president of OIKOS, the Netherlands research school in classical studies. Key publications: M. Flohr, S.T.A.M. Mols, T. Tieleman (eds.) *Anchoring Science and Technology in Greco-Roman Antiquity (*Leiden: Brill 2024); *Chrysippus' On Affections. Reconstruction and Interpretation* (Philosophia Antiqua 94, Brill: Leiden/Boston 2003); 346 pp.

Index Locorum

Alexander of Aphrodisias

De anima

In Metaph.

On the principles of the Universe (De Principiis)

Quaestiones

Aristotle

Atticus

Diogenes Laertius

Lives and Opinions of Eminent Philosophers

Dissoi logoi

Eusebius

Praeparatio Evangelica

Galen

Gorgias

Heraclitus

Hippocratic Corpus

Airs, Waters and Places

Epidemics

On ancient medicine

On diet

Homer

Iliad

Odyssey

Philoponus

In De anima

In De Gen. et Cor.

In Phys.

Plato

Porphyry

On Principles and Matter

Proclus

In Parmenidem

In Rem publicam

In Timaeum

Pseudo-Aristotle

De mundo

Simplicius

In De caelo

In Phys.

Thukydides

Histories

Xenophon

Memorabilia

Index Nominum et Rerum